AF886644

Ius Gentium: Comparative Perspectives on Law and Justice

Volume 73

Series editors

Mortimer Sellers, University of Baltimore
James Maxeiner, University of Baltimore

Board of Editors

Myroslava Antonovych, Kyiv-Mohyla Academy
Nadia de Araújo, Pontifical Catholic University of Rio de Janeiro
Jasna Bakšic-Muftic, University of Sarajevo
David L. Carey Miller, University of Aberdeen
Loussia P. Musse Félix, University of Brasilia
Emanuel Gross, University of Haifa
James E. Hickey Jr., Hofstra University
Jan Klabbers, University of Helsinki
Cláudia Lima Marques, Federal University of Rio Grande do Sul
Aniceto Masferrer, University of Valencia
Eric Millard, West Paris University
Gabriël A. Moens, Curtin University
Raul C. Pangalangan, University of the Philippines
Ricardo Leite Pinto, Lusíada University of Lisbon
Mizanur Rahman, University of Dhaka
Keita Sato, Chuo University
Poonam Saxena, University of Delhi
Gerry Simpson, London School of Economics
Eduard Somers, University of Ghent
Xinqiang Sun, Shandong University
Tadeusz Tomaszewski, Warsaw University
Jaap de Zwaan, Erasmus University Rotterdam

More information about this series at http://www.springer.com/series/7888

Pia Letto-Vanamo · Ditlev Tamm
Bent Ole Gram Mortensen
Editors

Nordic Law in European Context

Springer

Editors
Pia Letto-Vanamo
University of Helsinki
Helsinki, Finland

Bent Ole Gram Mortensen
University of Southern Denmark
Odense, Denmark

Ditlev Tamm
University of Copenhagen
Copenhagen, Denmark

ISSN 1534-6781 ISSN 2214-9902 (electronic)
Ius Gentium: Comparative Perspectives on Law and Justice
ISBN 978-3-030-03005-6 ISBN 978-3-030-03006-3 (eBook)
https://doi.org/10.1007/978-3-030-03006-3

Library of Congress Control Number: 2018958929

© Springer Nature Switzerland AG 2019
This work is subject to copyright. All rights are reserved by the Publisher, whether the whole or part of the material is concerned, specifically the rights of translation, reprinting, reuse of illustrations, recitation, broadcasting, reproduction on microfilms or in any other physical way, and transmission or information storage and retrieval, electronic adaptation, computer software, or by similar or dissimilar methodology now known or hereafter developed.
The use of general descriptive names, registered names, trademarks, service marks, etc. in this publication does not imply, even in the absence of a specific statement, that such names are exempt from the relevant protective laws and regulations and therefore free for general use.
The publisher, the authors and the editors are safe to assume that the advice and information in this book are believed to be true and accurate at the date of publication. Neither the publisher nor the authors or the editors give a warranty, express or implied, with respect to the material contained herein or for any errors or omissions that may have been made. The publisher remains neutral with regard to jurisdictional claims in published maps and institutional affiliations.

This Springer imprint is published by the registered company Springer Nature Switzerland AG
The registered company address is: Gewerbestrasse 11, 6330 Cham, Switzerland

Preface

Nordic law is often referred to as something different from other legal systems. At the same time, it is a common belief that the Nordic countries share more or less the same legal tradition and are very similar as to their approach to the law. This book engages with both of these points of view. It tells a story of how Nordic law and Nordic legal thinking differ from other legal systems. It also tells how many particularities exist in the law of each of the Nordic countries, making them different from each other. Thus, the idea of "Nordic" law also conceals national features.

The basic idea of this book is that even if there is no such thing as a Nordic common law, strictly speaking, it still makes sense to speak of "Nordic" law, and that achieving more than a basic knowledge of this law is interesting not only for comparative lawyers but also helpful for others who are working with Nordic lawyers and dealing with questions involving law in the Nordic countries.

Most of the following chapters, which together aim at providing an introduction to Nordic legal thinking, are written by more than one author in order to cover different national aspects of the law. The fact that only a few articles could be written by one author also demonstrates how a variety of legal solutions can be found in these countries, even if they may look very much alike from the outside. The editors have chosen legal topics in which a specific Nordic approach can be appreciated.

The volume starts with an introduction to Nordic cooperation within the law and the Nordic way of legal thinking. Chapter "Nordic Model of Welfare States" contains a more detailed description of one of the key elements of modern Nordic societies, namely the development of the welfare state. The following series of chapters starts with the Nordic constitutions and different constitutional approaches in each country (Chapter "Constitutional Mentality"), leading to questions regarding autonomies and minorities (Chapter "Respecting Autonomies and Minorities") and gender equality (Chapter "Promoting Gender Equality"). Marriage and family relations is the theme of Chapter "Marriage and Family Relations", followed by chapters on contracts (Chapter "Contracting with a Social Dimension"), property (Chapter "Property and Its Limits"), labour relations (Chapter "Labour Market and

Collective Agreements"), public administration (Chapter "Public Administration and Good Governance"), crime and punishment (Chapter "Crime and Punishment") and the courts (Chapter "Courts and Court Proceedings").

As a general rule, the authors have endeavoured to include a reasonable amount of necessary detail. However, the main aim is to present a more general outline of what is common among the different Nordic countries and what is peculiar to each of them within the legal fields listed above. Stress is also placed on what we see as specifically Nordic culture as compared to other legal cultures. A bibliography at the end of each chapter will enable the reader who seeks more details to find relevant material. References to the most important legislation can be found both in English and in national languages.

The editors wish to thank the publisher for engaging with the idea of a book on Nordic law and express the hope that it will provide a useful tool for both law students as well as comparative and other lawyers who may be interested in experiencing what—to quote from Shakespeare—may be found in a Nordic "lawyer's skull".

Helsinki, Finland — Pia Letto-Vanamo
Copenhagen, Denmark — Ditlev Tamm
Odense, Denmark — Bent Ole Gram Mortensen
July 2018

Contents

Nordic Legal Mind

Pia Letto-Vanamo and Ditlev Tamm

Abstract In the following, peculiarities of the Nordic legal systems and legal thinking, are discussed. Common features of the legal systems are based both on history (on a certain historical delay in comparison to many other European countries) and legal cooperation. The active legal cooperation, started in the 1870s, not only has a long history. It has also achieved many concrete results, common legal norms as an example. Often, Nordic peculiarities of legal thinking are described by using such expressions as pragmatism, realism, absence of formality, transparency and equality. These values have also been cornerstones of the Nordic cooperation. They also explain a certain reluctance towards trends and policies within the EU. Even today, Nordic lawyers prioritise flexibility in law-making (with discrete acts) above creating a codified private law system (with a civil code).

1 Nordic Law

There is no such thing as Nordic law, but you may talk of a Nordic legal mind. The Nordic countries, Denmark, Finland, Iceland, Norway, and Sweden (including the autonomous regions of Greenland, and the Faroe and Åland islands) all have their own law and their own legal institutions. However, to speak of Nordic law may be useful as we need a concept that covers those peculiarities and similarities which, with certain reservations, can be considered as such characteristic and common features in dealing with the legal systems of these countries, which constitute the Nordic legal mind.

Comparative lawyers trying to grasp European legal systems have traditionally put the Nordic countries together as one legal "family" or group, or at least as a

P. Letto-Vanamo (✉)
Faculty of Law, University of Helsinki, Helsinki, Finland
e-mail: pia.letto-vanamo@helsinki.fi

D. Tamm
Faculty of Law, University of Copenhagen, Copenhagen, Denmark
e-mail: ditlev.tamm@jur.ku.dk

© Springer Nature Switzerland AG 2019

P. Letto-Vanamo et al. (eds.), *Nordic Law in European Context*,
Ius Gentium: Comparative Perspectives on Law and Justice 73,
https://doi.org/10.1007/978-3-030-03006-3_1

subfamily of the continental European so-called "civil law family".[1] This classification can at least partly be explained by reference to history. Still, the idea of "Nordic-ness" is more recent.

In a comparative analysis, the peculiarities of development seen in the Nordic legal system(s) are often explained by reference to a certain historical delay in accepting such ideas and institutions which are considered as belonging to the "European mainstream". We may also speak of the centre and the periphery, to which the Nordic countries belong due to their geographical position.

However, only in the 19th century did the idea of a specific "Nordic law" become a current notion to substitute the old division between Danish-Norwegian law on the one hand and Swedish law (including Finland) on the other, and then especially as a tool to promote cooperation in the field of law. Since then, Nordic unity, or the Nordic legal family, was formed by active cooperation through which former differences were bridged: "Nordic law" resulted from those efforts. It started in 1872, when several prominent Nordic lawyers were invited to the first meeting between lawyers from all the Nordic countries with the aim of discussing common answers to the challenges, which the Nordic countries and their laws were facing at a time of still early industrialisation. The inspiration for the meeting came from similar German and English institutions.[2]

One of the main arguments put forward in favour of Nordic cooperation by those invited to this first meeting of Nordic lawyers[3] referred to what was considered a common way of legal thinking. That was based on an ideology that stressed more similarities than differences by looking back on the historical origins of law in the Nordic countries. Understanding of the characteristics of Nordic legal thinking therefore requires taking into account both the idea of historical similarities between the legal systems of the Nordic countries along with advanced legal cooperation.

Nordic legislative cooperation has featured significantly in framing legal systems in the Nordic countries as they are today. Nordic cooperation as it developed and gradually covered many fields of law has also been seen as an ideal model for legal cooperation elsewhere because of its informal and voluntary nature and its success,[4] especially at a time when European legal cooperation was still in its very early stages.[5]

This fruitful cooperation started in the 1870s, and has perhaps been the most enduring result of the so-called Scandinavian movement of the early 19th century,

---

[1]Zweigert and Kötz (1998), Husa (2004) and Husa (2015); see also Husa et al. (2007).

[2]Tamm (1972) and Carsten (1973).

[3]Since the first meeting of Nordic lawyers in Copenhagen in 1872, these have been held every three years except for the periods between 1903–1918 and 1938–1947. The latest meeting (Helsinki 2017) was attended by around 900 lawyers—judges, civil servants, practising lawyers and legal scholars—from all the Nordic countries. To enhance their importance for general debate on law, since the first meetings conference papers, talks and partly also discussions among participants have been printed and published. See http://www.nordisktjuristmote.org/.

[4]Smits (2007) and Matteucci (1956).

[5]Matteucci (1956).

which after the experience of centuries of warfare between the Nordic countries pleaded for unity, collaboration and friendship among the nations of the North. Scandinavism, as this movement is called, however, failed completely as a political movement that might lead to unification of the Nordic countries, an idea that proved to be utopian.

All the Nordic countries were and are rather small, and many at that time topical questions were unknown to their scholars. Lawyers experienced in commercial matters did not abound, especially not such as could really be considered experts in new and complicated legal fields. Working together and using the potential from several states was the obvious solution, and became an immediate success. Not only Nordic lawyers' meetings but also harmonization of Nordic law experienced their beginnings in the 1870s. Since then, active legislative collaboration has been a decisive feature in classifying the Nordic countries as a legal family closer to civil-law countries (countries with statutory law) than to so-called common law countries (countries with case law), or even as a family of its own.

The purpose of Nordic legal cooperation was to find a Nordic way of jointly approaching questions posed by the rapid development of international commerce. Challenges were posed by new instruments of payment in commercial life, changes in methods of communication, and, in general, issues attached to industry on a greater scale and to questions of international trade.[6]

Since that time, the way the cooperation works is that common new legal solutions are discussed among representatives of the different countries, but at the same time it is left to the lawmakers of each country and thus to a political decision whether and to what degree any such new legislation will actually be drafted and adopted in their country. Nor does cooperation mean that common courts or other organs have been established to create what could be called a "Nordic common law"[7] based on Nordic legislation. At the same time, national lawyers, judges or law professors are free to make their own interpretations of the law.

Thus, in contrast to the European Union (EU) regime, there is neither such a thing as a common Nordic judiciary nor any other kind of common legal organs, nor any common legal thinking. Court decisions, legal rules or legal literature are national, while those of other Nordic countries may be and will regularly be cited, but basically they only serve an advisory function in the same way as any other foreign law or can be used as sources of inspiration when making decisions. Also quite rarely, law students will be familiar with legal literature from other Nordic countries than their own.

---

[6]When the first Nordic lawyers' meeting was convened, the invitation stressed that because of a common understanding of law and of the common origin of many legal institutions, it was only natural that development of those institutions would need common action. The topics mentioned for cooperation were the law of commerce and issues of court procedure in civil and penal matters. During the first meeting in 1872, the question was raised of common Nordic legislation on commercial instruments of payment such as the bill of exchange, which was a means of getting short credit. This was successfully followed up by Nordic statutes; Carsten (1993).

[7]Common law here in the meaning of Glenn (2005).

Nonetheless, this "soft" method of harmonizing the law, which does not aim at unification but which respects local peculiarities and wishes, has led to an impressive series of important statutes within basic fields of law, such as commercial law especially with common statutes on the law of buying and selling and the law of contracts,[8] but also within fields often considered more national and culturally sensitive such as family law.[9] Based on some of these statutes, general principles of law have also been developed which in other continental legal systems are found in the general part of the civil code.

In the 1970s, Nordic legal cooperation suffered a crisis, as will be mentioned later, when the Swedish minister of justice declared at the 1972 Nordic lawyers' meeting that Sweden might decide to go its own way, especially in economic and family law matters, and not wait for the other Nordic countries.[10] Moreover, within the field of law of obligations problems have arisen in finding a common path to follow. Thus, the Nordic law of sale of goods that was discussed and drafted in the 1980s was not accepted in all the Nordic countries. Sweden and Finland preferred identical laws, and Norway had a very similar one. However, in Denmark the Nordic Sale of Goods Act was not accepted and the Danes preferred to amend the old Sale of Goods Act of 1906.[11]

For some decades now, great challenges to Nordic law and legal cooperation have been posed by the much wider cooperation taking part within the EU. Indeed, from time to time the issue whether Nordic cooperation has seen its heyday comes under discussion. In particular, the 1990s witnessed a boom of seminars and meetings on "Nordic legal identity" and its future. The main reason for this was the upcoming or recently achieved Finnish and Swedish membership in the European Union. The laws of the Nordic countries were compared with other European (EU) countries with the aim of determining what could be considered similarities between the Nordic legal systems on the one hand, and differences between them and other Western European countries on the other. In effect, this was an effort to foresee whether a kind of so-called "convergence" on a greater scale would happen through EU membership, and also what would be the impact on Nordic cooperation.[12]

Undeniably, Nordic cooperation within the field of law has been challenged by cooperation within the EU, based on institutions and the creation of obligations much more effective than the soft guidelines and voluntary arrangements that form the basis of Nordic cooperation. At that time, the EU and the development of EU law also seemed to many a more attractive field of study than the more limited Nordic cooperation. One might therefore say that since Swedish and Finnish

---

[8]See further Bärlund and Moegelvang-Hansen in this volume.

[9]See further Lund-Andersen and Kronborg in this volume.

[10]Lidbom (1973) and Modéer (1998).

[11]Se further Bärlund and Moegelvang-Hansen in this volume. On differences in regulation of registred partnership see further Lund-Andersen and Kronborg in this volume.

[12]See e.g. Letto-Vanamo (1998) and Bernitz (2000). See also Letto-Vanamo (2013).

accession to the EU in 1995 (Denmark has been a member since 1973), it was Europe, and not "Nordic-ness", that came into the focus of Nordic political and legal debates.

Today, the situation seems to have changed, at least partly. The economic-political crisis within the European Union has produced discussions on different ways of organizing societal life in the North and South of Europe, but also on the future of the so-called Nordic model with social welfare as a key element. Awareness of the Nordic countries as model societies has been strengthened and, at the same time, new openings for cooperation between the Nordic countries have been presented—even a modest relaunch of the proposal for a Nordic federal state.[13] It may also be maintained that there seems to be more external interest in "Nordic law" and ways to continue Nordic cooperation than some years ago, when the Nordic countries were considered more peripheral.[14] That said, however, it should be stressed that Nordic cooperation in the field of law is not as obvious a feature as it used to be. Revitalization is definitely needed.[15]

2 The Impact of "Old" Unions

The Nordic countries are in fact five countries with different histories, but also with different laws. Law is always national, even if national law itself needs not be of national origin: it can be a result of borrowing law or legal institutions from other countries or other legal systems. Indeed, the law of the Nordic countries—even if Roman law was never the law of the land—is firmly based on principles within private law that have their origin in a common European past in the field of law.

Ever since the Middle Ages, the Nordic countries have thus been exposed to influences from Canon law and Roman law. The law of the Church, Canon law, and scholars educated at universities in Southern Europe and Germany were important in forming legal thinking in the Nordic countries in the Middle Ages. They also played a significant role in the process of writing down local law, which mostly occurred in the 12th and 13th centuries. Thus, there is a long tradition of written law.

The early wave of Roman law influence (that of the *ius commune*), typical of many western European countries since at least the 16th century, did not have the

[13] See Wetterberg (2010) and Wenander (2014).

[14] The explorer spirit of Nordic cooperation, active in the 1870s–1930s and again when Nordic legislative cooperation was revitalized after World War II, is no longer present on the same scale. At the meeting of Nordic lawyers in 2005 the question whether Nordic legal cooperation had any further role to play actually came under discussion, with the conclusion that more fuel was necessary if this "Nordic dimension" was to maintain its position, Dahl (2005). Four years later a proposal was launched for more effective Nordic cooperation in implementing European (EU/EEA) legislation. Buskjær Christensen and Fenger (2009).

[15] The newest initiative Backer (2018).

same impact in the Nordic countries as elsewhere in Europe. Since end of the 15th century it was possible to study law also at a Nordic university, but students were few, and for a full study of law it was necessary to go abroad. A university-trained legal profession (with an exam) and legal science in the North are phenomena of the 18th or 19th centuries.[16] Since that time, the scholarly legal tradition has been that of continental Europe, with Nordic lawyers actively applying legal concepts and ideas from other countries. However, it was only rather late that so-called learned law and professional educated lawyers started to have an impact on law-making.

In the Middle Ages, important principles of local law were written down in all the Nordic countries, and even if many similarities can be found in the texts, significant differences also arose due to local peculiarities. In order to understand how law and legal contacts developed and functioned between the countries of the North, it is important to stress how the remains of earlier unions between the countries are still visible.

In fact, we may talk of a western Nordic group consisting of Denmark, Norway and Iceland, and of an eastern group consisting of Sweden and Finland. Denmark and Norway were united under the same King from 1380. Finland formed part of Sweden until 1809. The Danish-Norwegian monarchy (also including Iceland) and its law developed differently from the Kingdom of Sweden (of which Finland at that time formed part). In the late 17th century, Danish and Norwegian laws were unified on the basis of two major law books or codes (in principle containing basic rules in all fields of law), the Danish Code of 1683[17] and the Norwegian Code of 1687, the Norwegian Code being based on the Danish Code, leaving aside much of old Norwegian law.[18] Thus, Danish and Norwegian law were for centuries to a high degree virtually identical.

To a certain extent this idea of common Danish-Norwegian legal science also survived after 1814, the year Norway entered into a union with Sweden (until 1905)—but without adopting Swedish law. Sweden and Finland have always had a common legal basis, with its most material form in the shape of the Swedish Code of 1734.[19] Swedish law also remained the law of Finland and the Swedish language the official language[20] even after 1809, when Finland became an autonomous Grand Duchy (until 1917) within the Russian Empire. Still, the relation to Russia has had an impact on Finnish society as well as on societal and legal thinking, which may differ from that of the other Nordic countries. Especially, attitudes

[16]Tamm and Slottved (2009) and Björne (2002). See also Tamm et al. (2011).

[17]See Tamm (1984).

[18]Tamm (2011).

[19]See Wagner (1986).

[20]Today, Finland has two official languages, Finnish and Swedish; For instance, legislation is always published in both languages. Thus, in the following chapters references to the legislation in Finland can be found both in Finnish and Swedish.

towards law, have been more legalistic[21] in Finland than in the other Nordic countries. In addition, so-called Scandinavian Legal Realism played a less important role than in Sweden and Denmark. Furthermore, Finland became involved in Nordic cooperation later than the other Nordic countries, in fact only after becoming a sovereign state.

Nonetheless, strong links exist between Sweden and Finland, for example as to preparation of new legislation. In Swedish legal tradition, including judicial argumentation, preparatory works for new legislation (*travaux préparatoires*)[22] play an important role, as indeed they do in Denmark and Norway.[23] Reference to Swedish material has often been used when drafting new Finnish legislation. Indeed, the fact that legislation in Sweden and other Nordic countries is taken into consideration and referred to forms part of the preparatory procedure for new laws in Finland.

If such a development, which aimed at harmonizing the law, had not been counterbalanced by active legal collaboration since the 19th century, the Nordic countries might have continued as two or more clearly distinct legal groups within the civil law family. This cooperation, discussed later in more detail, was based not only on common histories and on the idea that the Nordic countries share a common idea of the law, but also on the conviction that the need for necessary legal reforms due to rapid developments, especially in international trade and commerce, could best be met by common efforts. Hence, Nordic legal collaboration not only has a long history. It has also achieved many concrete results, with common legal norms as examples, contributing to the feeling that such thing as a common Nordic "core" of the law does exist.[24]

Moreover, this active cooperation is a characteristic feature of what in a broader sense could be called "Nordic legal culture". A sense of coming from and having studied the law of a Nordic country is part of a Nordic lawyer's identity. The Nordic lawyers' meetings, which as we have seen started in 1872, have since then continued at different stages. Matters of common legal interest remain on the agenda. At the same time, these meetings, which are in principle only conducted in Nordic languages, have still contributed to the feeling among Nordic lawyers of having something more in common amongst themselves than with lawyers from other countries. At these meetings, participants are supposed to speak the language of their own country,[25] and to adapt their way of speaking to an audience which—not always without difficulty—is supposed to understand you. This means that the

[21]In the so-called Russification period during the decades before and after 1900, still during the autonomous period, legalism was a concept that referred to retaining Swedish legislation that was (still) in force in Finland as a symbol of "the rule of law".

[22]See further Husa in this volume.

[23]Wilhelmsson (1985).

[24]Carsten (1993).

[25]For participants from Finland, however, this means only the Swedish language. The Finnish language belongs among Indo-European languages and cannot be understood on the basis of knowledge of the other Nordic languages.

meetings also form part of a common Nordic legal identity across language borders.[26]

3 Common Ways of Legal Thinking

If we compare Nordic societies, many relatively well-known similarities clearly exist—indeed, some of these still play a role in the development of legal institutions and legal thinking. The countries are all rather small, and their societies quite homogenous and egalitarian.[27] For a long time, great majority of population was living on the countryside. Social and legal cultures have therefore been characterized as determined by a peasant or rural culture, as distinct from urban culture. At the time, you cannot neglect impacts of the strong Monarchy introduced in the waves of the Lutheran Reformation, which took place in the 16th century.

Both are rightly and often mentioned as important factors in understanding Nordic society and its legal institutions.[28] Here, so the argument goes, at least some reasons exist for the dominance of the Nordic idea of a "good" state and for implementing the idea of the social state, characterised not only by ways of organising conflict resolution[29] or institutions public law[30] but also by fundamental ideas of private law. A social dimension has been typical of Nordic legal thinking, for example with a focus on protecting the weaker party in contract law, especially in labour or consumer contract relationship.[31] One can also speak of one-norm societies with their interplay between state and church that could provide fruitful soil for modern, universal practices in Nordic welfare states.[32]

The Nordic countries were modernized relatively recently, generally speaking only during the 19th century, with the first wave of industrialization. In this process the state played an important role. At the same time, the Nordic countries are often characterized as countries in which the borders between civil society and the State are blurred. Indeed, the concepts of state and society do seem to be interchangeable in many ways. Hence, many societal and legal institutions have in a way been corporatist by nature in order to ensure representation of various social interests—for instance, boards with conflict-solving functions or committees for drafting

---

[26]Early results of this Nordic identity included the Nordic legal encyclopaedia (*Nordisk Retsencyklopedi* 1878–1899) and the Nordic journal *Tidskrift for Retsvidenskab* (today *Tidsskrift for Rettsvitenskap*, 1888–).

[27]See further Petersen and Niemi in this volume.

[28]Tamm (2010).

[29]See further Sunde and Nylund in this volume.

[30]See further Mäenpää and Fenger in this volume.

[31]Wilhelmsson (1994). See also further Bärlund and Moegelvang-Hansen in this volume.

[32]Stenius (2013).

new legislation.[33] At the same time, popular control and a common sense of justice have to varying degrees been brought into court proceedings through participation by laymen. Mention can also be made of state supervision of the legality of public administration by the (parliamentary) ombudsman—an institution with its origin in Sweden.

In all Nordic countries the public sector and public administration occupy a huge dimension and play an important role. The system of conflict resolution between public authorities and citizens varies to a high degree. Litigation between the administration and the citizen in Sweden and Finland is dealt with by specific administrative courts organized in a hierarchy which differs from that of ordinary courts. Other Nordic countries have no such organised administrative court system. For example, administrative cases in Denmark are dealt with by a plurality of different organs or boards. Most of these are set up for specific administrative complaints such as taxes, social legislation,[34] competition, environmental protection, energy providers, and consumer affairs, while the ordinary courts (with notable exceptions) normally have the last word in these matters.

4 Pragmatism and Realism

4.1 Against a Civil Code

Often Nordic legal peculiarities are described by using expressions: pragmatism, realism, absence of formality, an uncomplicated and understandable legal style, transparency, equality, and avoidance of extremes. These peculiarities of legal thinking can be forceful when maintained not by the Nordic countries individually but in common. The Nordic countries still feel that in these respects they are closer to each other than to other countries. This also explains a certain reluctance towards what is seen as trends in over-administration and centralization within the European Union. These values were also cornerstones of the original Nordic project of legal cooperation.

"Nordic-ness" is in some ways a consequence of the late professionalization of legal culture in these countries. For a long time one could speak of non-professional or lay-dominated legal cultures. This again has defined court systems and legal procedures,[35] but could also explain at least partly why Nordic legal culture is even today characterized by the term "pragmatism".[36]

[33]Letto-Vanamo (2014a, b).

[34]Tax law and social security complaints in Denmark and Norway are also decided by organs similar to ordinary courts. In these fields more similarities exist between the Nordic countries than in other parts of the complaints system.

[35]See further Sunde and Nylund in this volume.

[36]Zweigert and Kötz (1998).

In all the Nordic countries the most important source of law—and the key instrument for legal-societal changes—has been parliamentary legislation. Thus, the most important legal actor is the legislator. The countries do not have constitutional courts, and only seldomly the authority of the legislator is questioned by the judiciary.[37]

Ongoing European discussion of law addresses the question whether it is appropriate to collect rules in wide fields of law in written law books, so-called codifications or codes in the shape of systematic collections of law covering general principles and more detailed rules in several areas, and which are supposed to be the main source of law. In particular, the question has been raised whether codifications covering civil law, i.e. the law of obligations (in contract and tort), property law, family law, and law of succession, should be seen as a positive feature, or as one that complicates finding the law and causes stagnation in law-making.

Modern civil law codifications, including more or less detailed rules on general doctrines (principles) of civil law such as the French *code civil* (1804) or the German *Bürgerliches Gesetzbuch* BGB (1900), have been models for many countries covering all traditional fields of private law. After the fall of communism in 1991, work on codification was intensified in former Eastern-bloc countries. Indeed, the great majority of European countries today have a new or totally revised code on private law, considered as a national civil code which forms the basis of the law. Some countries even have a specific commercial code, which is also unknown in the Nordic countries even if some individual acts may have specific rules on commercial relations between professionals.

The Nordic countries, however, have been resistant to these large-scale law projects. They have chosen to enact the necessary legislation separately in discrete statutes, many of which were drafted on the basis of Nordic initiatives and discussions. Exceptions are found within penal[38] and procedural law. In Denmark, a code of procedure with more than a thousand articles came into force in 1919. The realistic, pragmatic approach, together with general democratization tendencies, led to reforms of legal procedure and the Swedish court system in 1948,[39] while similar reforms in Finland were realized only as late as the 1990s.

Within civil law, issues such as contracts, marriage or succession have been regulated by more or less independent acts, many of which are the result of common Nordic drafting and exchange of ideas. Indeed, the non-existence of broad, complex civil codes has enabled Nordic legislative cooperation. In Denmark, some important areas of law such as the general principles of tort law (on liability for non-contractual damages) are more or less exclusively based on the practice of the courts. At the same time, general doctrines (principles) of law have been developed, mainly by legal scholarship, while active cooperation with Nordic colleagues even today forms an important part of the daily work of many legal scholars.

---

[37] Wind and Føllesdal (2009); see also further Husa in this volume.

[38] See further Lappi-Seppälä and Nuotio in this volume.

[39] See further Modéer (2005).

There are also Nordic associations and/or yearly meetings for scholars and other lawyers within different disciplines, e.g. administrative law, criminal law, contract law and family law.

The idea that Nordic law should be codified in a complete Nordic code gained currency in 1896, when this work was carried through in Germany in the shape of the BGB, which came into force in 1900. German legal thinking and the drafting of the BGB were well known in the Nordic countries, and revived the old discussion of codifying civil law. In 1899 one of the more outstanding Nordic lawyers of the time, the Danish professor Julius Lassen, took the opportunity to launch the idea of creating a modern Danish civil code.[40] He was much driven by his interest in German systematic legal thinking but was also critical of the way the German Code was drafted. In this connection he mentioned that a common Nordic civil code should be the final goal. In Norway especially, this idea was seen as driven by some sort of megalomania, but in Sweden it was taken as a chance to revive Nordic legal cooperation, which after a very active start had somehow come to a halt. Inspired by Lassen, a member of the Swedish parliament took the initiative and proposed that Nordic legal cooperation should be extended to new fields.

This did not lead, nor was it intended to lead, to the drafting of a Nordic code. The scope was narrower when so-called civil law committees were set up in Denmark and Sweden (1901) and later in Norway as well. The first Nordic legislative programme was accepted, and legal problems concerning contract, sales and securities were seen as suitable subjects for cooperation. In the 1909 programme even family law issues were mentioned, with planned cooperation in the fields of marriage and economic relations between spouses.[41] There have been two standing committees, a civil law committee and a family law committee, in each country.[42]

The idea of creating a new Nordic civil law book was never seriously seen as a realistic option. Indeed, drafts were drawn up but the endeavour was never accomplished and these drafts never led to a Nordic civil code.[43] Creating a code, and even more a Nordic code, is a big issue, and much harmonization would be needed before such a project could seriously be considered. Nordic lawyers did not see such a project useful, and prioritised flexibility in law-making above creation of a coherent codified private law system including both general principles and detailed rules of several fields of private law.

---

[40]Tamm (2011), pp. 135–139.

[41]In family law especial objects of cooperation were marriage and divorce, property relations between spouses, guardianship and the relationship between parents and children. See further Lund-Andersen and Kronborg in this volume.

[42]In the field of civil law the most important results of Nordic cooperation were nearly identical statutes on sale, agency, and on the conclusion and nullity (non-validity) of contracts. See further Bärlund and Moegelvang-Hansen in this volume.

[43]Still, in 1948 the Danish law professor, Frederik Vinding Kruse, also acting on his own initiative, presented to the Nordic lawyers' meeting a draft of a Nordic civil code, and in 1962 a second draft.

Later proposals for a common European civil code also met attitudes among Nordic legal professionals that were more sceptical than enthusiastic. Even today, Nordic lawyers prefer discrete acts, which are easier to formulate and more flexible to amend, and which do not govern the law and legal thinking too much but allow pragmatism and judicial and scholarly interpretations to meet practical ends.

4.2 Realism

Nordic law and especially Nordic legal scholarship are heavily indebted to tremendous efforts, especially in Germany in the 19th century, to create a method of developing the law based on profound thinking on coherence in law and legal concepts. However, this thinking never became dominant and was gradually superseded by the idea of the law as serving social purposes, and thus having to be not only theoretically on a high level but also available as a tool for practical purposes. Great German lawyers such as F. C. von Savigny, Rudolf von Jhering and Bernhard Windscheid were familiar to leading Nordic lawyers, who might even have been among their students at some time.

Thus, it is important to stress that those lawyers who were instrumental within Nordic legal cooperation would have had a common background of legal knowledge based on German authorities, even if they represented different Nordic legal systems.[44] This was clearly the case in Finland and Denmark, whereas 19th century Norwegian lawyers were more critical towards the German approach. Still, when national legal scholarship[45] emerged in the Nordic countries during the late 18th and 19th centuries, this happened to a high degree based on German inspiration by adapting German legal ideas and relying heavily on textbooks by German legal authors. In this way, Nordic law became influenced by a Roman Law-based terminology and systematization, still visible today in the Nordic legal systems. At the same time, ideas of German legal scholarship and state theory played an important role in the development of public law in the Nordic countries.

However, it must be stressed that German legal thinking was not accepted uncritically. In particular, the work of the courts did not involve too much theoretical reasoning. We often talk of Nordic pragmatism in law. In other words, practical solutions have been preferred to those based on what in the Nordic countries is often seen as too much theoretical thinking or exaggerated abstraction. This tradition traces its roots back to the 19th century.

In Denmark one highly influential lawyer was Anders Sandøe Ørsted (1778–1860). In an impressive output of books and legal studies, to a high degree inspired

[44]Links do exist between Nordic law and the so-called "civil law family" represented e.g. by German law. But Nordic cooperation was still an important feature in creating and maintaining a way of legal thinking—and legal style—different from the highly abstract German approach.

[45]E.g. Montgomery (1889) and Lassen (1892).

by his reedling of contemporary German legal scholarship, Ørsted laid a basis in Danish and Norwegian law for a practical way of looking at the law.[46] From the 1920s, Nordic legal philosophy was influenced by the school of so-called Scandinavian Realism. This was mostly a Swedish and Danish phenomenon. In Sweden the main influence was the so-called Uppsala School, which made Scandinavian Realism as a philosophical school well known abroad, through such names as Axel Hägerström and Vilhelm Lundstedt. The Uppsala School had a significant impact on the thinking and argumentation of many Nordic lawyers, too. The Swedish lawyer Karl Olivecrona and the Danish lawyer Alf Ross are often seen as the most representative and internationally known legal scholar of the realistic movement. However, in Norway natural law thinking also came to play a role, while in Finland a more conceptual way of legal thinking truer to its German inspirations predominated.

Realism meant that legal theory was reluctant to recognize the importance of general legal concepts for argumentation and stressed that reflection on how the courts would actually reach their decisions was the proper object of the law. In this connection the concept of "*forholdets natur*" (the nature of the matter) or "*reella överväganden*" (real considerations) formed part of the basis of the Danish and Swedish doctrine of legal sources. At the same time, the idea of law as an instrument of "social engineering" formed a crucial element of Scandinavian realism.[47]

The dominance of German (conceptual) jurisprudence diminished in Finland, above all through influences from Analytical Philosophy and the so-called Analytical School of Law since the 1950s.[48] Analytical criticism focused mainly on "conclusions from concepts". But concepts were not neglected. They played a heuristic role—concepts were necessary for clarifying and classifying legal problems.[49] Today, legal principles have become important, but concepts are still in focus: they prepare the way for principles-based legal argumentation. Nevertheless, Finnish legal scholarship can be characterised as more theoretical than in the other Nordic countries.

At the same time, Finnish legal scholars share a view of three—almost equally powerful—legal actors (the legislator, the judiciary and legal scholarship), and the *ethos* of the active role of legal science as a means of changing the law and society.

---

[46]Tamm (1978).

[47]Pihlajamäki (2004) and Björne (2007).

[48]Influences in legal thinking were closely connected to Finnish philosophy of the 1960s and 1970s (e.g. von Wright and Hintikka), which was strongly influenced by Anglo-American analytical philosophy.

[49]The most important changes in Finnish society can be dated to as late as the 1970s. Since then it has become possible to speak of a welfare (social) state. The decade was characterised by various democratization and modernisation procedures: for instance, reforms to the school system, university education, and part of the court system. Approximation of legal science to other social sciences was required in terms of legal education at universities. Moreover, trends in legal research changed, visible e.g. in dissertations and other academic works pointing out the "social dimension" of law.

Legal scholarship, at least in the meaning of legal dogmatics, is understood as one—but just one—of the legal practices that continuously produce and reproduce the legal order. According to modern Finnish legal theorist Kaarlo Tuori, legal scholarship contributes to the development of the legal order through its very results, such as systematization of law. After a scholar's proposals have found general acceptance, for instance systematic divisions or new concepts, form an integral part of "legal-cultural pre-understanding" and also unfurl their heuristic effects in other legal practices such as law-making and adjudication.[50]

5 Towards Common Legislation

In general, the (early) procedure for creating common Nordic legislation could be described as follows. Work towards a common Nordic statute could start when one of the countries took on the task of preparing a written proposal that could be discussed by the national committees. After that the committees would meet regularly and conclude their work with a draft statute. With that in mind, each country prepared its own draft with necessary explanations. After that the draft could be submitted to the national parliament, and eventually be issued as a statute. The statutes were and are considered national law. Moreover, a national statute can easily differ from statutes on the same subject issued in the other Nordic countries. Nordic harmonization does not mean that statutes or legislation are necessarily identical, but on the other hand differences would normally not be too obvious. It should also be remarked that even if statutes are identical, national courts are free to arrive at their own interpretations of the law concerned.

Thus, the main players in achieving legal goals were the national committees or working groups. In each country, a committee was nominated to prepare a national draft. In the case of bills of exchange, a German statute on this theme was chosen as the model. The national committees worked and held meetings both separately and together before presenting their respective parliament with a draft statute. In the case of bills of exchange, the committees had worked so closely together that identical drafts could be presented and accepted as statutes in the 1880s. The next steps for legislative cooperation were common laws on commercial registration and statutes on registered trademarks. In the decades from 1872 to the 1890s, notable results were achieved in this way in terms of creating a common Nordic commercial law.

Nordic cooperation originated in a spirit of collaboration as something positive and useful in the field of law. Based on private initiatives and common, voluntary efforts, many concrete results were achieved. Active cooperation continued after World War II. In 1948, however, cooperation took on a more official dimension when the Swedish, Danish and Norwegian Ministers of Justice decided on a

[50]Tuori (2010), pp. 151–153.

common legislative programme including ten topics, and invited Finland and Iceland to take part in cooperation. At the same time, a permanent organ, the Nordic Committee for Legislative Cooperation (*Nordisk udvalg for lovsamarbedje*), was founded.[51] Later legislative cooperation was based on these programmes.

In 1962, Nordic cooperation acquired a written foundation in a treaty concluded in Helsinki. From a legal perspective, the Helsinki Treaty could be seen as a codification of former cooperation. But it has also been seen as a result of Denmark's and Norway's interest in cooperating with the European Economic Community (EEC). Thus, the Treaty would make Nordic cooperation visible in the eyes of "more formalistic Germans and Frenchmen" in negotiations on European cooperation.[52] According to the Helsinki Treaty, the Nordic countries would work for legal unity, for "uniformity of regulation throughout the Nordic countries in as many respects as possible". The aim is to attain the greatest possible uniformity in private law as was traditionally the scope of cooperation. However, the Treaty also mentions as a goal the promotion of unity as regards penal (criminal) law and penal sanctions.

In fact, close cooperation has long existed between Nordic researchers in penal (criminal) law,[53] while the capacity of criminologists has played an important role when execution of punishments has been under discussion. A Nordic journal of criminal law (*Nordisk Tidsskrift for Kriminalvidenskab*) was founded more than a hundred years ago. However, national politics often follow other lines: criminal policy has been an important political issue in most Nordic countries. This often leads to gaps between popular understanding and political goals, and recommendations by penal lawyers and criminologists.[54]

According to the preamble to the Treaty, the governments of the Nordic countries agreed that the provisions stemmed from a desire "to promote and strengthen the close ties existing between the Nordic peoples in matters of culture, and of legal and social philosophy, and to extend the scale of cooperation between the Nordic countries." In any case it was, and still is, important to point out that legal cooperation should be promoted within a community of common values. Secularism, democracy, respect for the individual, social considerations, and protection of the weaker party are often mentioned as Nordic values. These are also influential in legal matters.

At the same time, cooperation should be based on the principle of "Nordic utility" (in Swedish *nordisk nytta*), which means that cooperation should only take place where the common good of the Nordic countries can be achieved. The activity concerned should not only develop a Nordic feeling of unity but should also strengthen Nordic competence and competitive abilities. Thus, it is important to

---

[51]Boucht (1999).

[52]Wiklund (1987) and Petrén (1983). See also Wiklund (2000).

[53]See further Lappi-Seppälä and Nuotio in this volume.

[54]Träskman (2012).

consider whether the goal in a specific case tends towards achieving Nordic unity or simply exchanging information or more superficial harmonization.

In the 1970s, Nordic cooperation was formalized further with the founding of the Nordic Council of Ministers. Today, government cooperation in the area of legislation is led by the Nordic ministers of justice, who make up their own "Law Council". The key actor in practical work and in preparations for meetings of the Council of Ministers is the Committee of Senior Officials for Legislative Affairs, which consists of representatives of all the Nordic countries and autonomous territories. More generally, Nordic cooperation has been seen as part of intergovernmental cooperation based on Nordic conventions—covering issues of Nordic mobility of citizens, such as taxation, family relations, or social security.[55]

However, no conventions have been agreed in justice affairs, so that legal cooperation has continued on a traditional—informal and voluntary—basis. Still missing, though, are Nordic organs with supranational functions, such as the EU Court, or a Nordic *acquis*, or a binding set of common Nordic legal norms. Moreover, legislative cooperation is seen as a tool for the Nordic countries in their work in promoting the fundamental common principles of Nordic legislation.

6 Perspectives for the Future

After Sweden and Finland joined the EU in 1995, Nordic cooperation was seen as endangered, as already noted above. However, according to changes to the Helsinki Treaty (1995) Nordic cooperation is also seen as part of broader cooperation within the European Union. Nonetheless, the wish remains "further to renew and expand cooperation between the Nordic countries in the light of the greater participation by the Nordic countries in the process of European cooperation." Nordic cooperation lost some of its momentum after the 1990s, and it remains to be seen whether the recommendations of the Helsinki Treaty can be maintained. In many fields of law, Nordic cooperation seems to be merely a supplement to European Union regulation.[56] But, at the same time, unity between the Nordic legal orders was never so widespread earlier as it is today.

An important Nordic-related question today, therefore, is the future of Nordic legal cooperation, especially within the framework of the European Union.[57] Norway and Iceland are not members of the European Union but they are closely associated with the Union through their membership in the European Economic Area (EEA). Many tend, however, to underrate the impact of the European Union in this respect by pointing to Nordic cooperation as based on common tradition(s) and values rather than on specific economic goals (like that of the common market).

[55]Wenander (2014).

[56]Wilhelmsson (2005).

[57]Dahl (2005). See also Olsen and Svedrup (1998).

Others are more concerned that Nordic cooperation—based on goodwill, informality and ad hoc meetings among civil servants in Brussels—has lost its drive and its proactive nature, and that it needs to be revived; otherwise it will decline completely.[58] What remains is the fact that Nordic lawyers to a great extent belong to a Nordic legal community, even if many of them have lost their conviction of the importance of Nordic cooperation.

However, much has changed during recent decades. European legal harmonization has touched many fields of law. Consumer protection, once one of the main topics of Nordic cooperation, has been fully harmonized by EU legislation. Even criminal law has been partly Europeanised, with considerable impact on the one-time "Nordic rational and human criminal policy". Danish professor Ole Lando and the commission he chaired were successful in initiating the European Principles of Contract Law (PECL), thus furthering ideas towards a European civil code. Nordic legal scholars have participated in several European harmonisation projects (i.e. Draft Common Frame of Reference: Principles, Definitions and Model Rules of European Private Law, DCFR), EU jurisprudence has produced new legal principles, such as protection of legitimate expectations and proportionality, which have had an impact on Nordic legal thinking. More often, too, the English language is used even in communication between Nordic legal professionals.

In recent decades, Nordic legislative cooperation has also lost much of its former dynamism. At least, its nature has changed due to the fact that many important areas of law have been taken over by legislation within the European Union. Today, Nordic legislative cooperation can be characterized as "reactive" as opposed to "proactive". Thus, the agenda for discussions on Nordic uniformity of laws is mostly defined by the EU legislator and focused on proposals drafted in Brussels, or on national implementation of EU regulation. Moreover, legislative details are discussed instead of common legal principles.[59]

At the same time, Nordic attitudes to the European Union have been characterized as sceptical. In all the Nordic countries the democratic deficit, and problems of transparency in the EU, have been on the agenda. Today, the economic and political crisis has even increased criticism against the EU in Finland, which has been the only Nordic country to accept the Euro. Still, the real challenges to Nordic cooperation today do not seem to come from the European Union but from a weakening of the Nordic spirit. The tradition and also the framework including Nordic meetings, associations, journals, as well as legislative drafting procedures and the provisions of the Helsinki Treaty concerning Nordic legal cooperation still exist even in much wider fields than a hundred years ago. The main challenge today is how to maintain the Nordic spirit and to revitalize interest in protecting, or even furthering, common Nordic values.

[58]Backer (2018).

[59]Buskjær Christensen and Fenger (2009).

References

Backer IL (2018) Styrket nordisk lovsamarbeid: Muligheter og utfordringer. Nordisk ministerråd, Copenhagen

Bernitz U (2000) Nordic legislative cooperation in the new Europe—a challenge for the Nordic Countries in the EU perspective. Stockholm Inst Scand Law 39:39–45

Björne L (2002) Den konstruktiva riktningen—Den nordiska rättsvetenskapens historia, Del III, 1871–1910. Institutet for rättshistorisk forskning, Lund

Björne L (2007) Realism och skandinavisk realism—Den nordiska rättsvetenskapens historia, Del IV, 1911–1950. Institutet for rättshistorisk forskning, Lund

Boucht J (1999) De nordiska juristmötena och rättsgemenskapen i Norden. Defensor Legis 5:748–775

Buskjær Christensen M, Fenger N (2009) Nordisk samarbejde om gennemførelse af EU- og EØS-lovgivning. Realiteter og perspektiver. TemaNord 2009. Nordisk ministerråd, Copenhagen, p 575

Carsten G (1973) Hundert Jahre Nordischer Juristentag: 1872–1972. Rabels Zeitschrift für ausländisches und internationales Privatrecht (Rabel J Comp Int Priv Law), pp 80–100

Carsten G (1993) Europäische Integration und nordische Zusammenarbeit auf dem Gebiet des Zivilrechts. Zeitschrift für europäisches Zivilrecht, pp 335–348

Dahl B (2005) Har det nordiske lovsamarbejde udspillet sin rolle? In Árnason RT (ed) Forhandlingerne ved, Det 37. nordiske jurismøde i Reykjavík, Band 1, 18–20 Aug 2005, pp 155–173

Glenn HP (2005) On common laws. Oxford University Press, Oxford

Husa J (2004) Classification of legal families today. Rev Droit Comp 56:11–23

Husa J (2015) A new introduction to comparative law. Hart Publishing, Oxford

Husa J, Nuotio K, Pihlajamäki H (eds) (2007) Nordic law—between tradition and dynamism, Ius commune: European and comparative law series, vol 66. Intersentia, Cambridge

Lassen J (1892) Haanbog i obligationsretten—Almindelig Del. Gad, Copenhagen

Letto-Vanamo P (ed) (1998) Nordisk Identitet. Institutet för internationell ekonomisk rätt, Helsinki

Letto-Vanamo P (2013) Nordische Rechtsgeschichte—eine europäische variante? Z Neuere Rechts 35:112–124

Letto-Vanamo P (2014a) Nordic democracy facing the EU: traditions, myths and challenges. In: Fichera M, Hänninen S, Tuori K (eds) Polity and crisis. Reflections on the European Odyssey. Ashgate, Farnham, pp 217–234

Letto-Vanamo P (2014b) Judicial dispute resolution and its many alternatives: the Nordic experience. In: Zekoll J, Bälz M, Amelung I (eds) Formalisation and flexibilisation in dispute resolution. Brill, Leiden, pp 151–164

Lidbom C (1973) Den nordiska rättsenhetens problem idag. Svensk Juristtidning, pp 273–278

Matteucci M (1956) The Scandinavian legislative co-operation as a model for a European co-operation. In The Swedish Branch of the International Law Association, The Swedish Association for International Maritime Law (eds) Liber Amicorum to Algot Bagge. Stockholm, Norstedt, pp 136–145

Modeer KÅ (1998) Nordisk juristkultur en del av rättskulturen—Förändring och stabilitet. In: Letto-Vanamo P (ed) Nordisk identitet. Nordisk rätt i europeisk gemenskap. Institutet för internationell ekonomisk rätt, Helsinki, pp 1–14

Modéer KÅ (2005) Renässans för den nordiske juristen? Tidskrift utgiven av Juridiska Föreningen i Finland, pp 58–70

Montgomery R (1889) Handbok i Finlands allmänna privaträtt I. G. W. Edlund, Helsinki

Olsen JP, Svedrup BO (eds) (1998) Europa i Norden: Europeisering av nordisk samarbeid. Oslo, Tano

Petrén G (1983) Helsingforsöverenskommelsens tillkomst. Nordisk Tidskrift för vetenskap, konst och industri, pp 62–72

Pihlajamäki H (2004) Against metaphysics in law: the historical background of American and Scandinavian legal realism compared. Am J Comp Law 52(2):469–488

Smits J (2007) Nordic law in European context. Some comparative observations. In Husa J, Nuotio K, Pihlajamäki H, Nordic law—between tradition and dynamism, Ius commune: European and comparative law series, vol 66. Cambridge, Intersentia, pp 55–64

Stenius H (2013) A Nordic conceptual universe. In: Haggren H, Rainio-Niemi J, Vauhkonen J (eds) Multi-layered historicity of the present—approaches to social science history. University of Helsinki, Department of Political and Economic Studies, Helsinki, pp 93–104

Tamm D (1978) Anders Sandøe Ørsted and the influence from civil law upon Danish private law at the beginning of the 19th century. Scand Stud Law 22:243–265

Tamm D (1984) The Danish code of 1683: an early European code in an international context. Scand Stud Law 28:163–180

Tamm D (2011) The history of Danish law: selected articles and bibliography. Copenhagen, Djøf

Tamm D, Andersen P, Vogt H (eds) (2011) How Nordic are the Nordic medieval laws: proceedings from the first Carlsberg conference on medieval legal history. Copenhagen, Djøf

Tamm D, Slottved E (2009) The University of Copenhagen: a Danish centre of learning since 1479. University of Copenhagen, Copenhagen

Tamm H (1972) De nordiske juristmøder 1872–1972—Nordisk retssamvirke gennem 100 år. Nyt nordisk Forlag Arnold Busck, Copenhagen

Tuori K (2010) Ratio and Voluntas: the tension between reason and will in law. Ashgate, Burlington

Träskman P (2012) Finsk, svensk och nordisk straffrätt—och den europeiska—några reflektioner. In Hyttinen T (ed) Rikoksesta ja rangaistuksesta. Juhlajulkaisu Pekka Viljanen 1952. Turku, Turun yliopisto, 26 Aug 2012, pp 257–270

Wagner W (1986) Das schwedische Reichsgesetzbuch (Sveriges Rikes Lag) von 1734. Klostermann, Frankfurt am Main

Wenander H (2014) Fri rörlighet i Norden. Nordiska gränshinder i rättslig belysning. Juristförlaget, Lund

Wetterberg G (2010) The United Nordic Federation, Tema Nord 583. Copenhagen, Nordiska ministerrådet. Available www.norden.org/fi/julkaisut/julkaisut/2010-583. Accessed 21 June 2108

Wiklund C (1987) Helsingforsöverenskommelsens tillkomst. Nordisk Tidskrift för vetenskap, konst och industri, pp 328–343

Wiklund C (2000) 1962 års Helsingforsavtal—den första heltäckande nordiska samarbetstraktaten. In: Sundelius B, Wiklund C (eds) Norden i sicksack—Tre spårbyten inom nordiskt samarbete. Santérus Förlag, Stockholm, pp 91–103

Wilhelmsson T (1985) Den nordiska rättsgemenskapen och rättskälleläran. Tidsskirft for rettsvitenskap, pp 181–197

Wilhelmsson T (1994) Social contract law and European integration. Aldershot, Dartmouth

Wilhelmsson T (2005) Det bristfälliga nordiska lagstiftningssamarbetet och Helsingfors-fördraget. Nordiska ministerrådet, Lagstiftningspolitik—Nordiskt seminarium om lagstiftningspolitik, TemaNord 516. Nordiska ministerrådet, Copenhagen, pp 117–127

Wind M, Føllesdal A (eds) (2009) Nordic reluctance towards judicial review under siege. Nord J Hum Rts 27(2):131–141

Zweigert K, Kötz H (1998) An introduction to comparative law. Oxford University Press, Oxford

Nordic Model of Welfare States

Jørn Henrik Petersen

Abstract Characteristics, similarities and differences of the Nordic welfare states are developed based upon an analysis of a number of input, output and outcome measures. It is demonstrated that familiarity between the countries has to be established by outcome measures like the Gini coefficient and poverty ratios both mirroring aspects of the income distribution subsequent to taxation and transfer payments. It is argued that the Nordic countries share the basic value of equality, may be even 'equal dignity in hut and palace'. Irrespective of different choices with regard to instruments to achieve equality, the underlying ethos of the Nordic welfare states is the same. The chapter is closed by discussing a number of challenges facing the Nordic welfare states.

1 Introduction

In 1936 the Danish poet Hans Hartvig Seedorff Pedersen wrote a poem *Svanerne fra Norden* (The Nordic Swans) to be made public on 'the 1936-day of Norden' together with a poster illustrating the five swans.[1] The first verse of the poem runs as follows:

[1]Seedorff Pedersen (1951). The poem was printed in a private edition in 1946. In 1985 the poem inspired Finnish artist Kyösti Varis to draw a logo symbolising Nordic cooperation.

J. H. Petersen (✉)
Department of Political Science and Public Management,
University of Southern Denmark, Odense, Denmark
e-mail: jhp@sam.sdu.dk

© Springer Nature Switzerland AG 2019

P. Letto-Vanamo et al. (eds.), *Nordic Law in European Context*,
Ius Gentium: Comparative Perspectives on Law and Justice 73,
https://doi.org/10.1007/978-3-030-03006-3_2

On Northern shores they once did come to rest,
the five wild swans, in coats of silver shimmer.
A tinge of daybreak coloured every breast,
ere sunlight's fiery flame caused all to glimmer.
The mists' last wisps were gone. A mighty dome,
with dawn clouds' mountain splendour o'er waves' foam,
lowered its azure into depths of ocean,
where young, bright Northern lands rocked in slow motion.

The poem[2] illustrates the time-honoured idea of a commonality between Denmark, Finland, Iceland, Norway and Sweden. They are all swans. But a swan is not simply a swan. Different species exist, though they all belong to the genus Cygnus. In his fairy tale *The Ugly Duckling*, Hans Christian Andersen wrote: "Being born in a duck yard does not matter, if only you are hatched from a swan's egg". Were the Nordic countries' welfare states hatched from a swan's egg? Do they belong to the same species or are they only related by belonging to the same genus? To be or not to be—that is the question. Are the Nordic countries welfare states and in what sense? What are the commonalities and in which ways do they differ? These questions are investigated in this chapter by studying different input, output and outcome measures.

In 1993 Francis Castle[3] edited a book entitled *Families of Nations* based on the idea that it is possible to identify distinct families of nations, defined in terms of shared geographic, linguistic, cultural and/or historical attributes and leading to distinctive patterns of public policy outcomes. The idea followed from two observations: (1) groupings of nations exist that to varying degrees share common historical and cultural experiences and (2) families of nations defined in this sense appear, at least in some areas, to manifest rather similar policy outcomes.[4]

Denmark, Finland, Iceland, Norway and Sweden—until recently small ethnically and religiously homogeneous states each characterised by a strong sense of national identity—are frequently grouped together as the Nordic countries and seen as representing a particular Nordic Model of welfare states.

These countries share a tradition of democracy mirrored by an ingrained respect for popular participation, respect for civil, political and social rights as well as the rule of law. Taken together, these characteristics mirror what might be termed governance by compromise and consensus.[5] Seen in an international perspective they are characterised by high standards of living, a large public sector,[6]

---

[2]I am most grateful to the poet and translator John Irons for the translation.

[3]Castle (1993).

[4]"Civil law family" as a concept is discussed in Chap. "Nordic Legal Mind".

[5]These are the prerequisites for relying on an implicit, unwritten social contract.

[6]Debates on the difference between 'public' and 'private', so crucial in many other countries, have from olden days been of minor importance in the Nordic countries.

a comprehensive public system of cash benefits and services financed dominantly by taxation, an autonomous labour market working smoothly with the state, equality of status, limited stigmatisation, individually-based rights to benefits (as an aspect of citizenship), universality,[7] basic security for all, reliance on the tax-transfer-principle, emphasis given to services compared to in-cash benefits, investment in and provision of high-quality services for all, irrespective of ability to pay, poverty reduction and equal income distribution as important objectives, social solidarity and strong individualism going hand in hand, and so on.[8] The status of the countries as developed welfare states mirrors the goal of social cohesion as part of the self-understanding of the Nordic countries.[9] The characteristics mentioned cover partly institutional characters, partly outcome measures. The following arguments show that delimitation of the Nordic family has to focus on outcome measures.

Despite their similarities it is important to keep in mind that, strictly speaking, each social security system is a model of its own, since the societal environment and unique historical and political contingencies always enter into the making of a model.[10] It is reasonable, therefore, to regard the concept of "Norden" (the Nordic countries) as a model with five exceptions.[11] Thus, the relationship within the 'families-of-nations model' is more analogous to that of cousins than of siblings.

It ought to be mentioned that explicit Nordic cooperation in the field of social policy has taken place during the last hundred years.[12]

2 Welfare States and Expenditures

Whether examining the size of the public sector measured by general government expenditures (Fig. 1[13]) or social expenditures (Fig. 2[14]) as a share of gross domestic product, it is difficult to discern a family of Nordic countries. At least

---

[7]Universality is a contested concept. In this chapter it simply means that everyone is entitled to the same services and that basic services are largely provided free. Genuine universality is found in particular in provision of services in health and education.

[8]The Nordic countries obviously satisfy the Sandmo criteria for being developed welfare states. Individuals and families are guaranteed a minimum income irrespective of the market value of their endowments; at least part of individuals' loss of income due to social contingencies is offset; a basic level of services (health care and education) is provided free of charge to all citizens. But the criteria are met in such a manner that inequality and poverty are reduced to a greater extent than in most other countries. For the Sandmo criteria, see Sandmo (1991).

[9]Many Social Democratic-oriented researchers argue that the 'Nordic model' is a Social Democratic model. This view, however, is overly simplistic.

[10]Ólafsson (1999), p 75.

[11]Christiansen and Petersen (2001).

[12]Petersen (2006, 2011).

[13]OECD.stat, https://stats.oecd.org/Index.aspx?DataSetCode=NAAG#.

[14]OECD.stat, https://stats.oecd.org/Index.aspx?DataSetCode=SOCX_AGG.

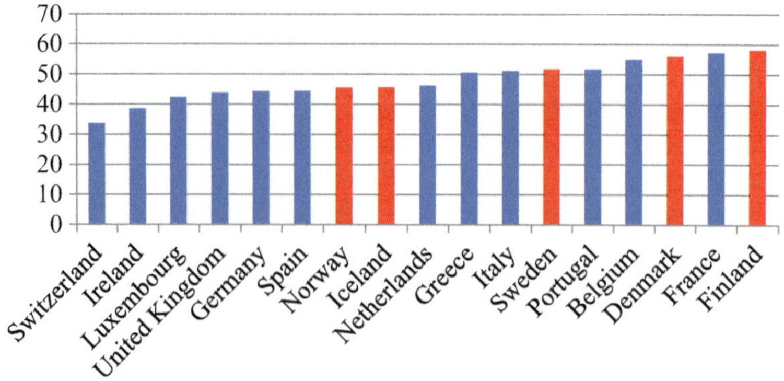

Fig. 1 General government expenditures as a share of GDP 2014

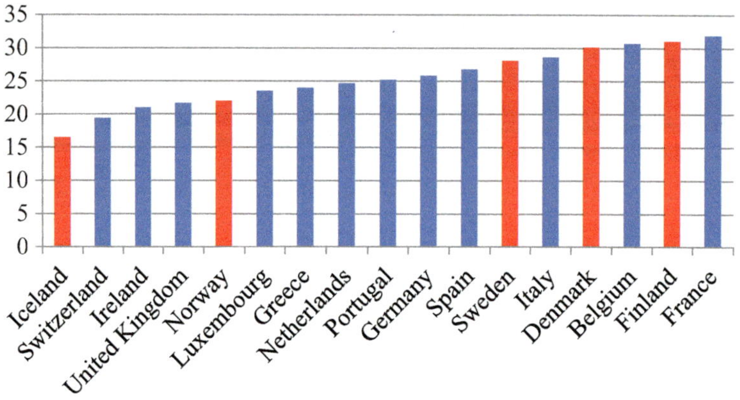

Fig. 2 Social expenditures as a share of GDP 2014

Norway and Iceland appear as outliers in terms of general expenditures, and the more so if one looks at the share of social expenditures.

This tells us little, however, because aggregate expenditures are a poor proxy for outcomes. The size of the public sector measured in one way or another does not pick up the impact on, say, poverty, equality or security, i.e. the very outcomes which social policy measures aim to modify. The number of elderly relative to the active population, the labour force participation rate, the number of unemployed, the number of single parents, income distribution prior to taxes, benefits and services, and so on, influence the expenditures necessary to achieve the desired post-tax-benefit distribution as well as the poverty level.

Nor do expenditure measures take into account how expenditures are spent. The redistributive impact of a given amount of expenditures depends on the manner in which expenditures are spent (and financed).

Expenditure levels, therefore, are not good indicators of family relations in Castle's sense across countries.

3 The Timing of Social Legislation

It is outside the scope of this chapter to examine the historical origins and developments of the Nordic welfare states in detail.[15] Let it be mentioned, however, that social security systems and public welfare services were established in several waves, all of them based on extensive planning regarding coverage, funding, benefit levels and administration.

A first wave, prior to and around the turn of the twentieth century, brought basic protection legislation, health insurance and pensions, but coverage and benefit levels remained low. Denmark was the prime mover, followed by Sweden and Finland. The second move followed around the great depression. A system based on 'social help', to some extent relying on discretionary measures, was replaced by 'social security', to a great extent relying on individual rights. The third wave occurred from the 1950s turning the 'social security state' into a 'welfare state'. Presently the countries seem to be placed in a transition phase in which elements of the classic welfare state are being eroded. One might speak of a gradual but slow journey with the so-called competitive state as the destination.

Although the timing of social security reforms differs across the Nordic countries, it is worth emphasising the weight given to the principle of universality as a contrast to reliance on targeting and status. Danish sociologist Gösta Esping-Andersen has developed a welfare-state typology partly relying on the understanding of labour as a 'fictitious commodity'. Therefore, he stresses de-commodification, i.e. the individual's greater independence from the labour market.[16] From another perspective, Finnish historian Pauli Kettunen has given weight to the idea of "a virtuous circle between efficiency, solidarity and equality" as a hallmark of the Nordic welfare states.[17]

Table 1 presents a chronology of legislative reforms in social security in the Nordic countries[18] as an illustration of the chronology of the development and a picture of the roots of the Nordic welfare states.

Industrial accident insurance was in place—with Iceland as an exception—around the turn of the previous century. Regarding sickness insurance, the laggards are Finland and Iceland. Denmark was the prime mover in pension

[15]For such a discussion see Christiansen et al. (2006), Baldwin (2001).

[16]Esping-Andersen (1990).

[17]Kettunen (2006).

[18]Flora (1983), p 337.

Table 1 Year of introduction of major social insurance laws in the Nordic countries

	Industrial accident insurance		Sickness insurance		Pension insurance	Unemployment insurance	
	Employers' liability	Compulsory	Subsidised, voluntary	Compulsory		Subsidised, voluntary	Compulsory
Denmark	1898	1916	1892	1933 (semi comp.) 1971	1891	1907	
Finland		1895		1963	1937	1917	
Iceland		1936		1936	1936	1956	
Norway		1894		1909	1936	1906	1938
Sweden	1901	1916	1891	1953	1913	1934	

insurance[19] followed by Sweden, whereas the three other Nordic countries were late-comers. Unemployment insurance saw Norway and Denmark as first movers with Sweden, and particularly Iceland, as laggards.

These observations do not make it easy to state familiarity between the Nordic countries and in principle it appears dubious to construct welfare state developments based on chronology, because timing cannot catch the relations between social policy discourses and institutions. Development in the seemingly laggard countries had in many cases to do with temporally long distances between the first definitions and debates of a problem and the solution, along with the concomitant practical consequences and applications.[20] It is for example interesting that all Nordic countries in the 1880s set up commissions to scrutinise aspects of the rising 'social question'.

A chronological perspective and distinctions between first movers and laggards do not rule out a family resemblance between the Nordic countries.

Despite scepticism with regard to expenditure measures mentioned above, Fig. 3[21] presents the growth of social expenditures over six decades (percentage point growth). In 1950 Iceland had the lowest expenditure rate (6.2%) along with Norway (6.3%). Finland was placed in the middle (7.3%) with Denmark (8%) and in particular Sweden (8.5%) being front-runners. During the 60s and 70s the growth

[19]Even though the Danish 1891 Act was a law on public support for the deserving old outside the law on poverty, it did represent introduction of the basic features of long-term benefits in the country: Universality, tax-financing and benefits related to current earning from other sources. It was basically different from the German 1889 Act, which actually served as a negative foil for Danish thinking on social policy. Denmark was marked by strong anti-German sentiments due to defeat in the 1864 war and the loss of Schleswig. It is important also to note that 'the Nordic model' was strongly dependent upon the international economy of the day. In fact early Danish social security was inter alia a response to globalisation of the economy. Petersen (1985).

[20]As an example Kettunen points to the very late passage of the Sickness Insurance Act *Sairausvakuutuslaki* 364/1963 in Finland, adopted as late as 1963. However, the topic had been on the agenda since the 1880s, and Ólafsson presents a number of examples from Iceland, see Kettunen (2001) and Ólafsson (1999).

[21]Nordisk Socialstatistisk Komité (1998).

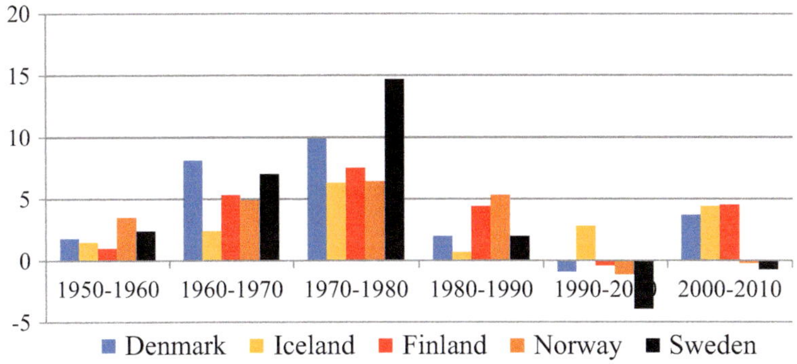

Fig. 3 Percentage point growth in social expenditures as share of GDP

of expenditures into solidarity and social security was strong indeed, in particular in Sweden and Denmark. Whereas the difference between the lowest and the highest spender-country in 1950 was 2.3% points, this had grown to 16.2% points in 1980. The figure shows that the growth pattern has been different across countries, but in 2010 those 16.2% points had been narrowed to 8.3 points.

Comparatively low Icelandic growth between 1960 and 1990 mirrors a desire to keep to a "Beveridge/New Zealand" model of low benefit levels with significant use of income-testing. This in turn mirrored the interest of restraining public expenditures and buttressing the embedded ethos of self-help. Ólafsson (1999) emphasises a strong work ethic, a strong sense of self-help and other individualistic values as characteristic of Icelandic society.

4 Financing the Welfare State and the Role of In-Kind Benefits

Frequently emphasised as a hallmark of the Nordic welfare state model is that it is funded by taxation. The correctness of this assertion, however, depends on how one defines taxation. Figure 4[22] shows social protection receipts by type. It reveals that almost 80% of Danish social receipts are funded by general government followed by Iceland collecting 56%. The three other countries rely to a greater extent on contributions paid in particular by employers. Nor does the pattern of social protection receipts suggest a close familiarity between the Nordic countries.

In a broader perspective one may—based on Fig. 5[23]—argue that the Nordic countries, Norway being a minor and Finland a major outlier, to a greater extent than most other welfare states spend social expenditures on institutional benefits.

[22]Eurostat, http://ec.europa.eu/eurostat/web/products-datasets/-/tps00108.

[23]OECD.stat, https://stats.oecd.org/Index.aspx?DataSetCode=SOCX_AGG.

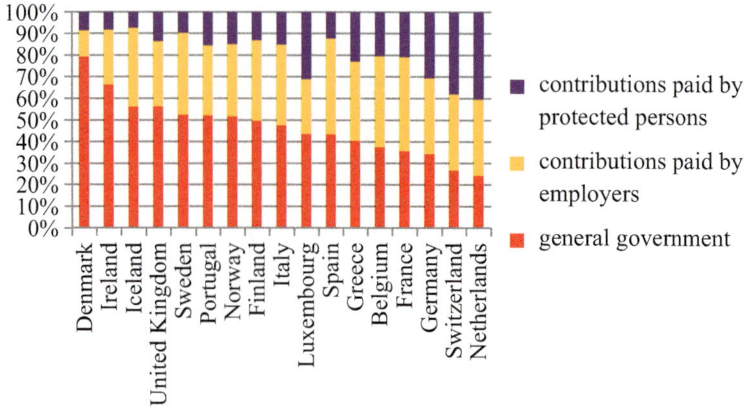

Fig. 4 Social protection receipts by type 2012

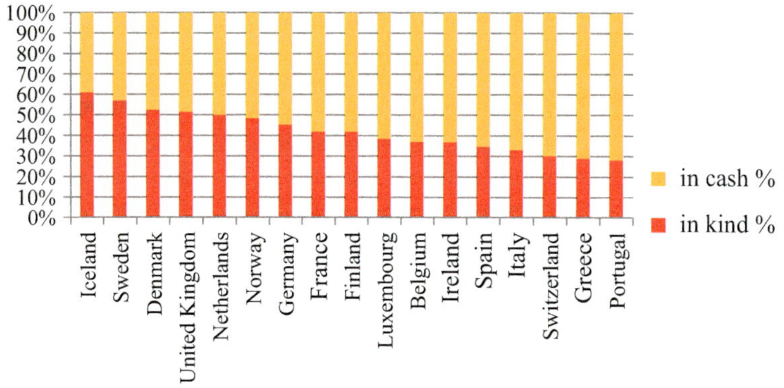

Fig. 5 Social expenditures on resp. in-cash and in-kind benefits 2014

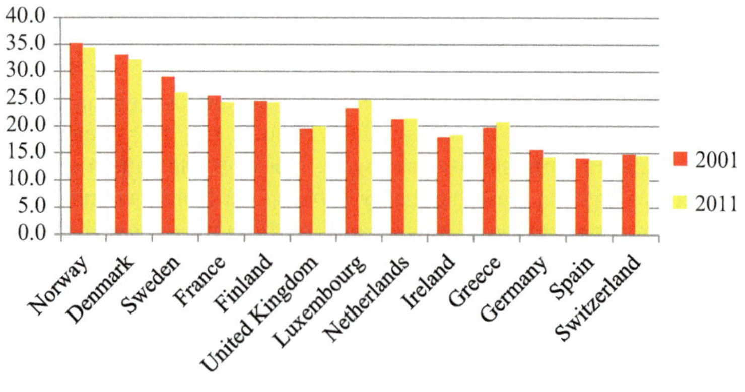

Fig. 6 Share of employment by general government and public corporations

These are by nature more universal than most cash benefits, and the observation is indicative of the weight attributed to universality in the Nordic countries.

A similar conclusion follows from Fig. 6,[24] which illustrates the share of employment by general government and public corporations. Norway, Denmark and Sweden are ranked as the three countries with the largest public employment. France sneaks in before Finland, but clearly the figure underlines a familiarity between the Nordic countries.[25]

The welfare sector (e.g. education, care-giving, upbringing) has a slow increase in productivity in comparison with other economic sectors. Assuming equal wage developments across sectors, this means that unit costs increase more rapidly in the production of welfare services than in the economy as a whole. At the same time, demand for not least welfare services tends to increase faster than income. The corollary is that total spending on welfare services tends to rise faster than GDP over time. The tax level, therefore, follows the same pattern. Obviously this is a problem of the service-intensive welfare state, which in a perspective of the future may increase the 'trade-off' between efficiency, competitiveness, growth on the one hand and reliance on equality on the other.

However it may be, the reasoning so far suggests that familiarity between the Nordic nations has to be established by measures more closely mirroring the outcome of different levels of general government (e.g. equality, the poverty ratio) rather than social expenditures, different timing in introducing social legislation, different financing structures and different patterns of expenditures spent on cash benefits and services (the characteristics of welfare state institutions).

5 Equality

Figure 7[26] shows the Gini coefficient both before and after taxes and transfers. Looking at the coefficient post-taxes and post-transfers, four of the Nordic countries rank first and only Belgium slips in before Sweden, ranked six. Equality of income distribution is a hallmark of the Nordic family.

---

[24]Government at a Glance 2013—© OECD 2013, http://www.oecdilibrary.org/docserver/download/4213201ec032.pdf?expires=1470922942&id=id&accname=guest&checksum=AA439A072DF1BD0CB617DD7A774FAE0B. Data for Iceland are not available. Data on public corporations for Belgium, Italy and Portugal are not available and thus these countries are not presented. Data for the Netherlands are from 2005 and are expressed in full-time equivalents. Data for Germany, Ireland, Sweden and the United Kingdom are from 2010. Data for Finland and Greece are from 2008 and data for Norway from 2007. Data for France are from 2006.

[25]Between 1970 and the mid-80s employment growth in the Nordic countries first of all took place in the public sector, in particular in Denmark and Sweden. The expansion of the service sector was mainly a welfare state phenomenon opening the path towards a strong increase in the women's labour force participation rate.

[26]OECD (2016), Income inequality (indicator). https://doi.org/10.1787/459aa7f1-en, https://data.oecd.org/inequality/income-inequality.htm.

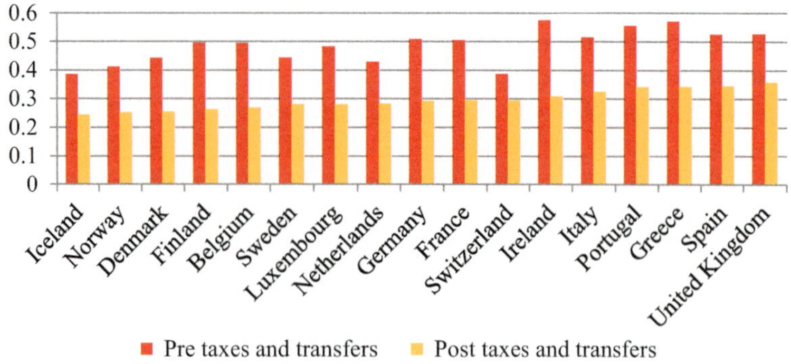

Fig. 7 Gini coefficients before and after taxes and transfers

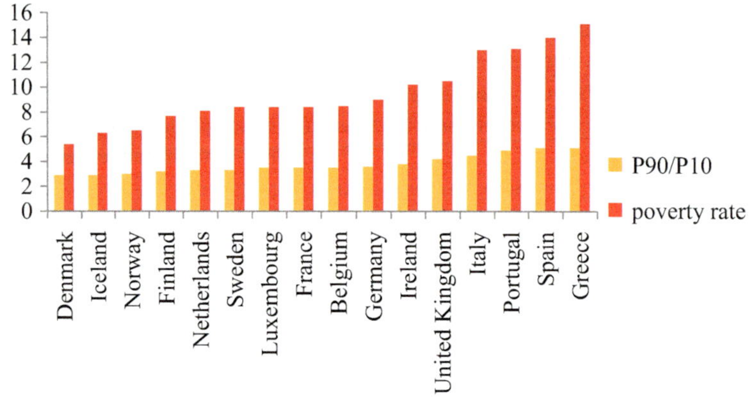

Fig. 8 Poverty ratio after taxes and transfers and P90/P10 most recent data

This finding is further strengthened if we take a look at two other outcome indicators: the poverty ratio[27] and the P90/P10-ratio.[28] Figure 8[29] also ranks four Nordic countries first, with only the Netherlands slipping in before Sweden, ranked number six.

[27]The poverty rate is the ratio of the number of people whose income falls below the poverty line; taken as half the median household income of the total population.

[28]The P90/P10 ratio is the ratio of the upper bound value of the ninth decile (i.e. the 10% of people with the highest income) to that of the first.

[29]OECD (2016), Income inequality (indicator). https://doi.org/10.1787/459aa7f1-en; http://www.oecd-ilibrary.org/social-issues-migration-health/data/oecd-social-and-welfare-statistics/income-distribution_data-00654-en.

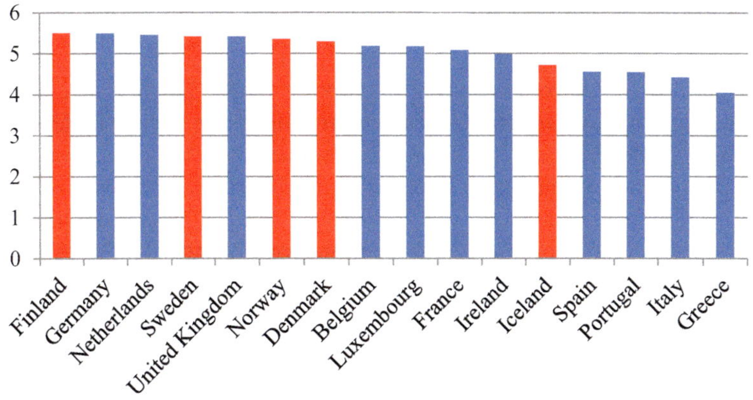

Fig. 9 The global competitive index 2014–15

Scrutinising two important outcome measures substantiates the view that it makes sense to talk about the family of Nordic countries sharing the basic value of equality, i.e. the underlying ethos of the Nordic model irrespective of the use of different instruments is to ensure equality, mirroring a belief that all people are of equal value.

A frequent claim is that a 'trade-off' occurs between equality and efficiency. However, part of the thinking of the Nordic family is that it is possible to combine the two, i.e. equalisation and competitiveness go hand in hand in Nordic thinking. Figure 9[30] shows the overall competitive index as measured by the World Economic Forum and based on 12 pillars. Among 144 countries, Finland ranks 4, Sweden 10, Norway 12, Denmark 13 and Iceland 30. With Iceland something of an outlier, the Nordic countries seem highly competitive despite their endeavour to promote equality. A similar picture emerges if one looks at data on GDP per capita.

The equal distribution of income and the security perceived by the single individual have facilitated adjustments to new technology and changes in the market. The low risk of poverty means that people are more willing to adjust to changed circumstances, which in turn promotes efficiency and competitiveness. Nordic thinking encompasses a belief in a 'virtuous circle' between equality, efficiency and social solidarity as important values. The Nordic model generates political support for growth-enhancing technological change, free trade and open markets because collective sharing of risks means that 'the winners' from structural changes compensate 'the losers', at least to some extent.

Despite the presumably weak economic incentives following from high tax wedges, a generous social security system and an equal distribution of income, the Nordic countries actually seem to succeed better than many other countries in terms of combining economic efficiency, growth, a peaceful labour market, equitable distribution of income and social cohesion.

[30]World Economic Forum (2014).

6 Challenges Facing the Nordic Family

During recent (and upcoming) years the Nordic family has had to cope with a number of challenges threatening fiscal sustainability. The common features of the challenges are that they are in one way or another related to labour force participation. The Nordic welfare state depends on a sufficiently high share of the population being employed. On the one hand social security ensures all unemployed transfer incomes, but the welfare state is simultaneously dependent on collecting its financial basis by taxation, the tax base being strongly dependent on the amount of work supplied. The Nordic welfare state, therefore, is preconditioned by high levels of employment for men as well and in particular for women. The Nordic model is an employment model simultaneously demanding modesty (among actual receivers of benefits), generosity (among actual contributors) and a strong willingness to work.

Figure 10[31] shows four of the Nordic countries placed among the five highest-ranked countries in terms of the labour market participation rate. Germany and the United Kingdom sneak in before we meet Finland.

Figure 11 presents a rough illustration of the social contract's ability to function. Its function depends on the relation between the area ABCD and that part of EFGH lying outside ABCD, i.e. the number of 'dependants' relative to the number of contributors. The size of EFGH depends on longevity/life expectancy, the number of immigrants and fertility and development of these variables over time, whereas ABCD is reduced by a rising average age of entry to the labour market, a lower average age of retirement and a reduced labour force participation ratio/ employment. The balance between those contributing to, and those benefiting from, the welfare state must be kept currently as well as over time.

Looking ahead to the future, the number of elderly will grow absolutely as well as relative to the active population. The first means rising expenditures for pensions, care and health services. The latter means that 'the implied burden' has to be distributed between the generations in one way or another. The change is driven by two factors: the "baby boom" effect as the large cohorts of the 1940s and 1950s reach retirement age and the effect caused by a continued increase in life expectancy.

Figure 12[32] shows a rough measure of the old-age dependency ratio for the Nordic countries. It seems that in particular Denmark and Finland are strongly affected, but the ratio is also increasing in the other countries—but to not such a high level.

Lengthening working careers must go hand in hand with increasing longevity, if the "social contract" is not to be based on the assumption that the "burden" can be shifted to future generations in the form of rising future tax rates. Work careers, therefore, have to begin earlier and be prolonged by a rising retirement age possibly

---

[31]OECD.stat, https://stats.oecd.org/Index.aspx?DataSetCode=LFS_SEXAGE_I_R.

[32]Nordisk Socialstatistisk Komité (2009).

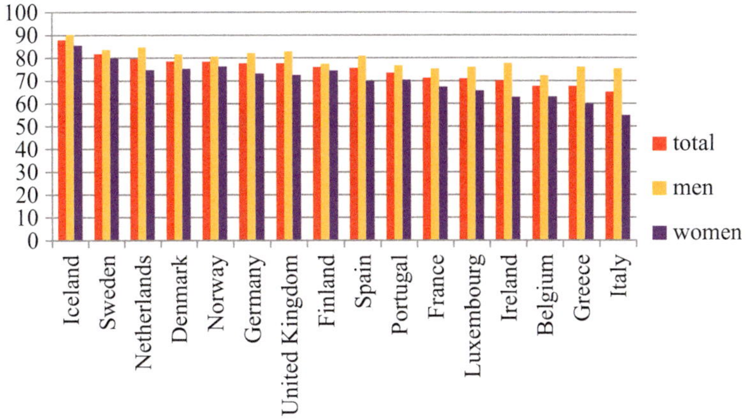

Fig. 10 Labour force participation rates 2015

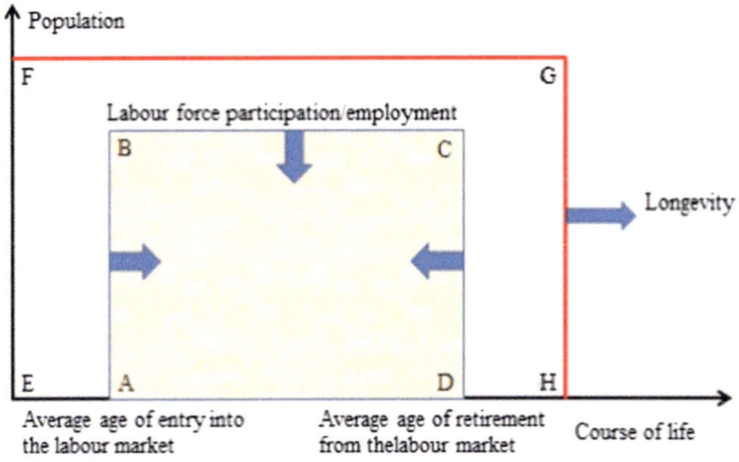

Fig. 11 Determinants of the social contract's ability to function

related to longevity by a mechanism of indexation. In addition, pensioners could be encouraged to continue working.

This problem related to rising old-age dependency ratios is not specific to the Nordic countries—on the contrary. This is seen from Fig. 13,[33] which shows the number of citizens over and above 65 relative to the number of citizens between 15 and 64 calculated to be in employment. The countries are presented ranked according to the increase of the dependency ratio from 2013 to 2050.

[33]See http://ec.europa.eu/economy_finance/publications/european_economy/2014/pdf/ee8_en.pdf. Data for Iceland were not presented.

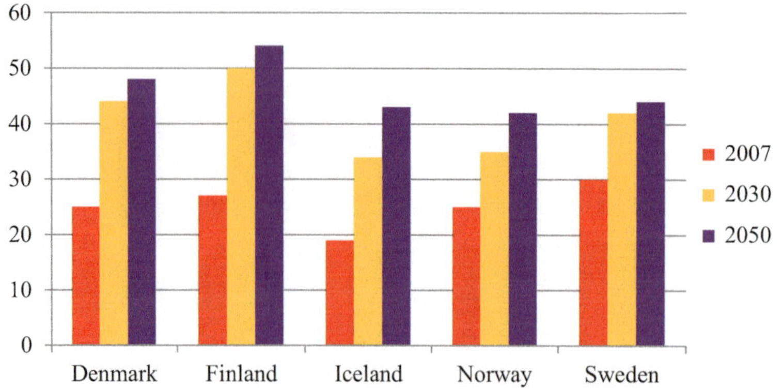

Fig. 12 Number of persons aged 65 and over in relation to the number aged 20–64

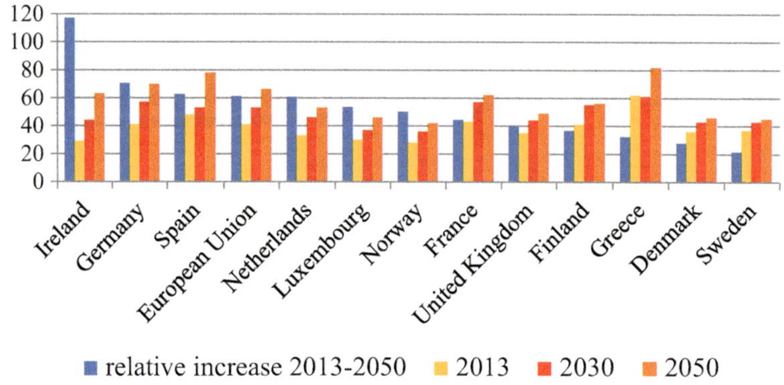

Fig. 13 Number of 65+ relative to the employed population 15–64

These alternative figures show many other European countries appearing with higher 'burdens' than the Nordic countries.

A second factor is increasing incomes and wealth. This is a challenge because it causes partly rising demands for services provided by the public sector and partly a stronger demand for leisure. The first means increased public expenditures, whereas the latter weakens the tax base.

Thirdly, technology and innovation—in particular in the health care sector—create new requirements and needs, and thus pressures on public expenditures.

Fourthly, globalisation creates requirements for continuous adjustments and reconfigurations, in particular in the labour market.[34] Open global markets benefit economic growth. The returns to production factors increase due to international

[34]Increased mobility of capital and labour across national boundaries may imply that adjustments of wages, working conditions, social benefits and tax rates are subjected to downward pressure.

exchange of goods and services and/or via international factor mobility. But the gains are not equally distributed. In the wake of globalisation will be 'winners' as well as 'losers'. Continued political support for open markets does not call for a dismantling of the Nordic model. Globalisation, in contrast, calls for preserving a security system based on a collective pooling and sharing of labour market and other risks.

Fifthly, increased levels of immigration as well as emigration cause a challenge. The Nordic welfare state model is a genuine national model in the sense that it presupposes that people are born in a territory, live their lives in the territory and die in the territory. The welfare state was designed on the basis of a culturally similar citizenry. Therefore, the model is threatened by migration.

Cultural belonging and political rights are intertwined, and "equality" is interpreted to mean two different things simultaneously: "cultural similarity" and "political sameness" (with regard to civic rights). Cultural homogeneity on the one hand, and the universal structures and ideological presumptions of the Nordic welfare state on the other, are central to understanding reactions to immigration and integration in the Nordic countries.

Immigrants from poor countries stand to reap the benefits, while the native population is exposed to a loss, i.e. the gains from migration are distributed asymmetrically. Immigrants from non-western countries and their descendants have generally been net beneficiaries of the Nordic countries' welfare states, because of lower labour market participation, higher unemployment and concomitantly more intensive use of the income transfer system compared to immigrants from western countries as well as native citizens.

To some extent this is an implication of the welfare state institutions themselves working from the supply side as well as from the demand side. The supply side builds on rather generous social benefits and small differences compared to minimum wages. This weakens economic incentives for labour market participation, in particular among low-skilled labourers. At the same time, generous social benefits exert upward pressures on minimum wages, which in turn reduces the demand for low-skilled labourers.

In terms of emigration, the important point is that entitlements to all kinds of benefit—in cash or in kind—are a prerogative of all citizens as individuals, whereas the costs of entitlements are collectively financed. In principle, this involves the risk that youngsters may take advantage of a tax-financed educational system and move to a country with a more advantageous tax regime and, similarly, citizens who have spent their working lives abroad may re-enter their home country after retirement to benefit from free hospital treatment and care-giving.

Figure 14[35] shows the number of foreign-born individuals from countries that are not members of the EU as a share of the total population. It is easily seen that

[35]Eurostat, http://ec.europa.eu/eurostat/statistics-explained/index.php/Migration_and_migrant_population_statistics.

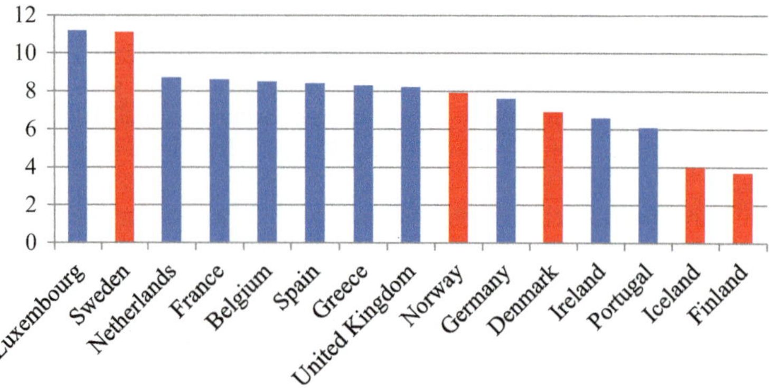

Fig. 14 Share of foreign-born population born in countries that are not members of the EU 2015

Sweden in particular is facing a problem, whereas the problem seems to be minor in Iceland and Finland.

In particular, Danish society and Danish politics have had difficulties adjusting to a different, multiethnic population compared to the situation only 20 years ago. The issue became heavily politicized throughout the 1990s, receiving extra impetus through the establishment in 1995 of the Danish People's Party, which mobilised electoral support on the immigrant issue above all others. In the wake of the recent influx of foreigners to Europe, the problem has become of crucial importance in Sweden.

To an increasing extent, immigrants are seen as an unwelcome presence because cultural assimilation has been more difficult than originally expected, and awareness has been growing of the financial burden that newcomers place on the welfare system. At the same time, negative stereotypes of immigrants ("welfare scroungers"/"refugees of convenience") have become common. In the opinion of many, they are seen as unfairly taking advantage of a system never intended for their benefit.

Even though the challenges with regard to sustainability are substantial, the solution to these problems is to a large extent—at least in a technical perspective—politically controllable, but taken together they give rise to a sixth and more basic challenge, namely how to reform the system without losing the basic values of promoting equality and combating poverty. From this point of view the challenges represent the greatest threat to maintaining the Nordic model.

The Nordic countries have all responded to these challenges by introducing reforms of numerous social welfare schemes. I shall not enter into a discussion of these changes but will instead close the chapter by some reflections more of principle in nature.

7 From Welfare State Towards Competitive State?

The problems of the Nordic welfare states have to do with a number of tensions embedded from day one—self-destructive mechanisms.[36] The most important of these—from which others follow—is the tension between, on the one hand, the generous, modest and work-willing 'welfare-state man' disregarding his own wishes and interests so as to help the needy and, on the other hand, 'economic man', who is always insisting on a return for his efforts and always having an incentive to free-ride, to engage in rent-seeking and to take advantage of possible asymmetric information.

Economic man is always tempted to insist on reciprocity (deservingness) as a basis for support at the cost of the ethically-based unilateral demand, and he is tempted to take advantage of unconditional benefits. This was and is the basic dilemma of the Nordic welfare state.

In Nordic mythology, one comes across Særimner the pig, which was slaughtered and eaten every day, but recreated every evening. The welfare state mirroring the societal community is not Særimner and is not an inexhaustible well; but motivated as economic men we all tend to think that it is all about getting as much as possible in return for a given effort or achieving a given result for the least possible effort.

Therefore, a basic tension exists between the ethical demands raised by the welfare state as characterized in Sect. 1—the welfare state's order of being—which it cannot guarantee itself, and the private economic rational incentives imbibed with one's mother's milk. A welfare state realising its underlying normative standards demands that men behave irrationally in a private economic sense.[37] The welfare state is facing a clash between the well-known *homo oeconomicus* and *homo generosus*—private versus societal man.

It is reasonable to see the aim of Social Democratic policies of culture preceding and during the building of the classic welfare state as an endeavour to develop welfare-state man. As written by former Danish minister of education and minister of foreign affairs K.B. Andersen as early as 1954[38]:

> If in the name of individualism we give too much emphasis to personal self-realisation, a competition mentality and egoism as societal driving forces, we have to give up the hope of moving away from existing society and its anxiety and insecurity. If we do not dare to make sense of community, solidarity and the cooperating will to decisive views we have no hope of building a society by a basically different structure than the one we have.

Similarly, Danish theologian and Social Democrat Hal Koch[39] would develop a school for citizens who cared for 'the common cause' and were willing to take

[36]On the idea of self-destructive mechanisms, see Petersen (2014), in particular, pp 175–189.

[37]Andersen (1983, 1984a, b).

[38]Andersen (1954).

[39]Koch (1956).

responsibility for life among fellow-beings in the family, neighbourhood, workplace, parish, the municipality and in society. Men had to be educated to engage in common affairs, for societal understanding and development of character. Common and shared responsibility was a precondition for a true democracy and for living in compliance with the welfare state's order of being. Too many people saw the state as an enemy and thought and acted antisocially. This revealed a societal immaturity which called for training of citizens' character. Too many acted as "private individuals", whereas only a few acted as "societal individuals".

The welfare state's dilemma is about economic incentives versus habits of the heart. The issue at stake is whether ethics can govern one part of society and selfishness another.

In principle, it is the acts of individuals that determine whether we live up to the welfare state's order of being. A unilateral welfare state is a morally demanding project which we as individuals have not been able to honour. When politicians to a growing extent adopt regulations on *quid pro quo* principles, when unilateral benefits are abolished, when societal responsibility is toned down in favour of personal responsibility, when solidarity with the needy is displaced by solidarity with the working, when contractual arrangements are extensively used, and so on, it signals their understanding that we are not acting as welfare-state citizens but are deviating from the straight and narrow path. It looks as if the classic welfare state suffers from embedded self-destructive forces.

Where do these observations lead us? The political rhetoric seems to rely on a tacit—rarely spoken—assumption that no room exists in society for dependent people—those outside the labour market. Dependence has become a bogey word—a position which decent people should avoid. But this very underlying assumption neglects the point that dependence and ethics go hand in hand.

Despite the disciplining work-fare line, the gap between the working and the dependent group is widening, and it is difficult not to see the initiative as being primarily motivated by a concern for the independent and employed group. In the competition state paradigm, keeping the needy in a decent human condition does not make much 'economic sense'.

From a perspective of declining rights and increasing obligations, the political rhetoric and the implications of activation policies for citizenship are negative. Where administrations use activation measures to discipline the marginalised, activation even becomes a punitive measure which may deter people from seeking help.

The political rhetoric has further had the side-effect that people talk without batting an eyelid about those who sponge, cheat and abuse societal benevolence and that the needy are seen as inept and lazy idlers who are not only unable, but unwilling to work, preferring to live at the expense of hard-working taxpayers. They are simply seen as a 'burden on society' whose disappearance seems to be the eventual aim of so-called welfare policies. The needy are not, as in former days, objects of pity and compassion. Rather they are turned into objects of resentment and anger. Adoption of the competition state paradigm as a belief beyond doubt means that the welfare state is on the defensive and that ethical thinking is experiencing hard times.

References

Andersen KB (1954) Folkeoplysning og samfund. In: Krag JO (ed) Tidehverv og Samfundsorden. Forlaget Fremad, Copenhagen

Andersen BR (1983) Two essays on the Nordic welfare state. AKF's Forlag, Copenhagen

Andersen BR (1984a) Kan vi bevare velfærdsstaten? AKF's Forlag, Copenhagen

Andersen BR (1984b) Rationality and irrationality of the Nordic welfare state. Daedalus 113(1): 109–139

Baldwin P (2001) The politics of social solidarity: class bases of the European welfare state 1875–1975. Cambridge University Press, Cambridge

Castle F (ed) (1993) Families of nations. Dartmouth Publishing House, Aldershot, Brookfield, Hong Kong, Singapore, Sidney

Christiansen NF, Petersen K (2001) Preface. Scand J Hist 26(3):153–156

Christiansen NF, Petersen K, Edling N, Haave P (eds) (2006) The Nordic model of welfare. A historical reappraisal. Museum Tusculanum Press, Copenhagen

Esping-Andersen G (1990) The three worlds of welfare capitalism. Polity Press, Cambridge

Flora P (1983) State, economy, and society in Western Europe 1815–1975. A data handbook. Volume I: the growth of mass democracies and welfare states. Campus Verlag, Chicago

Hichs A, Misra J, Ng TN (1995) The programmatic emergence of the social security state. Am Sociol Rev 60(3):329–349

Jonsson G (2001) The Icelandic welfare state in the twentieth century. Scand J Hist 26(3):153–267

Kettunen P (2001) The Nordic welfare state in Finland. Scand J Hist 26(3):225–247

Kettunen P (2006) The power of international comparison: a perspective on the making and challenging of the Nordic welfare state. In: Christiansen NF, Edling Ni, Haave P, Petersen K (eds) The Nordic model of welfare. Museum Tusculanum Press, Copenhagen, pp 31–66

Klaus S (ed) (2014) The global competitiveness report 2014–2015. World Economic Forum, Geneva

Koch H (1956) Staten en fjende. Politiken, 2 Dec

Nordisk Socialstatistisk Komitė (1998) Social tryghed i de nordiske lande. In: Nordic statistical yearbook. Nordisk Socialstatistisk Komité, Copenhagen

Nordisk Socialstatistisk Komité (2009) Old-age pension systems in the Nordic countries. In: Report 35. Copenhagen Schultz Information

Ólafsson S (1999) The Icelandic model. In: Bouget D, Palier B (eds) Comparing social welfare systems in Nordic Europe and France. Maison des Sciences de l'Homme Ange-Guépin, Nantes, pp 61–81

Petersen JH (1985) Den danske alderdomsforsørgelseslovgivnings udvikling I. Odense Universitetsforlag, Odense

Petersen JH (2014) Pligt & Ret, Ret & Pligt, Refleksioner over den socialdemokratiske idéarv. Syddansk Universitetsforlag, Odense

Petersen K (2006) Constructing Nordic welfare? Nordic social political cooperation 1919–1955. In: Christiansen NF, Petersen K, Edling N, Haave P (eds) The Nordic model of welfare. A historical reap-praisal. Museum Tusculanum Press, Copenhagen, pp 67–98

Petersen K (2011) National, Nordic and trans-Nordic: transnational perspectives on the history of the Nordic welfare states. In: Kettunen P, Petersen K (eds) Beyond welfare state models, transnational historical perspectives on social policy. Edward Elgar, Cheltenham, Northampton, pp 41–64

Sandmo A (1991) Economists and the welfare state. Eur Econ Rev 35:213–239

Seedorff P (1951) Svanerne fra Norden. Gyldendal, Copenhagen

Constitutional Mentality

Jaakko Husa

Abstract Nordic Constitutions have both differences and similarities. This chapter explains certain key differences by reflecting legal-cultural and historical dimensions of living Nordic constitutional law. The underlying idea is to offer a thematic and comparative overview. First, the general comparative context of Nordic constitutions is explained shortly. Secondly, chosen key feature of each constitution is thematically highlighted. In Finland's case, the focus is on the role of the parliament's Constitutional Committee as the guardian of constitutionality. When it comes to Sweden, the focus is on the exceptionally central position of its parliament. Section for Norway explains the central role of the Supreme Court. Discussion on Denmark centres on national sovereignty. In the case of Iceland, the new creative manner of reforming constitution is addressed. Final section speaks of the Nordic experience—or "Nordicness"—and questions its future in the world of expanding judicial review.

1 Introduction

If we focus on constitutional law, the macro-conceptualisations of mainstream comparative law have very little to say. In other words, the general characterisations of comparative law are virtually useless in terms of constitutional law. If and when Nordic systems are viewed from a comparative constitutional perspective, however, certain commonalities are discernible. But there are also differences. The following analysis in this chapter is not doctrinal but, rather, reflects legal-cultural and historical dimensions of living Nordic constitutions.[1]

[1]This is a rational choice in the comparative constitutional approach because written constitutional documents are not really power maps. Instead, they may be inaccurate or, as Mark Tushnet puts it, "The realities of power may not be fully reflected in a constitution", Tushnet (2015), p 11.

J. Husa (✉)
Faculty of Law, University of Helsinki, Helsinki, Finland
e-mail: jaakko.husa@helsinki.fi

© Springer Nature Switzerland AG 2019
P. Letto-Vanamo et al. (eds.), *Nordic Law in European Context*,
Ius Gentium: Comparative Perspectives on Law and Justice 73,
https://doi.org/10.1007/978-3-030-03006-3_3

The underlying idea of this chapter is to offer a thematic overview of the Nordic constitutions. Because of limited space there is no point in trying to describe constitutions descriptively in such a manner that would be easy to replace by internet searches or reading English translations of constitutional documents. Instead, this chapter briefly explains the context and generalities of the Nordic constitutions comparatively and then quickly moves to thematically highlight and characterise chosen key features of each constitution. Crucially, the stress in this chapter is placed on distinctive features; the observations are general and should thus be treated with some caution.

In the case of Finland the focus is on the role of the parliament's Constitutional Committee as the guardian of constitutionality. As for Sweden, the focus is on the exceptionally central position of its parliament. As for Norway, this paper discusses the central role of the Supreme Court. In the case of Denmark, discussion centres on national sovereignty. When it comes to Iceland, the new creative manner of reforming constitution is highlighted. Moreover, this chapter shortly addresses the protection of human rights in the Nordic systems, especially in dialogue with the European Convention on Human Rights (ECHR). However, before individual country discussions, the following section offers a general comparative overview of the Nordic constitutional landscape.

2 The Nordic Constitutional Landscape

2.1 Constitutional Mentality

Even while the abovementioned classifications offered by comparative lawyers are not especially fruitful in the case of Nordic constitutional law, certain useful comparative notions may be utilised in this context. To begin with, Nordic legal systems clearly possess some features of the continental legal tradition.[2] These features are, however, not completely identical: legal systematics is—basically—continental in upholding the division between private and public law. Key constitutional documents (constitutional or equivalent Acts) in the Nordic countries are written or codified even though they are supplemented in various ways by other formal Acts, amendments, constitutional conventions or customary constitutional rules and praxis. Crucially, Nordic systems favour a specific idea of the constitutional Act with *lex superior* status, where constitutional Acts are located at the peak of the national hierarchy of legal norms. This feature separates Nordic constitutions from such common law constitutional systems as the UK and New Zealand.

In comparative overview, the question of safeguarding constitutionality holds an important position. Nordic systems employ some kind of mechanisms for reviewing

---

[2]This part of the chapter draws on Husa (2002), see especially Chap. 6.

the constitutionality of legislation.[3] Accordingly, these systems presuppose some form of separation of powers. Nevertheless, there are different constitutional arrangements as to how judicial review is organised. Denmark does not have an explicit constitutional provision concerning judicial review. However, it hesitantly recognises judicial review as part of its systems. Finland and Sweden have explicit written constitutional provisions concerning judicial review, although in practice judicial review is resorted to cautiously. Norway added judicial review by an amendment to its Constitution Act in 2014.

A significant general difference nevertheless exists between levels of judicial activism. Sweden, Finland, Denmark and Iceland all accommodate de facto judicial self-restraint, whereas Norway's judicial self-restraint is clearly less cautious. Differences in judicial review are also reflected elsewhere: Sweden and Finland do not strictly follow the principle of separation of powers, whereas Norway and Denmark are perhaps inclined more towards separation of powers, although in a parliamentary form.

Given these points, we may speak of a Nordic constitutional mentality which is visible, among other things, in the ways that supreme courts take into account the will of the legislator. The Nordic conception of democracy is of utmost importance in this context. In effect, Nordic judicial systems hold great respect for their national parliaments as democratically chosen legislators. This is reflected in the use of preparatory legislative works as a recognised source of law. Even though the Norwegian Supreme Court has been the most active, it prefers to seek to avoid open power conflicts with the Norwegian parliament.

Some common law-type features can also be found in the Nordic systems. For instance, all Nordic systems have room for norms or doctrines that are unwritten but still hold a notable constitutional position. To illustrate, in Norway the case law of its Supreme Court occupies a focal position.[4] Additionally, certain parts of the constitutional Act that deal with the monarch are de facto in a state of *desuetudo*, especially in Norway. Likewise, the Finnish system contains some customary elements such as the de facto binding force of opinions of the Constitutional Committee of Parliament and the position that (external academic) constitutional specialists enjoy in the a priori form of control.

Consequently, all this provides a view to a legal thinking that is more pragmatic (lacking formalism and deductive and scholarly nature of German-style *Juristenrecht*) than in the civil law legal family. However, the distinction between public and private law stemming from Roman law is clearly a common feature with civil law, although the distinction is not sharp in the Nordic systems as, for example, may be seen by the fact that Denmark, Norway and Iceland have no separate administrative courts, which is regarded as one of the hallmarks of the continental notion of law. Besides, all the Nordic systems are parliamentary.

---

[3]See also Hautamäki (2007).

[4]According to Svein Eng, the Norwegian Supreme Court may become closer to the "discursive English style" in the future, Eng (1997), p 214.

Denmark, Norway, Iceland and Sweden are plainly parliamentary systems, as indeed is Finland, especially after the total reform of its Constitution in 2000. Notably, in Finland the president's role was diminished when the position of the parliament and the cabinet was strengthened, so that Finland moved closer to other Nordic systems in this respect.

Correspondingly, the fact that the Nordic parliaments play such a crucial role is one of the reasons for the cautiousness of Nordic forms of judicial review (with the possible exception of Norway): not much room is available for courts to quarrel with a highly legitimate national parliament. Moreover, the contextual constitutional landscapes are generally quite close to each other: relatively small Evangelical-Lutheran populations, multiparty systems, a high standard of living, an ideology of gender equality, a high level of development, and generally shared ideas about the modern welfare state.[5]

2.2 *The Key Position of the Parliament*

As already noted above, the parliament holds a central position in the Nordic systems as the legislative organ representing the people. However, respect for the will of the legislator does not take the same form as, for example, in France, where the judicial style of the courts is less argumentative than in the Nordic systems; Nordic forms of judicial decision-making do not stick so closely to the written statutory text but seek a rather more general argumentative base for justificatory purposes. Similarly, a certain general Nordic doctrinal openness of argumentation is discernible; in this way it differs from sparse French and German lengthy pedantic style. Furthermore, none of the Nordic supreme courts plays such a clearly political role as do continental constitutional courts. With this in mind, the implicit doctrine of the 'political question' is to be found in all Nordic systems; the politicisation of courts is not applauded in the Nordic systems since it is the national parliaments that hold the role of legislator. Accordingly, none of the supreme courts or other controlling organs possesses the competence to formally nullify parliamentary Acts.

Under these circumstances, Nordic supreme courts and other constitutional control organs have traditionally played a stabilising and mediating role between various branches of state public power. In short, "[i]n Nordic countries, it is universally accepted that it is elected politicians who should take the most important decisions in the public sphere".[6] For these reasons, courts generally speaking fulfil only a minor role as constitutional players; courts perform their judicial functions but that is mostly all that there is to it.

---

[5]For more detailed, though slightly outdated, analysis of Nordic constitutionalism see Scheinin (2001).

[6]Cameron (2009), p 72.

On the whole, constitutional law in the Nordic sphere is not all about codified or written rules. For instance, in Norway and Denmark, constitutional Acts are held as important national symbols, not merely a collection of written rules. However, in Finland, Sweden and Iceland, constitutional Acts do not perform equally strong symbolic functions, so that interpretation of the constitution is slightly more pragmatic.

All in all, the Nordic version of constitutionalism contains a few common macro-elements, including legal, cultural and political elements. These can be listed as follows: a parliamentary system with a mixture of separation of powers as political meta-ideology; consensual democracy (avoidance of open conflict, multi-party system); cautious systems of judicial review (judicial self-restraint, no strong culture of rights); respect for the will of the legislator (avoidance of conflict between the parliament and supreme courts; significance of preparatory works as a source of law); the political question doctrine in use by the courts[7]; no separate constitutional courts; a combination of written and unwritten rules and principles (constitutions also contain customary material); a spirit of constitutionalism and rule of law (general respect for the rules of the constitution within parliamentary frames; effective hierarchy of rules, i.e. constitutional Acts are not political manifestos; doctrine of separation of powers); and a pragmatic and practical legal style.

Finally, we may also note that Nordic constitutions seem to maintain a certain degree of flexibility: although constitutional Acts are written, alteration takes place in various forms, i.e. by formal amendment, custom, convention, and case law.[8]

The greatest differences appear between the eastern and western members of Nordic law; by extending the family metaphor one might say that Sweden and Finland are the eastern brothers of Denmark, Norway and Iceland in the west. Sweden and Finland are (or at least have been) closer to each other than the country-pair of Denmark and Norway. Denmark, Norway and Iceland are NATO members whereas Finland and Sweden are militarily neutral countries, although this neutrality should be seen in a different light than before due to membership of the EU and more recently a loose partnership with NATO. Furthermore, the level of political isolationism varies from Norway's relatively high level of isolationism to (present-day) Finland's relatively high level of internationalism.

What is more, parliamentarism is reflected on the protection of fundamental rights. Essentially, the Nordic countries have three dimensions in their systems: domestic constitutions, European conventions, and global conventions. Constitutional protection varies from country to country, but a common feature is that the ECHR is the most important human rights instrument. All the Nordic countries have incorporated the ECHR into their domestic legal systems. The brief analyses in this chapter focuses in particular on the dialogue between the European

---

[7]Cf. Elo Rytter (2000), pp 46–47.

[8]See also the conclusions drawn by Italian constitutional comparatist Duranti (2009), pp 243–245.

Court of Human Rights (ECtHR) and national courts because this sheds light on the special quality of each Nordic constitution.[9]

Altogether, it seems that significant doctrinal, functional, political, cultural and historical similarities can be pointed out even though there are institutional differences. Moreover, Nordic constitutions may be characterised as socially and politically successful constitutions because they have provided a stable framework for democratic governance. In summary, Nordic constitutions appear to be systems operating with similar foundational values, although differences exist in constitutional rules, institutions, and cultures.[10] As a result, we may speak of "Nordicness" in terms of constitutional law. In the following sections we will highlight and discuss the distinctive constitutional-cultural dimensions of the Nordic constitutions which are not similar.

3 Constitutional Variations on a Nordic Theme

3.1 Finland's Constitution

The Finnish Constitution is technically enshrined in a single Act, i.e. the Finnish Constitution,[11] which entered into force in 2000.[12] Before the present Constitution Act there were four separate constitutional Acts—following the Swedish tradition—which were: the Form of Government Act (1919), the Procedure of Parliament Act (1922), the Ministerial Responsibility Act (1922), and the Act on the High Court of Impeachment (1922). In essence, the Constitution Act provides a catalogue of constitutional rights and provisions about the principles for the exercise of public power by government, the organisation of the government and the relationships between the highest organs of the state. In 2012 the Constitution Act was amended. These amendments clarified the division of powers between the President of the Republic and the government. Moreover, provisions were added on membership in the EU—Finland has been a member of the EU since 1995—and on the citizens' initiative.

Generally speaking, Finland is a parliamentary democracy with certain semi-presidential elements i.e. it has a president as the head of state and with certain competences which are listed in the Constitution Act. On a day-to-day basis the Finnish system functions as a parliamentary system and the president stays in the background. As a general remark we can say that Finnish governance normally

[9]The discussion on fundamental rights in this chapter benefited from the paper provided by Jonas Christoffersen, Director, The Danish Institute for Human Rights—Denmark's National Human Rights Institution.

[10]And yet we may see that Norway and Denmark (west-Nordic) are closer to each other than Sweden and Finland (east-Nordic).

[11]*Suomen perustuslaki/Finlands grundlag* 731/1999.

[12]This section is based on Husa (2011).

works so that it seeks consensus rather than partisan solutions backed by a temporary majority, i.e. the constitutional culture strives towards consensus. This produces a certain rigidity, i.e. the Constitution changes relatively slowly, both in a legal and in a political sense.

The Finnish system is based on core principles according to which power is vested in the people, who are represented by deputies assembled in the parliament. Crucially, legislative power is exercised by the parliament whereas the President of the Republic plays a minor role. According to the Constitution Act, the top level of governance is the Council of State (i.e. the government) which is headed by a prime minister and a requisite number of other ministers. Following the principle of parliamentary systems, the government and its individual members must enjoy the confidence of the parliamentary majority. Another key point is that judicial power is vested in independent courts of law, at the highest level in the Supreme Court and the Supreme Administrative Court.

In comparative constitutional analysis the most distinctive feature of the Finnish system is the manner in which it guards the constitutionality of statutory laws. Even in a global comparison this feature stands out as a unique quasi-judicial arrangement.

As already mentioned above, Finland has no constitutional court but courts are allowed to perform judicial review of legislation to a certain limited extent. After the total reform of the Constitution Act in 2000, it became possible for courts to perform judicial review of legislation. The idea of constitutionality, however, is not limited to judicial review only because, in addition to the courts, other public authorities are also obliged to interpret legislation in such a manner that adheres to the Constitution and to respect constitutional and human rights.

According to the Constitution Act (Article 106), the courts must give preference to the Constitution when they decide a case if the application of a parliamentary Act would be in manifest conflict (in Finnish "*ilmeinen ristiriita*") with the Constitution Act.[13] In a handful of cases, starting from 2004, the courts have applied Article 106 but in the overall picture judicial review by the courts plays a minor role in terms of guarding the constitutionality of parliamentary Acts.[14] However, certain signs are discernible of the gradually growing constitutional role of the judiciary.[15]

In practice, the constitutionality of laws is examined in advance i.e. before an Act enters into force. Review mainly takes place in the parliament's influential Constitutional Law Committee (*Perustuslakivaliokunta*). The function of this parliamentary-bound control is advance prevention of laws conflicting with the Constitution being enacted in the ordinary legislative procedure. From the constitutional point of view, the Committee's key function is to issue statements on bills sent to it for consideration and on the constitutionality of other legislative matters

---

[13]This Article was adopted as an alternative to establishing a Constitutional Court, Government Proposal (*Hallituksen esitys* 1/1998), pp 53–54.

[14]See Husa (2011), pp 186–187.

[15]See Ojanen (2009).

and their bearing on international human rights. Even while the Committee's members are ordinary members of the parliament, the Committee calls experts (on the basis of constitutional convention) to give evidence, and the Committee itself operates in a non-party-political manner in reporting to the parliament. These reports are official statements and are respected by the government, which seeks to amend the provisions of a bill that the Committee has found to be unconstitutional before the bill is passed. If the unconstitutionality is significant it means, in practice, that the bill is withdrawn and the government has to think of another way to proceed because in a multiparty-system governments do not have the required qualified majority to change the Constitution Act.

From a comparative point of view the fact that the Constitutional Committee functions in a non-political quasi-judicial manner (e.g. statements are based on the evidence given by constitutional experts, the Committee follows its own "precedents", there is no party-political discipline) is particularly significant. All this results in a unique system of controlling the constitutionality of legislation in which an abstract *ex ante* and concrete case-bound review mechanism are combined. Importantly, the significance of the *Perustuslakivaliokunta* is reflected in the whole legal system and its statements hold a special status as a source of law as de facto precedents.[16] Only with slight exaggeration one may characterise the weight of these statements as de facto "constitutional precedents".

During years 2012–2016 Finland has been found by the European Court of Human Rights (ECtHR) to have violated the European Convention on Human Rights (ECHR) in fourteen cases. One of the main issues has been application of the principle of *ne bis in idem*. In five cases the Finnish courts were found by the ECtHR to have convicted the parties of the same matter in two different sets of proceedings: Finland had thereby violated Article 4 of Protocol no. 7.[17] Another main challenge appears to be striking a balance between freedom of expression and protection of other interests, as in four cases the ECtHR found that Finland had violated Article 10.[18] In three cases, the ECtHR found a violation of Article 8 concerning private and family life.[19]

[16]See Husa (2011), pp 78–88.

[17]*Nykänen v Finland*, no. 11828/11, ECHR 2014; *Glantz v Finland*, no. 37394/11, ECHR 2014; *Kiiveri v Finland*, no. 53753/12, ECHR 2015; *Rinas v Finland*, no. 17039/13; *Österlund v Finland*, no. 53179/13, ECHR 2015.

[18]*Lahtonen v Finland*, no. 29576/09, ECHR 2012; *Ristamäki and Korvola v Finland*, no 66456/09, ECHR 2013; *Niskasaari and Otavamedia Oy v Finland*, no. 32297/10, ECHR 2015; *M.P. v Finland*, no. 36487/12, ECHR 2016.

[19]*X v Finland*, no. 34806/04 (the case also concerned a violation of Article 5 concerning freedom of liberty), ECHR 2012; *Laakso v Finland*, no. 7361/05, ECHR 2013; *Röman v Finland*, no. 13072/05, ECHR 2013.

3.2 Sweden's Constitution

Sweden has five key constitutional documents. These are the Instrument of Government (1974),[20] the Act of Succession (1810),[21] the Freedom of the Press Act (1949),[22] the Fundamental Law on Freedom of Expression (1991),[23] and the *Riksdag* (i.e. Swedish parliament) Act (1974).[24] Alongside these constitutional documents, EU laws hold significant constitutional weight in the Swedish system, as in Finland and Denmark. In constitutional essence, Sweden is a constitutional monarchy with a parliamentary system. Like Finland, Sweden has been an EU member since 1995.[25] And, again like Finland, Swedish constitutional practice tends (at least so far) strongly to strive towards consensus, which produces significant constitutional stability.[26]

The Instrument of Government contains the written basic principles of the form of government, dealing with such issues as how the government functions, fundamental freedoms and rights, and how elections to the *Riksdag* are to be implemented. When the Instrument of Government came into force it reduced the powers of the monarch. For this reason, the monarch remains as the head of state but with stripped political powers. The Act of Succession stipulates who is to inherit the throne. Until 1979 the succession was through the male bloodline but two years after the birth of Princess Victoria the *Riksdag* decided that a female could also inherit the throne.

The Freedom of the Press Act was adopted in 1949, although the freedom of the press was already established by law in 1766. This Act provides the right to disseminate information in printed form but it also concerns the principle of public access to official documents. The Law on Freedom of Expression contains provisions on free dissemination of information and prohibits censorship. These abovementioned Acts are constitutional Acts, which means they are more difficult to amend or repeal than other Acts. Similarly, according to the hierarchy of norms, no other Acts or ordinances may—in principle—conflict with these constitutional laws.

Alongside the abovementioned documents, also of constitutional importance is the *Riksdag* Act, which contains detailed provisions on the parliament and its workings. This Act enjoys a curious status between a constitutional Act and an ordinary Act. To amend this Act requires only one *Riksdag* decision but it must be adopted by a qualified majority of at least three-quarters of votes and the support of more than half the members. Now, in comparative constitutional analysis one of the

[20] *Kungörelse* (1974: 152) *om beslutad ny regeringsform.*

[21] *Successionsordning* (1810: 0926).

[22] *Tryckfrihetsförordning* (1949: 105).

[23] *Yttrandefrihetsgrundlag* (1991: 1469).

[24] *Riksdagsordning* (2014: 801).

[25] For a general informative overview see Nergelius (2011).

[26] Cf. Bull (2014), p 12.

most striking general features of the Swedish system is the central position of the *Riksdag*.[27] Notwithstanding, this is not to suggest that parliaments in other Nordic countries would not be in a central position. However, centrality seems to be legally-culturally emblematic in terms of the Swedish Constitution.

So, we must be cautious when underlining the role of the *Riksdag* because all Nordic constitutions rely on the foundational idea and doctrine of parliamentary democracy and a representative form of government. Be that as it may, the Swedish system in particular seems to grant de facto a distinctly focal constitutional weight to its parliament. To be sure, the Instrument of Government provides (Article 4.1) that "the *Riksdag* is the foremost representative of the people". However, as a written constitutional provision this article is in line with the rest of the Nordic constitutions.

From a comparative point of view, the actual highlighted constitutional position of the *Riksdag* can be seen in the doctrine of sources of law. In practice, Swedish lawyers routinely use *travaux préparatoires* when they try to obtain more information about a law i.e. they seldom use the text of the law alone. This is not only a Swedish legal cultural feature but applies to all Nordic systems, although there are clear national variations. Basically, the underlying idea of this kind of source-of-law doctrine is to be found from the constitution in the broad sense of the word i.e. not only does the text of the constitutional document play a significant role but also constitutional practices and conventions have a strong foothold in moulding the legal mentality of Swedish lawyers.

Notably, the final justification for giving so much weight to *travaux* is the understanding of constitutional democracy itself; as Peczenik and Bergholz say "*travaux préparatoires* should be taken into account because they form a part of a democratic and rationally justifiable legislative procedure."[28] At the same time, one might perhaps sometimes claim that the heightened role of the *Riksdag* shadows the legal function of the constitution. One telling indication of the role of the *Riksdag* is the cautious tradition of judicial review, which is the constitutional flipside of the coin; the great respect for the parliament—as in Finland—seems to hinder the courts from taking a more active role in controlling the constitutionality of parliamentary Acts.

In any case, in 1979 the Instrument of Government was reformed and a cautious form of judicial review was taken as a part of the written Constitution. The provision on judicial review (in Swedish "*lagprövningsrätt*") stated that a court could declare a parliamentary Act to be in violation of the Constitution or a government decree and, thus, inapplicable but only if the error was of manifest/evident nature. This provision—which was worded similarly to the Finnish model—has had very little practical effect on the behaviour of the courts.

---

[27]As Ola Zetterquist says "The traditional position in Swedish constitutional law is that courts are not to exercise any political power of significance since such a position is atypical of the Swedish constitution where political power should rest with the Riksdag", Zetterquist (2008), p 98. See also Bull (2014), p 16, holding basically a similar view.

[28]Peczenik and Bergholz (1991), p 328.

Since 2011 provisions no longer need to be in evident conflict with a constitutional rule in order to be set aside by a court or other public body. However, this reform did not mean a startling break from the centrality of the *Riksdag* because the provision in question also contains a second part which states that: "In the case of review of an Act of law under paragraph one, particular attention must be paid to the fact that the Parliament is the foremost representative of the people and that fundamental law takes precedence over other law." In other words, even while giving into pressure for stronger judicial review, the Swedish system in fact sought to fuse together the old *Riksdag*-centred thinking and more recent separation of powers with a stronger judicial review doctrine.[29] As shown above, the strong position of the *Riksdag* is still a fundamental key feature of the Swedish Constitution, especially if placed in a comparative analytical framework.

Sweden has also been found by the ECtHR to have committed violations of the ECHR. In years 2012–2016, five of the cases concerned violations of Article 3 in relation to expulsion of asylum-seekers.[30] Four cases were about application of Article 6 on fair trial.[31] Three cases concerned Article 8 (on protection of private and family life).[32]

3.3 Norway's Constitution

The Norwegian Constitution Act[33] was adopted in 1814. This means that it is the second oldest written constitutional document in the world still in force. Although technically it is like any constitution Act, its characteristic significance seems to be more central than in other Nordic countries because for Norwegians it symbolizes freedom, independence and democracy. In addition, because of the considerable age

[29]In Government's proposal (*Regeringens proposition* 2009/10: 80, 145–147) it is explained that reform strengthens the constitutional control after the legislative phase and this, in turn, actually secures the key position of the *Riksdag*. The risk that this would politicize the courts is expressly deemed as ungrounded.

[30]*F.N. and others v Sweden*, no. 28774/09, ECHR 2012; *S.F. and others v Sweden*, no. 52077/10, ECHR 2012; *I v Sweden*, no. 61204/09, ECHR 2013; *J.K. and others v Sweden*, no. 59166/12, ECHR 2016; *F.G. v Sweden*, no. 43611/11, ECHR 2016.

[31]*Olsby v Sweden*, no. 36124/06, ECHR 2012; *Karin Andersson and others v Sweden*, no. 29878/09, ECHR 2014; *Naku v Lithuania and Sweden*, no. 26126/07, ECHR 02016; *Arlewin v Sweden*, no. 22302/10, ECHR 2016.

[32]*Strömblad v Sweden*, no. 3684/07, ECHR 2012; *Rousk v Sweden*, no. 27183/04, ECHR 2013; *Söderman v Sweden* [GC], no. 5786/08, ECHR 2013. There were also three cases dealt with violations of Article 4 of Protocol no. 7 (*Lucky Dev v Sweden*, no. 7356/10, ECHR 2014), Article 1 of Protocol no. 1 (*Rousk v Sweden*, no. 27183/04, ECHR 2013), and the right to an effective remedy under Article 13 (*Lindstrand Partners Advokatbyrå AB v Sweden*, no. 18700/09, ECHR 2016).

[33]*Kongeriket Norges grunnlov* 1814 no 17.

of the constitutional document the role of customary constitutional law is greater than in the other Nordic systems.[34]

The constitutional system of Norway is, like Sweden and Denmark, a constitutional monarchy with a parliamentary democratic system of governance. According to the constitutional provision, the king is the country's head of state and can select his council. But, according to constitutional practice the government may govern only with the confidence of the *Storting* (i.e. the parliament). In fact, the king has very little actual political power. However, the king still seems to hold a crucial symbolic function as the head of state and official representative of Norway. According to a constitutional provision, public power is distributed between three institutions: the parliament, holding the legislative power; the government, holding executive power; and independent courts holding judicial power. In 2014 the parliament passed some significant amendments by including provisions on human rights. In contrast to Denmark, Finland and Sweden, Norway is not an EU member.

In a comparative Nordic view, Norway's individual constitutional characteristic can be seen linked to the fact that it actively exercises an *ex post* system of judicial review of the constitutionality of legislation. This fact is closely connected to the central role of the Supreme Court (*Høyesterett*) and also appears to reflect the symbolically central role of the constitution and the Supreme Court as its final guardian. With this in mind, to become a justice of the Supreme Court seems to be a more significant accomplishment in Norway than in the other three systems.

Of all the Nordic countries Norway maintains the strongest tradition of judicial review of statutory laws. In effect, although decentralised, this control function or power is exercised by the Supreme Court, which reviews whether a statute is in conflict with the Constitution. As in the US, in Norway, too, this competence was originally not expressly vested in a written constitutional document before 2015. But this is certainly not a novelty in Norwegian constitutional law. Judicial review of constitutionality emerged as long ago as the 19th century.[35] However, today's living tradition can be traced to 1976 and the famous *Kløfta* judgment.[36] In this case, which concerned compensation for expropriation of property, one can see clearly the effect of US constitutional law and ideas which are more alien to other Nordic systems. However, even the Norwegian system does not fully follow the American model but has instead formulated its own approach, which combines strong American judicial review and the Nordic tradition of a softer or parliamentary-friendly approach.

---

[34]According to the leading classic book about Norway's constitutional law, the role of customary law is characterised as follows: "Not in any other area of law has customary law greater significance than in the area of constitutional law", Andenæs and Fliflet (1995), p 40.

[35]See Slagstad (1995).

[36]*Kløfta*. Norsk Retstidende, 1976, p 1. The precedential outcome of this case is that when the courts are asked to decide on the constitutionality of an Act, the parliament's view of the matter inevitably plays a crucial role. However, if any doubt arises as to how a statutory provision should be interpreted, the courts have a right and a duty to apply the Act in the manner which best accords with the Constitution.

In other words, the effects of the Nordic approach can be seen in the fact that the Supreme Court does not quash an Act or a particular provision of that Act, i.e. it does not declare an Act null and void but, rather, merely sets aside the provision in question. Moreover, there is very little similarity with the continental European approach, relying on constitutional courts, because the *Høyesterett* eliminates the legal-normative power of a provision only in the actual concrete case before the Court. But, of course, because of the de facto precedential power of the *Høyesterett*, its decision actually means that its case-bound elimination leads to a situation in which the provision loses its de facto authority in other cases too. By the same token, the *Høyesterett* does not seem to seek to replace or challenge the democratically-chosen legislator, although it may set legal limits on its legislative competence.

In comparison to other Nordic supreme courts, we can argue that Norway's Supreme Court holds the most prestigious position in its own legal context and constitutional culture. From a comparative point of view, this means that in this particular regard Norway's Constitution is actually quite close to the US Constitution, where the constitutional document and the highest court guarding it perform not only a legal function but also a strong symbolic function. And, curiously, the relevant old constitutional documents in the US and in Norway were both silent (the US Constitution is, of course, still silent) on whether the courts can review an Act, or a particular provision in an Act, in regard to its constitutionality.

However, in the reform of 2015 a novel provision was added. This provides that "[i]n cases brought before the courts, the courts have the power and obligation to review whether Acts and other decisions by the state authorities are contrary to the Constitution".[37] Basically, from a comparative point of view we can see that the heightened role of the *Høyesterett* is also connected to the Norwegian mentality of constitutional conservatism.[38] In practice, this means that the constitutional Act also performs an important symbolic function, so that, as a result, the *Høyesterett* gains a special position as the guardian of the nationally-enshrined symbol of the statehood —and ultimately the sovereignty—of Norway.

In seven cases (in 2012–2016) Norway has been found by the ECtHR to have committed violations of the ECHR. Also in them, application of Article 8 and Article 6 haven been in focus. Two cases related to expulsion of criminals in violation of Article 8 protecting the right to private and family life,[39] three cases

---

[37]This looks like a significant amendment but, in fact, it merely confirmed an established customary constitutional rule allowing—and expecting—judicial review. Preparatory materials underline the importance of constitutionality by stressing the priority of human rights (Rapport fra Menneskerettighetsutvalget om menneskerettigheter i Grunnloven, avgitt 19. desember 2011, pp 79–81). Preparatory materials also explain that constitutional judicial review has been part of the Norwegian Constitution for 150 years (Innst. 263 S, Innstilling til Stortinget fra kontroll- og konstitusjonskomiteen 2014–2015, p 6).

[38]For a more detailed analysis see, e.g., Smith (2011).

[39]*Butt v Norway*, no. 47017/09, ECHR 2012; *Kaplan and others v Norway*, no. 32504/11, ECHR 2014.

involved violations of Article 6 on fair trial.[40] The last case involved violation of the right to property protected by Article 1 of Protocol no. 1.[41]

3.4 Denmark's Constitution

By and large, Denmark's constitutional law is based on the Constitutional Act of the Kingdom of Denmark in 1849. Although still the basis of the system, this old Act has been amended many times, most importantly in 1953. Like other Nordic constitutional Acts it enjoys heightened legal status, i.e. it stands at the top of the hierarchy of laws. Now, the Act provides for the supreme institutions of the state. These are the *Folketing* (i.e. Danish parliament) holding legislative power; the government, holding executive power; and the independent courts, holding judicial power. Besides, like so many other modern constitutional documents, the Act contains provisions on a number of fundamental freedoms and human rights.

Like Sweden and Norway, Denmark is also a constitutional monarchy that relies on the parliamentary system, which in turn means that the power of the monarch is limited by the Constitutional Act[42] and customary rules. Generally speaking, the Danish system "reflects a legal system and a separation of powers model with a strong Parliament" and it has "very few constitutional constraints on the content of legislation".[43] In fact, parliamentary precedence has been a feature of the Danish legal mentality and legal practice for quite some time.[44] It is also noteworthy that Denmark has been a member of the EU since 1973 (EEC at that time) which means that it took part in European integration 22 years before the other two Nordic countries joined the Union.

In a comparative Nordic view, Denmark's distinctive constitutional characteristic has been its almost paradoxical will—despite taking part in European integration—to guard its national sovereignty, and later its constitutional identity, in relation to the EU. In comparison to Sweden and Finland, this feature (i.e. constitutionally motivated reluctance) seems to some extent to distinguish the Danish constitutional mindset from the other two Nordic EU member states. On the other hand, this fact means that Denmark and Norway are close to each other in this particular respect.

The Danish constitutional conception of sovereignty seems to be more distinct and outspoken than is the case with the two other Nordic EU member states.

---

[40]*Kristiansen and Tyvik As v Norway*, no. 25498/08, ECHR 2013 (the case concerned civil proceedings); *Hansen v Norway*, no. 15319/09, ECHR 2014 (the case concerned civil proceedings); *Kristiansen v Norway*, no. 1176/10, ECHR 2015 (the case concerned criminal proceedings).

[41]*Lindheim and others v Norway*, nos. 12331/08 and 2139/10, ECHR 2012.

[42]*Danmarks Riges Grundlov* 1953 no 169.

[43]Krunke (2014), p 29.

[44]See Schaumburg-Müller (2009).

This is by no means to say that sovereignty and, especially, transfer of national competence outside the country would be a walk in the park in Sweden and Finland. However, one can grasp the profound extent of the Danish conception when this specific feature is highlighted in the context of the EU. Now, from a narrow constitutional point of view the Danish approach seems in certain respects similar to that in Finland.

So, Denmark can basically transfer sovereignty to international organisations in two distinct ways. First, powers vested in the authorities of the realm may be delegated "to such extent as shall be provided by statute" (Article 20). This is a challenging path because it requires a five-sixths majority of all members of the parliament. In practice it means that at least 150 of the 179 members of the parliament need be present and vote in favour of delegation. But, if delegation of powers is not provided by statute, or if they are not vested in the authorities of the state, sovereignty can only be transferred by amending the Constitution itself. Yet, the Constitution Act still has Article 19, allowing the Government to sign international treaties that do not transfer sovereignty. This kind of signature requires the consent of the parliament by an ordinary majority.

Notwithstanding—and here is the main point—Danish reluctance to transfer national competences outside the country does not stem from written constitutional provisions but, rather, from the Danish constitutional mentality. It is important to realise that this reluctant form of constitutionalism seems to be rooted in the constitutional culture of the country but is not an outcome of specific constitutional provisions. In practice, the Danish courts are sometimes reluctant to refer questions of EU law to the ECJ but probably not more than the national courts of other EU countries. However, a comparatist may see a slight difference between the Danish approach to the ECHR and to the case law of the ECJ, even if the difference should not be exaggerated. The Danish courts may, generally speaking, have been more open to implementing ECtHR decisions, whereas the attitude towards the ECJ can be seen as somewhat more cautious. This difference may be connected to the fact that the EU goes further—regarding sovereignty—than the ECHR, which is basically an international treaty. Moreover, this can be seen as a consequence of the lack of a modern catalogue of human rights in the Danish Constitution.[45]

Clearly, the Nordic constitutional systems place a high value on the primacy of parliament. However, Denmark's uneasy relation with the EU seems to indicate an ingrained constitutional vision of a strong national parliament, at least in relation to external "competing powers". This is also reflected in the fact that in "the Danish constitutional context with strong Parliaments, courts do not play…an active role".[46] It has been pointed out, by a Danish scholar, that the underlying idea is that "the *Folketing* represents the people, and the people are sovereign".[47] Although this may be true, we need to be cautious about jumping to conclusions; in comparison to

[45]Cf. Elo Rytter and Wind (2011).

[46]Krunke (2014), p 35.

[47]Wind (2009), p 288.

Finland and Sweden, the difference is certainly not dramatic, but at the same time it seems to characterise the Danish constitutional mentality, in particular because it sets Denmark in a different position in the European context from the other Nordic member states.

Only one case (in 2012–2015) brought against Denmark before the ECtHR resulted in a finding of violation of the European Human Rights Convention. This happened in the case of Biao v. Denmark, in which the court found that an exception to Danish rules on family reunification—the so-called 28-year rule—violated Article 14 of the Convention taken in conjunction with Article 8.[48]

3.5 Iceland's Constitution

Iceland was part of Norway until 1814 and after that part of the Kingdom of Denmark. The present Constitution[49] was adopted in 1944, when Iceland decided not to continue the union with Denmark established in 1918. The Constitution is based on Iceland's first Constitution, given to Iceland in 1874 by the Danish king. This constitution again was based on the Danish Constitution of 1849.

The 1944 Constitution was amended several times but still it was felt by many that Iceland should have a modern constitution of its own. In an attempt to establish a new constitution, a very interesting experiment was undertaken: a major part of the Icelandic population would be involved in the constitutional work. In 2009, a coalition government opened a debate on a new constitution. A privately organized national assembly of 1500 members, partly chosen at random and partly representing different institutions and groups, started out with a discussion of the basic principles of a new constitution. A year later, the Government followed up by passing an Act on a constituent assembly of 25 delegates elected directly to discuss, among other things, the organization of the government and the legislator, the role of the president, judicial control, the democratic process and elections, and the use of natural resources.[50]

However, the election of this body was ruled void by the Supreme Court and instead a Constitutional Council (*Stjórnlagaráð*) was appointed by the Icelandic parliament (*Althing*) in 2011. A draft Constitution was finished on 29 July 2011 and presented to the parliament. A non-binding constitutional referendum was held in October 2012 with a positive result from around 2/3 of the voters. This reform, however, has so far come to a halt, as the later government of the country has not moved the proposal further forward.[51]

---

[48]*Biao v Denmark*, no. 38590/10, ECHR 2016.

[49]*Stjórnarskrá lýðveldisins Ísland* 33/1944.

[50]See Árnason (2011).

[51]Comparison between Icelandic and Irish experiences, see Suteu (2015).

In judicial review Iceland seems to have its own specific approach. Courts have been applying judicial review since 1944; however, the volume of cases has increased since 1995, when a human rights catalogue was included in the constitution. Basically, the Icelandic courts may disregard an Act but not formally invalidate it. Essentially, there seems to be relatively little hesitation by the courts, politicians, and constitutional theorists to accept the basic idea of constitutional judicial review. This can be seen, for instance, in the fact that Acts are more frequently held to be unconstitutional than in the other Nordic countries. Moreover, unlike in the other Nordic countries, there is relatively little doctrinal or theoretical discussion that would be genuinely critical concerning the role of the courts and there is hardly any political opposition to judicial review.[52] Be that as it may, generally speaking the Icelandic constitutional mentality fits reasonably well within the general Nordic framework i.e. there is a lack of judicial activism even though judicial review forms part and parcel of the Icelandic constitution.

Iceland has been found at fault in five cases of violations of the ECHR during 2012–2016.[53] All five cases concerned Article 10 of the convention on freedom of expression and were brought against the state by journalists who had been convicted by the national courts in defamation proceedings brought against them because of their journalistic work. Three of the cases were brought before the ECtHR by the same journalist.

4 Conclusion

This brief comparative discussion started from the assumption that, despite striking similarities between the Nordic constitutions, there are also peculiarities in terms of living constitutions. However, the question is: are these peculiarities so different after all? No doubt a deeper comparative analysis would reveal commonalities. Finland's peculiar doctrine on controlling constitutionality can be derived from the fact that constitutional practice involves a special role for the national parliament. At the same time, Finland has caved in concerning the European dimension in terms of the EU as well as with the ECHR and the case law of the ECtHR.[54] Sweden has also had its doubts both with the EU and with the ECHR. Even while Sweden today is relatively open to the European dimension, it still guards its Nordic-style understanding of the sources of law and assigns a particularly distinct role for legislative preparatory works. Moreover, it seems quite evident that this can be

[52]See Helgadóttir (2011).

[53]*Björk Eiðsdóttir v Iceland*, no. 46443/09, ECHR 2012; *Erla Hlynsdóttir v Iceland*, no. 43380/10, ECHR 2012; *Erla Hlynsdóttir v Iceland*, no. 54125/10, ECHR 2014; *Erla Hlynsdóttir v Iceland*, no. 54145/10, ECHR 2015; *Ólafsson v Iceland*, no. 58493/13, ECHR 2017.

[54]As pointed out by Markku Suksi, Nordic constitutional identity is under pressure both from the European Court of Justice and the ECtHR. See Suksi (2014), pp 83–84.

explained by Sweden's constitutional self-understanding, holding the *Riksdag* in a key position and shadowing the constitutional role of rights.

Comparatively speaking, Nordic constitutions are curious; they encompass both the idea of popular sovereignty (as a legitimate form of political democracy) and the idea of separation of powers. This probably partially explains the seemingly low political profile of their supreme courts—they do not willingly challenge the legitimacy of parliamentary Acts, although they are very much legally independent of direct (political) influence by legislators. On the whole, the highest Nordic courts seem to feel a great deal of loyalty toward their respective parliaments but they do so without direct parliamentary guidance (except statutory law, of course), so this is an outcome of a Nordic constitutional mentality growing from a certain notion of democracy and appreciation of the rule of law. As a result, Nordic constitutions are more governance-oriented than rule-oriented; more weight seems to be given to institutions than to rights. However, the growing significance of fundamental rights is slowly changing the overall picture.

More generally, the Nordic experience—or "Nordicness"—seems to imply that constitutional law is both "law" and "politics", i.e. written constitutional documents are insulated against "politics" because constitutions are themselves so deeply and profoundly of a political nature.[55] Moreover, the Nordic experience seems to be pragmatic in its tendency to admit that constitutions are about law and politics; written rules are interpreted, applied and de facto amended by constitutional practices and interpretations.

Yet it is beyond doubt that the Nordic countries take their constitutions seriously even while their constitutional styles are not identical. Even so, today many scholars and lawyers are seeking a stronger rights-based culture and a stronger position for judicial review in the Nordic countries. However, only time will tell how these pressures will transform the parliament-oriented Nordic constitutions. In a broad sense, it is clear that Nordic constitutions and "Nordicness" in constitutional laws are not isolated because they are affected by global and European legal developments—rights are also gaining more weight within the Nordic constitutional sphere. The rise of fundamental rights and especially the ECHR have grown in constitutional gravity.

Constitutional protection of fundamental rights varies significantly between the Nordic countries. Yet, from a comparative point of view it is easy to see that all Nordic systems take fundamental rights seriously. When the Human Rights Court decides against a Nordic country, these countries take measures to deal with the problem through legislation or, at least, through interpretation by the national judicial organs. The judicial dialogue they have had with the ECtHR reflects,

[55] However, it would be a mistake to assume that this connection would be openly admitted: indeed, quite the contrary. As Thomas Bull says about Sweden, there is "difficulty to acknowledge the close connections between law and politics [...] many participants and observers of the system still cling to the idea that law and politics is and should be sharply divided", Bull (2014), p 17. Yet, in constitutional comparison this connection looks evident.

however, the domestic special features of each system as the cases decided by the ECtHR clearly indicate.

To conclude, the recent Nordic expansion of judicial review may bring about a novel challenge to the traditional Nordic notion of democracy. It would seem that these systems are slowly gliding towards rule by judges instead of rule by parliamentarians. Moreover, if the ECtHR type of judicial activism extends to the traditional Nordic understanding of democracy (popular sovereignty in an important position) it may become difficult to avoid transformation of constitutional cultures favouring parliaments.[56] But, then again, resilience has always been an underlying feature of Nordic constitutions. It is safe to assume that parliamentary focus will not concede with haste.

References

Andenæs J, Fliflet A (1995) Statsforfatningen i Norge. Universitetsforlaget, Oslo
Árnason ÁT (2011) A review of the Icelandic constitution—popular sovereignty or political confusion. Tijdschrift voor Constitutioneel Recht 3:342–351
Bull T (2014) Constitutional identity—a view from Sweden. Retfærd 37:10–23
Cameron I (2009) The influence of European human rights law on national law. In: Hollo EJ (ed) National law and Europeanisation. Suomalainen lakimiesyhdistys, Helsinki, pp 63–84
Duranti F (2009) Gli ordinamenti costituzionali nordici: Profili di diritto pubblico comparato. Giappichelli, Torino
Elo Rytter J (2000) Grundrettigheder: domstolenes fortolkning og kontrol med lovgivningsmakten. Thomson-GadJura, Copenhagen
Elo Rytter J, Wind M (2011) In need of juristocracy? The silence of Denmark in the development of European legal norms. Int J Const Law 9:470–504
Eng S (1997) Precedent in Norway. In: McCormick ND, Summers RS (eds) Interpreting precedents. Dartmouth, Aldershot, pp 189–217
Hautamäki V (2007) The question of constitutional court—on its relevance on the Nordic context. In: Husa J, Nuotio K, Pihlajamäki H (eds) Nordic law in between tradition and dynamism. Intersentia, Antwerp, Oxford, pp 153–171
Helgadóttir R (2011) Nonproblematic judicial review: a case study. Int J Const Law 9:532–547
Holland KM (1991) Introduction. In: Holland KM (ed) Judicial activism in comparative perspective. Macmillan, London, pp 1–11
Husa J (2002) Nordic reflections on constitutional law: a comparative Nordic perspective. Peter Lang, Frankfurt am Main
Husa J (2011) The constitution of Finland—a contextual analysis. Hart, Oxford
Krunke H (2014) Constitutional identity—seen through a Danish lens. Retfærd 37:24–40
Nergelius J (2011) Constitutional law in Sweden. Kluwer, Alphen van den Rijn
Ojanen T (2009) From constitutional periphery toward the center—transformations of judicial review in Finland. Nord J Hum Rights 27:194–207
Peczenik A, Bergholz G (1991) Statutory interpretation in Sweden. In: McCormick ND, Summers RS (eds) Interpreting statutes. Dartmouth, Aldershot, pp 311–358

[56] It is a general comparative finding that "judicial activism tends to erode both the parliamentary system and majoritarian democracy", Holland (1991), p 5.

Schaumburg-Müller S (2009) Parliamentary precedence in Denmark—a jurisprudential assessment. Nord J Hum Rights 27:170–184

Scheinin M (ed) (2001) The welfare state and constitutionalism in the Nordic countries. Nordic Council of Ministers, Copenhagen

Slagstad R (1995) The breakthrough of judicial review in the norwegian system. In: Slagstad R, Smith E (eds) Constitutional justice under old constitutions. Kluwer, The Hague, pp 81–111

Smith E (2011) Old and protected? Isr Law Rev 44:369–388

Suksi M (2014) Markers of Nordic constitutional identity. Retfærd 37:66–91

Suteu S (2015) Constitutional conventions in the digital era: lessons from Iceland and Ireland. Boston Coll Int Comp Law Rev 38:251–276

Tushnet M (2015) Advanced introduction to comparative constitutional law. Edward Elgar, Cheltenham

Wind M (2009) When parliament comes first—the Danish concept of democracy meets the European Union. Nord J Hum Rights 27:272–288

Zetterquist O (2008) A European res publica. In: Cramér P, Bull T (eds) Swedish studies in European law, vol 2. Hart, Oxford, pp 77–103

Respecting Autonomies and Minorities

Bent Ole Gram Mortensen and Markku Suksi

Abstract The following chapter deals with Nordic territorial autonomies found in Denmark and Finland and with non-territorial cultural autonomy created for the indigenous Sami populations in Finland, Norway and Sweden. I addition minority situations in all Nordic countries will be discussed.

1 Introduction

In several Nordic countries there are areas where a form of autonomy[1] or other special arrangements for minority populations may be found to differing degrees. The reason behind the existence of, for instance, autonomy is that a group of persons that lives in a particular area differs ethnically or culturally from the dominant population group in the country. More often than not, this group has its own language or other particular cultural characteristics, or both. Some minority groups are called indigenous peoples. Autonomy is often, although not always, associated with protection of these minorities.

In this context, the term "minority" means a national or ethnic, linguistic or religious[2] minority with a historically long-lasting and permanent attachment to

[1]Autonomy is not a precisely defined concept in international law. For an attempt at a definition in constitutional law, see Suksi (2011), pp. 130–139.

[2]In addition to ethnic and linguistic minorities, religious minorities also exist in the Nordic countries. Their status is mainly catered for on the basis of freedom of religion. In Finland, in addition to the statutorily established Evangelical-Lutheran Church, the Finnish Orthodox Christian Church is also recognized as an official Church.

B. O. G. Mortensen (✉)
Department of Law, University of Southern Denmark, Odense, Denmark
e-mail: bom@sam.sdu.dk

M. Suksi
Department of Law, Åbo Akademi University, Turku, Finland
e-mail: markku.suksi@abo.fi

© Springer Nature Switzerland AG 2019

P. Letto-Vanamo et al. (eds.), *Nordic Law in European Context*,
Ius Gentium: Comparative Perspectives on Law and Justice 73,
https://doi.org/10.1007/978-3-030-03006-3_4

their country of residence.[3] Refugees and immigrant groups are not generally covered by the notion of a minority.[4] In the following chapter, the constitutional position of Nordic minorities will be analysed and discussed.

In Europe, a majority-minority constellation in a country is normally a product of the concept of the nation state, which from the 19th century and against the background of the ideology of nationalism started to claim that states be organized according to the maxim "one people, one language, one state". In the European context, autonomy for indigenous peoples came into particular focus in the 20th century, as most colonies received increased or full independence. Denmark, Finland, Norway and Sweden have signed and ratified the European Framework Convention on National Minorities and the European Charter on Regional or Minority Languages, while Iceland has only signed the two treaties[5] but not ratified them. Denmark and Norway have ratified ILO Convention No. 169 concerning Indigenous and Tribal Peoples in Independent Countries.

In this article, we are dealing with Nordic territorial autonomies found in Denmark and Finland, with non-territorial cultural autonomy created for the indigenous Sami populations in Finland, Norway and Sweden, and with minority situations in all Nordic countries.[6]

2 Nordic Territories with Special Status

2.1 Denmark and Finland: Differently Constructed States with Territorial Autonomies

Among the Nordic countries, Denmark occupies a special position by being constructed as a commonwealth (*rigsfællesskab*), usually referred to as either "the realm" or the Kingdom of Denmark,[7] while Finland is constituted as a more regular

---

[3]For a definition of minorities, see resolution of the United Nations General Assembly A/Res/47/135 with the Declaration on the Rights of Persons Belonging to National or Ethnic, Religious and Linguistic Minorities, in particular Article 2.

[4]But see General Comment No. 23: The rights of minorities (Article 27), para. 5.2., where the Human Rights Committee of the United Nations presents a more expansive view of what could constitute a minority.

[5]No actual national minorities or minority languages exist in Iceland. This is the likely reason for Iceland only having signed but not ratified the Framework Convention for the Protection of National Minorities (ETS No. 157) and the European Charter for Regional or Minority Languages (ETS No. 148).

[6]The special territory of Svalbard in Norway is under Norwegian sovereignty but is governed by a special treaty.

[7]In translations of the Self-Government Act into English the term "Realm" (*Riget*) is used. However, a more correct translation of the Danish wording in the Self-Government Act is "the Kingdom of Denmark". In this chapter the term "the Kingdom of Denmark" or "the kingdom" or "the realm" is used.

unitary state, although not as a pure unitary state. The Kingdom of Denmark is constituted as a sovereign state with two sub-state entities: the Faroe Islands and Greenland. Each part has its own ethnicity and official language. However, the Danish language may be used in relation to public authorities in all parts of the kingdom. In Finland, the Åland Islands is the sole sub-state entity, fashioned as a monolingual Swedish-speaking territory, although the Finnish Constitution identifies two national languages, Finnish and Swedish, for the rest of the country.

Danish legislation recognizes that the populations of the Faroe Islands and Greenland are distinct peoples. In contrast to Denmark, the Faroe Islands and Greenland are not members of the European Union (EU). However, Greenland is one of the overseas countries and territories (OTC) associated with the EU, while the Faroe Islands are not. In public international law (*jus gentium*), Greenland and the Faroe Islands are not considered independent states but parts of the kingdom, which means that the state of Denmark is ultimately responsible under public international law for the conduct of the public authorities of the Faroe Islands and Greenland.

By contrast, the Swedish-speaking population of Åland (or the Åland Islands) is not identified as a people under national or international law, but shows a distinct identity and is counted as part of the Swedish-speaking population of Finland. Åland is also within the EU, apart from certain exceptions concerning particular rights guaranteed to the Åland Islanders that are contrary to the provisions of EU law. In Protocol 2 to the Accession Treaty of Finland, Åland is granted exemptions from some features of the right of establishment and the purchase of real property, and Åland is also regarded as a third country with regard to indirect taxes. Thus, although Åland is a part of the EU, it has in some respects a position that moves it slightly towards the status of the Faroe Islands and Greenland. The state of Finland is responsible under both international law and EU law for the conduct of the public authorities of the Åland Islands.

The Kingdom of Denmark is characterised by a common constitution,[8] common citizenship[9] and the sharing of certain general functions (primarily foreign, security and defence policy, justice as well as currency and monetary policy).[10] In accordance with the Finnish Constitution,[11] Åland enjoys self-government, including legislative powers, the exercise of which is clearly defined in Section 18 of the

[8]See Danish Constitution, *Grundloven* 1953 no 169.

[9]The population figures in relation to Denmark; the Faroe Islands and Greenland in 2012 were respectively 5,580,516; 48,372; and 56,749. See http://www.stat.gl/sa/sad2014.pdf and http://www.dst.dk/pukora/epub/upload/16252/19faer.pdf.

[10]Greenland's area measures 2,166,086 km^2, while Denmark and the Faroe Islands are only 43,098 and 1399 km^2 respectively. When Greenland left the European Community in 1985, the EC lost 50% of its land mass.

[11]Finnish Constitution, *Suomen perustuslaki/ Finlands grundlag* 731/1999, § 75 and § 120. This is in contrast to the autonomy of the Faroe Islands and Greenland, which is not mentioned in the Danish Constitution.

1993 Self-Government Act of Åland.[12] In relation to those areas of competence where legislative powers have been granted to the Faroe Islands, Greenland and Åland, these autonomous entities can be considered as independent legal orders on a par with national legal orders, and in principle no supremacy or national pre-emption exists in relation to the legislation of the autonomous entities.

However, the courts of law applying the legislation of the Danish autonomies are the Danish state courts, with the Danish Supreme Court as the highest instance, and in Finland, too, the courts are state courts, with the Supreme Court and the Supreme Administrative Court as the highest instances. Competence control concerning legislation passed by the Åland Legislative Assembly is performed in the first instance by a particular body, the Åland Delegation, and if a potential *ultra vires* situation is detected, the matter is submitted to the Supreme Court for an opinion prior to a decision by the President of Finland on whether or not the Åland act or part thereof can enter into force. The Danish mechanism of competence control established in the 1948 Home Rule Act has never been used, and the competence control system has been latent also in relation to Greenland. This might mean that disputes over who is entitled to legislate on what have been resolved by means of negotiations.

In principle, Denmark proper has no "regional" parliament. The Danish parliament (*Folketing*) is the parliamentary assembly of the entire kingdom. Typically, with legislative acts passed by the Danish parliament, the extent to which the particular law also applies to the Faroe Islands and to Greenland is explicitly considered and stated in the act itself. The Finnish parliament does not enact its legislation with explicit mention of whether or not the enactment should apply within the jurisdiction of Åland (although *travaux préparatoires* might sometimes make such a reference). Instead, the competence line established in Sections 18 and 27 (and in 29) of the Self-Government Act is observed when legislation is implemented. The Danish constitution ensures that the Faroe Islands and Greenland each have two members in the Danish parliament, out of a total of 179 members, while according to the Finnish Constitution Åland has one member among the 200 in the Finnish parliament.[13]

Autonomy in relation to the Faroe Islands and Greenland is established by ordinary legislation[14] passed by the Danish parliament and not based on specific provisions in the Danish Constitution. The situation is different in Finland, where Sections 75 and 120 of the Constitution refer to Åland and its self-government, as defined in a particular Self-Government Act. This Act is of a constitutional nature and requires qualified majorities for its amendment, supplemented by the

---

[12]Self-Government Act, *Självstyrelselag för Åland* 1144/1991 in relation to Åland. By 2015, committee work was under way with a view to enacting a new Self-Government Act in around 2020 to mark the 100th anniversary of the autonomy of the Åland Islands.

[13]Danish Constitution § 28, and Finnish Constitution § 25(2). However, this is more a mechanism of guaranteed regional representation for citizens of Denmark and Finland, not tied to membership in a particular people or population.

[14]Act on Greenland's Self-Government, *Lov om Grønlands Selvstyre* 2009 no 473 and Act on Faroe Islands home rule, *Lov om Færøernes Hjemmestyre* 1948 no 137.

requirement that the Åland legislative assembly must adopt the amendments by the same qualified majority.[15] Theoretically, therefore, the Danish autonomies can be amended or abolished by a majority in the Danish parliament. In practice, however, it is unlikely that a political situation could arise in which it would be possible to limit the autonomy that the Faroe Islands and Greenland have already achieved, in particular as the basic acts concerning autonomy are based on agreements between the two entities on the one hand, and the Danish government, on the other. In connection with the Greenland self-government law, an advisory referendum was held in Greenland in 2008 in which 75.5% of the votes were in favour of introducing self-government.[16]

2.2 *Home Rule in the Faroe Islands*

The Faroe Islands consist of a group of 18 islands in the northern Atlantic Ocean, to the north of Scotland (Shetland) and to the west of Norway, with a population of around 50,000. The majority of the population is Faroese, a west-Nordic people of primarily Norwegian and Scottish/Irish descent. The Faroese language is related to Icelandic and Norwegian. From 1035, the Faroe Islands were under Norwegian rule. By the Treaty of Kiel in 1814, at the end of the Napoleonic wars, Norway entered into a union with Sweden. The treaty did not include the Faroe Islands, Greenland and Iceland, which therefore remained with Denmark.[17]

Until 1948, the Faroe Islands enjoyed the legal status of a county of Denmark and had only the same limited competence to govern their own affairs as other parts of Denmark according to the legislation on local government. In 1946, after the Second World War, a referendum held on the Faroe Islands showed a slim majority among voters for independence, but the Danish government refused to recognise this result. However, the Faroe Islands were granted widened autonomy through the Home Rule Act in 1948 in which the Faroe Islands took over legislative and executive power within a number of policy areas.

In 2005, the 1948 Home Rule Act was supplemented by the so-called Takeover Act[18] that extended the number of policy areas under Faroese self-government to include all policy areas in relation to internal affairs. After this time, Faroese

[15]See note 14 above.

[16]In an advisory referendum in 1979, a majority of 70.1% of the inhabitants of Greenland supported creation of home rule for Greenland.

[17]Iceland gained independence from Denmark in 1944.

[18]Act on the Faroese authority's take-over of cases and case-areas, *Lov om de færøske myndigheders overtagelse af sager og sagsområder* 2005 no 578. This Act did not revoke the 1948 Home Rule Act, which remains in force in amended form. Further, the Faroe Islands acquired a limited right to enter into international treaties although the kingdom remains responsible even for obligations entered into by the Faroe Island Government 579/2005.

autonomy is often described as a form of self-government instead of home rule.[19] By contrast to Greenland, the Faroe Islands are not guaranteed by law the right to make any decisions of their own on becoming fully independent. The Faroe Islands' home rule is constituted by their own legislative assembly (*Løgtingið*) and government (*landsstyret*), which is chosen by the legislative assembly and which is politically accountable to the legislative assembly.

It is an inbuilt feature of the system that the Faroe Islands can themselves decide when to take over a specific policy area from the legislative powers of Denmark proper. Certain policy areas are, however, established as areas that cannot be transferred to the Faroe Islands.[20] Takeover of policy areas is partly an economic question, since the costs associated with acquired policy areas are to be borne by the Faroe Islands. However, the kingdom does offer the Faroe Islands financial support in relation to a number of portfolios in health, education and the social spheres. These portfolios had already been taken over by the Faroese authorities before enactment of the Self-Government Act.[21] The extent of financial support is fixed by agreement between the parties and is given as a so-called block grant. This allows the Faroe Islands' government significant freedom in allocating funds within specific areas.[22] In relation to certain more complex portfolios, such as the police and the judiciary, the law provides that the timing of a takeover is fixed by negotiation between the Danish and Faroese authorities.

A number of portfolios have not yet been taken over. Such areas include banking, family and migration/refugee law, as well as the police and justice. Portfolios that have not been taken over fall within the Danish realm's competence and are financed by the realm.

Despite the general rule that the realm is responsible for foreign policy questions, a proxy system[23] is in place that enables the Faroese government to negotiate and conclude international law agreements in relation to policy areas that have been taken over by the Faroe Islands. This is not the equivalent of delegated power, because the Faroe Islands government, in principle, negotiates on behalf of the realm. The system similarly allows for the Faroe Islands to seek membership of international organisations and for representatives of the Faroe Islands government to be deployed at embassies of the realm. In 2005, an agreement was concluded whereby the Faroe Islands are involved in decisions on foreign and security policy

---

[19]The difference between home rule and self-government lies in the degree of autonomy. There is no definitive qualitative difference.

[20]According to Section 1(2) of the 2005 takeover act, the following policy areas cannot be taken over by the Faroe Islands: the Constitution, citizenship, the Supreme Court, foreign, security and defense policy, and foreign exchange and monetary policy.

[21]The Danish state has no immediate legal basis to support portfolios that are transferred to the Faroe Islands after the coming into effect of the takeover act.

[22]The block grant was for 2,014,644 DKK. It had previously been higher but was reduced following a request from the Faroe Islands.

[23]Act about the Faroe Islands government's conclusion of international law agreements, *Lov om Færøernes landsstyres indgåelse af folkeretlige aftaler* 2005 no 579.

of significance to the Faroe Islands (*Fámjin-erklæringen*).[24] The Faroe Islands have their own coat of arms and flag.

2.3 Greenland's Self-government

Greenland, which geographically belongs to North America, is populated by almost 57,000 inhabitants, some 88% of whom belong to the indigenous Inuit population. From the 17th and 18th centuries onwards, Greenland came under Danish authority. With the Constitution of 1953, Greenland's status was changed from a colony[25] to that of a municipality, albeit without consulting the indigenous population. At this point, Greenland achieved the same form of limited competence to govern its own affairs as the Faroe Islands had enjoyed until 1948. In 1979, the Greenland Home Rule Act[26] entered into force. With this act, Greenland achieved autonomy, albeit of a somewhat limited kind. Among other things, the opportunity was created allowing policy areas under state power to be transferred to Greenland. At the same time, Greenland achieved its own legislative assembly and government.

In 2009, the Self-Government Act[27] entered into force and replaced the 1979 Home Rule Act. The 2009 Act expanded on the autonomy that Greenland had been allowed under the home rule system, and it clearly resembles the system that applies on the Faroe Islands. The self-government authorities in Greenland comprise a legislative assembly (*Inatsisartut*) and a government (*Naalakkersuisut*). Greenland has its own coat of arms and flag.

The Self-Government Act has extended the number of political areas that may be taken over by the Greenland self-government. In practice, this includes all internal affairs. However, a large number of areas have not yet been taken over. This is partly so because self-government has not existed for very long. Again, this is partly explained by the fact that the Greenland self-government must finance these areas, while the areas that are not taken over are financed by the realm. One of the areas taken over is mining (taken over in 2010). This area was taken over because of expectations of considerable revenue from the extraction of raw materials, including hydrocarbons. However, these expectations have yet to be fulfilled.

---

[24]Common statement of principles of 29 March 2005 between the Danish government and the Faroe Islands government about the Faroe Islands' involvement in foreign and security policy.

[25]It has been argued (by Thorkild Kjærgaard, a Danish historian from the University of Greenland) that Greenland never had the status of a colony as the population of Greenland had Danish citizenship with the same rights and duties as other Danish citizens. However, Greenland is in general counted as one of the former colonies of Denmark (together with the Danish West Indies and colonies in Africa and the Indian subcontinent). See for instance The Danish Institute for International Studies (2007), p. 67.

[26]Act on Greenland's Home Rule, *Lov om Grønlands hjemmestyre* 577/1978.

[27]Act no. 473 of 12 June 2009 on Greenland's Self-Government. The Act revoked the previous Home Rule Act.

The Self-Government Act fixes an (indexed) yearly block grant from Denmark to Greenland of around 3.5 billion Dkr. (approximately euro 420 million). The grant is not earmarked for special projects. According to a special provision in the Self-Government Act, the block grant is reduced by an amount that is the equivalent of one half of the income that the self-government receives from mining revenue above 75 million Dkr. In contrast to the situation applying to the Faroe Islands, fixing the size of the block grant means that, for example, increased expenditure in the social sphere due to change in the age composition of the population will exclusively be covered by Greenland.

The kingdom is responsible for foreign and security policy. However, as with the Faroe Islands, a system has been established which, within the portfolios that Greenland has taken over, authorizes the Greenland government to negotiate and conclude international law agreements which only concern Greenland. The authorisation system is established in the Self-Government Act. Nevertheless, areas may exist where a conflict could arise about the extent to which a particular relationship falls under an area taken over by Greenland or falls under the kingdom's competence. In reality, disputes have arisen about the extent to which extraction and export of uranium is a common raw material issue (and thereby under Greenlandic competence) or a security policy concern (and thereby under the kingdom's competence). Similarly to the Faroe and Åland Islands, Greenland enjoys independent representation in Nordic cooperation.

The Self-Government Act contains a special provision that allows Greenland the right to decide about full independence at an appropriate time. This type of right is rare in the international context. The pre-conditions for full independence are approval of the independence plan in an advisory referendum in Greenland and the negotiated agreement between the Greenlandic and the Danish government as well as the consent of the legislative assembly of Greenland. The Self-Government Act does not address the situation where the Danish government refuses to give consent. The explanatory notes to the government proposal on the Self-Government Act state that the provision requires the government to commence negotiations with a view to actual conclusion of an agreement. Independence must finally be approved by a decisive referendum in Greenland whereas no referendum on Greenland's independence is foreseen for the other parts of the kingdom.

2.4 *Åland*

Åland is an archipelago comprising a main island and approximately 200 inhabited islands and more than 6000 islets and rocks in the Baltic Sea between Finland and Sweden. The islands are inhabited by some 30,000 persons, the majority of whom, linguistically and culturally, are Swedish-speaking (although around 5% of the population is Finnish-speaking). The islands are under Finnish sovereignty and are self-governing on the basis of the Finnish Constitution and the Åland Islands Self-Government Act.[28] The inhabitants of Åland are not, in Finnish legislation, identified as a people. The inhabitants of Åland have their own identity, and are, at the same time, a part of the Swedish-speaking population of Finland.

The connection to Finland can be traced back to the Treaty of Fredrikshamn in 1809, which ended the war between Sweden and Russia and which forced Sweden to surrender to Russia not only mainland Finland, which had been an integral part of the Kingdom of Sweden since the 14th century, but also Åland, which historically belonged to this eastern part of Sweden. The Åland Islands were thus part of Finland at the time of its independence in 1917. The population of Åland, however, petitioned the Swedish government to negotiate a secession of Åland and to join the territory with Sweden. As a consequence, a dispute arose between Finland and Sweden. This was resolved in 1921 through the intervention of the League of Nations, when Finland and Sweden agreed in the so-called Åland Islands Settlement that the archipelago should continue under Finnish sovereignty, but that autonomy, originally established in 1920 with a publicly-elected assembly, should continue and that the area should maintain Swedish as the sole language[29] and preserve its own Swedish culture.[30] The international guarantee of the Åland Islands' autonomy thus arises out of a conflict between the two states.[31] This Åland Settlement should not be confused with the Åland Convention on demilitarisation and neutrality of the Åland Islands (see below).

Åland enjoys competence in a number of areas that would generally come under state or regional administration. The areas of competence include municipal and regional tax law, municipal division, building, zoning and expropriation law, rental law, social and health law, nature conservation and environmental law, education, land, forestry and fisheries law, mining law, the police, and postal services. In general, the legislative assembly of Åland possesses legislative powers in the sphere of public law and that part of criminal law which is auxiliary to its competence in public law, while the Finnish parliament is competent to legislate for Åland mainly within the sphere of private law and criminal law. Because the self-governing institutions of the Åland Islands take care of public functions that the state otherwise would have to take care of, the Self-Government Act stipulates that Åland is entitled to an equalizing amount from the state budget. This is around 0.45% of state expenditure. In addition, the Åland Islands may receive some more or less discretionary transfers, including compensation for certain taxes. The Åland Islands have their own coat of arms and flag.

---

[28] *Ahvenanmaan itsehallintolaki/ Självstyrelselag för Åland* 1144/1991.

[29] Finland is in any event a bilingual nation, with Finnish and Swedish as national languages.

[30] This agreement is the so-called Åland Islands Settlement. It is not an international treaty, but the Settlement is still regarded by Finland as unilaterally binding under international law.

[31] The first act on autonomy was passed in 1920 (Act No 124/1920), but opposition from the local population initially blocked the functioning of autonomy. The Åland Islands Settlement was implemented by Act No. 189/1922, after which the autonomy arrangement started to function.

Legislative power under self-government belongs to Åland's legislative assembly (*lagting*), while executive power is held by Åland's government (*landskapsregering*). Areas that are not assigned to Åland self-government are assigned in the Self-Government Act to the competence of the Finnish parliament. This includes foreign relations, but the Åland Islands have a certain possibility to participate in treaty negotiations conducted by Finland. After conclusion of a treaty by Finland, the entry into force of the treaty in the Åland jurisdiction requires the consent of the legislative assembly if the contents of the treaty fall within Åland legislative competence. In contrast to the Faroe Islands and Greenland, the Åland Islands are a part of Finland's EU membership, which was agreed to by the population of the Åland Islands in a separate advisory referendum held prior to the decision on consent made by the legislative assembly in 1994. It has been stated that Finland's membership in the EU has meant that "Åland is autonomous in relation to Finland, but not in relation to the EU",[32] meaning that the legislative power of Åland's legislative assembly, as assigned in the Self-Government Act, is limited by EU law.

Åland self-government may be regarded as exclusionary, in that a special regional citizenship (*hembygdsrätt*) is a pre-requisite for voting and the right to stand as a candidate in elections to the legislative assembly. The Åland Islands also impose limitations on the right to own land in relation to persons without regional citizenship,[33] as well as the right to carry out commercial business operations. In addition, Åland islanders who hold regional citizenship are exempt from military service obligations. In contrast to Faroese and Greenland autonomy, permanent residence is not an insignificant feature in the Åland Islands, because regional citizenship, which is a platform for the free exercise of the special rights of the Åland islanders, requires Finnish citizenship and a five-year uninterrupted residence in the Åland Islands.

With the Treaty of Paris of 1856, which brought an end to the Crimean War, the Åland Islands became a demilitarised zone. Demilitarisation was supplemented by neutrality in 1921 in a separate Convention on the neutrality and demilitarisation of the Åland Islands, undersigned by altogether ten states, mainly in the Baltic Sea area. Russia is not a party to the 1921 Convention, but entered in 1940 into a bilateral treaty with Finland about the demilitarisation of the Åland Islands.[34]

---

[32]Suksi (2014a, b), p. 50.

[33]The right to own land is regulated by the *Ahvenanmaan maanhankintalaki/Jordförvärvslag för Åland* 3/1975. On the basis of this Land Acquisition Act concerning Åland, enacted by the Finnish parliament, the Legislative Assembly of the Åland Islands has enacted Åland legislation that specifies the provisions of the 1975 Act.

[34]See Björkholm and Rosas (1990).

3 Indigenous Peoples and Minorities

3.1 The Sami in Finland, Norway and Sweden

The Sami are an ethnic minority which traditionally resides in the northern parts of Finland, Norway and Sweden, as well as in the Kola Peninsula in Russia. It is assumed that they immigrated to the area at least 2000 years ago. They are recognised as an indigenous people in the north. It is assumed that there are around 70,000 Sami, of which at least one-half reside in Norway.

The Sami have their own culture and languages, which form part of the Fenno-Ugric language group. A part of the Sami way of life has traditionally been nomadic or semi-nomadic, with reindeer husbandry[35] as a characteristic feature. Agriculture and fishing are also traditional occupations for Sami.[36] The Sami languages are recognised by Finland, Norway and Sweden as coming within the protection of the Framework Convention and the Language Charter.

Neither in Finland, Norway or Sweden do the Sami enjoy territorial self-government, but instead a non-territorial cultural autonomy. However, various rights are conferred on them as indigenous peoples and as minorities, including a state obligation to protect their language and culture. In addition, in Norway and Sweden, the Sami enjoy particular grazing rights for their reindeer (in Finland, non-Sami can also own reindeer within the reindeer-herding area, which is much larger than the Sami homeland area).

In Norway, the right to use and develop one's own language, culture and lifestyle is constitutionally protected in Section 110a of the Norwegian Constitution and catered for by the Sami Assembly, an independent statutory body.[37] Despite this, it was not until the entry into force of the Finnmark Act of 2005[38] that the Sami's collective land rights were acknowledged in Norway.[39] A specific land area in the northernmost part of Norway, previously mainly owned by the state of Norway, was defined as a particular legal person managed by a board, membership of which consists equally of representatives appointed by the state authorities of Norway and by the Norwegian Sami Assembly.[40] The position conferred to the

---

[35]Reindeer husbandry consists of looking after animals (reindeer), which are moved around to different pastures during the course of the year, in the same way as wild deer would move around seeking grazing opportunities. Therefore, the flock remains partially nomadic.

[36]Ravna (2012), p. 261.

[37]The Norwegian Constitution, *Kongeriket Norges Grunnlov* 1814 § 110a. See also Act on the Sami Assembly and on other Legal Relations (the Sami Act) of 1987 no 56. In addition to creating the Sami Assembly as a national body for the interests of the Sami in Norway, the Act equalizes the Sami language with the Norwegian language.

[38]Law on legal matters and management of basic and natural resources in Finnmark County, *Lov om rettsforhold og forvaltning av grunn og naturressurser i Finnmark fylke* 2005 no 85. See § 5.

[39]For a description of the difficult process for formal acceptance of this right, see Ravna (2012), p. 263 ff.

[40]See Suksi (2008), pp. 76–78.

land area by the Finnmark Act is a consequence of Norway's ratification of ILO Convention No. 169 concerning Indigenous and Tribal Peoples in Independent Countries.

In Finland, the Sami are recognized as an indigenous people and their right to develop their own language and culture is similarly constitutionally protected (§ 17 (3), § 121(4)). As concerns language, the Sami Language Act creates certain guarantees for the three Sami languages spoken in Finland (Northern Sami, Inari Sami and Skolt Sami).[41] As for culture in the broad sense of the term, a Sami Assembly is elected on the basis of the Sami Assembly Act,[42] also often referred to as the Sami Parliament Act, which works for the improvement of the Sami languages and for the status of the Sami. The Sami Assembly is an independent statutory body, but it holds no legislative powers, nor any significant executive powers. Ratification by Finland of ILO Convention No. 169 is still pending after years of preparation.

Sweden acknowledges in its Constitution that the Sami are a people[43] and has established its Sami Assembly as a state agency.[44] An act passed in 2009 on National Minorities and Minority Languages[45] also covers the Sami. In addition, in Sweden's 2009 Language Act,[46] Sami is recognized as a minority language entitled to a certain status before the courts and public authorities, while the public authorities are tasked with protecting and promoting national minority languages. However, Sweden has not ratified ILO Convention No. 169, and in Sweden the Sami's land rights are presumed to be too weak for Sweden to be able to adhere to the Convention. Minority protection for the Sami under minority legislation operates in Sweden within a geographically delimited area (within specified municipalities).

Hence, in each Nordic state where the Sami exist, that is, Finland, Norway and Sweden, a publicly elected representative assembly has been established for the Sami (*Sameting*). Each *Sameting* has its own organisational structure; in Finland and Norway, the assembly is an independent statutory body, while in Sweden it is a state agency. The three *Sameting* cooperate in a collective organisation (the Nordic Sami Council). A common feature of the three *Sameting* is their limited competence. Typically, however, each of them is conferred special administrative functions in connection with, for instance, language, education, as well as collective representation of the Sami before public authorities.

In this respect, material legislation, such as the mining legislation of Norway and Finland, may open up avenues of participation to the Sami Assemblies as counterparts to state authorities when applications for mining permits are being dealt with. The law may also grant Sami Assemblies the right to file complaints against

---

[41]The Sami Language Act (Act No. 1086/2003).

[42]The Sami Assembly Act (Act No. 974/1995).

[43]Section 1(2), sub-section 6, of the Instrument of Government.

[44]*Sametingslag* 1992:1433.

[45]*Lag om nationella minoriteter och minoritetsspråk* 2009:724.

[46]*Språklag* 2009:600.

mining permits granted to companies.[47] Nevertheless, the circumstances surrounding these representative assemblies probably cannot be properly described as effective self-government because the assemblies possess few public powers.[48]

3.2 *German Minority in Denmark*

The two former Duchies of Schleswig and Holstein (between Denmark and Germany) which today form the German state of Schleswig and Holstein and a part of Southern Denmark previously belonged to the Danish Crown. After the Second Schleswig War, these regions passed to Prussia and Austria under the Vienna peace agreement in 1864, and later became a part of Germany. Following a referendum at the end of the First World War in the 1920s, the northern part of Schleswig became a part of Denmark, with the result that a German-speaking minority (currently approximately 15,000 to 20,000 persons) came to live in Denmark, whereas a somewhat bigger Danish minority live in the German state of Schleswig-Holstein.

The Danish Constitution contains no special minority rules concerning the German minority, who have no specific status, not even in relation to political assemblies. In contrast with the Faroe Islanders and Greenlanders, the German minority is not ensured a representative in the Danish parliament.[49]

In the period following the Second World War, the conditions for the German minority—after a short period of sanctions against the minority as a result of their broad cooperation with the German occupying power—have developed into peaceful co-existence with the Danish-speaking population, in exactly the same way as conditions for the Danish minority in Germany. This development can, in particular, be attributed to the so-called Copenhagen Declaration of 29 March 1955 (and the equivalent German Bonn Declaration of the same date),[50] though this involves no greater protection than that applicable under Danish law to any Danish citizen. However, it does involve a political obligation to ensure the German minority the continuing opportunity to be a minority with its own organisations. Within the normal legislative framework, the German minority has established its own schools and a political party, which is represented in several municipal councils.

---

[47]See Amatulli (2015).

[48]See Suksi (2015).

[49]By contrast, the Danish minority in Germany enjoys special minority protection in the state of Schleswig-Holstein's administration (*Verfassung des Landes Schleswig-Holstein in der Fassung vom 2. Dezember 2014*). Therefore, in accordance with article 6, a citizen may freely associate with a minority, without being detached from normal civil duties. In addition, the state must protect cultural uniqueness. Pursuant to article 12, the state is obliged to accept and co-finance Danish schools. Following voting legislation, the Danish minority is further exempt from the normal threshold to the states parliament in Schleswig-Holstein.

[50]Reprinted by executive order no. 24 of 7 June 1955 concerning the German minority's common rights.

In connection with ratification of the Language Charter, Denmark has acknowledged the German language as the only language covered by the Charter.

3.3 National Languages and Minority Groups in Finland

For historical reasons, Finland also has a Swedish-speaking population outside the Åland Islands, equivalent to approximately 5.4% of the total population of Finland. The official languages as stated in the Constitution are Finnish *and* Swedish (§ 17). The languages are, therefore, placed on an equal footing and there also exist special Swedish language institutions, including educational institutions. Therefore, from a constitutional point of view, the Swedish-speakers of Finland are not a minority population, but a linguistic group equal to the linguistic group of Finnish-speakers. However, from the point of view of public international law, the Swedish-speakers may be regarded as a minority, although, in relation to the Language Charter, Finland has chosen to identify Swedish as a less widely-used official language to which a large number of provisions of the Charter apply.

This set-up, with two national and thus official languages, is the foundation for the national legislation of Finland being enacted in two languages, Finnish and Swedish, on the basis of § 79(4) of the Constitution and in the application of that legislation by administrative authorities and courts of law in the two languages within the framework of a combination of the personality principle and the territoriality principle, as established in the Language Act.[51] This means that central government authorities are bilingual in relation to the entire country, while regional state authorities are bilingual only to the extent to which their jurisdictions contain bilingual municipalities or unilingual municipalities where the other national language is the language of the municipality. Municipalities are thus the basis of the system, and a municipality may be unilingually Finnish-speaking, unilingually Swedish-speaking or bilingual either with Finnish or Swedish as the language of the majority.

Within this framework, and with some variation on the basis of material legislation,[52] the individual right to service in a person's own language, Finnish or Swedish, is guaranteed, although not always implemented with complete success.[53] The Swedish-speaking Peoples' Assembly (*folktinget*), indirectly elected in conjunction with local government elections, is a statutory body of an advisory nature that has been created to promote the position of the Swedish-speaking population in Finland.[54]

---

[51]Language Act, *Kielilaki/Språklag* 423/2003. For comparative reviews, see Suksi (2012) and (2014a, b). In the Åland Islands, legislation is enacted in Swedish only.

[52]In addition to the Language Act, more than 200 different Acts and Decrees establish the manner in which a system with two national languages should operate. See also § 122(1) of the Constitution of Finland on administrative division on linguistic grounds.

[53]Ministry of Justice (2013).

[54]*Lag om Svenska Finlands folkting* 1331/2003.

In the 2015 Sign Language Act,[55] the point of departure is that there is both a Finnish and a Finland-Swedish sign language, each of which is entitled to protection by the public authorities. To varying degrees and in addition to the population groups mentioned above, Roma, Karelians, Tatars and Jews[56] are also recognised as minorities, and the languages of these groups are recognised under the Language Charter.

3.4 *Minorities in Norway and Sweden*

According to the 2009 Act on National Minorities and Minority Languages of Sweden,[57] Jews, Roma, the Sami, Sweden-Finns and Tornedal Finns are national minorities in Sweden. Thus two groups of Finnish-language origin are recognised as separate minorities in Sweden.

In addition, in the 2009 Language Act of Sweden,[58] the national minority languages Finnish, Yiddish, Meänkieli (a variant of Finnish spoken in the North of Sweden by the Tornedal Finns), Romani Chib and Sami as well as sign language are recognized minority languages entitled to a certain status before the courts and public authorities. At the same time, the public authorities are given a duty to protect and promote the national minority languages. Approximately four per cent of the population of Sweden is Finnish-speaking.

No particular language act or minorities act exists in Norway, but some provisions in material legislation take into account minority groups, often in a very extensive manner so as also to cover migrant groups. In addition to the Sami, it is possible to identify at least two minority groups of Finnish origin in Norway, the Kvens and the Forest Finns.

4 Conclusion

As in Europe generally, a number of minorities of varying sizes have a long-lasting connection to one or more Nordic countries.[59] In addition to the Sami, a number of other minority groups are recognised in Finland, Norway and Sweden and these enjoy various minority rights. To the extent that they use their own language, these languages have been acknowledged as being covered by the Language Charter.

---

[55] *Viittomakielilaki/Teckenspråkslag* 359/2015.

[56] Jews are deemed to be a religious minority, but in accordance with their own wishes are also recognised as a national minority.

[57] *Lag om nationella minoriteter och minoritetsspråk* 2009:724.

[58] Act No. 2009:600.

[59] Defining who belongs to a minority can be problematic. And who belongs to the group is especially relevant when the group acquires special rights.

Territorial autonomy is a distinctive feature of Denmark and Finland but an exception in the Nordic region in general, with Iceland, Norway and Sweden organized as pure unitary states. By contrast, many minority groups exist in the Nordic region. To varying degrees, these enjoy a recognized or special status in all Nordic countries but Iceland, where no minorities of this kind exist. For instance, the Sami are entitled to non-territorial cultural autonomy in Finland, Norway and Sweden. In relation to Denmark, it is noteworthy that Faroe Islanders and Greenlanders residing in Denmark are not regarded as minorities.

Denmark differs from Finland, Norway and Sweden in that protection of minorities and self-governing territories is not in any way founded upon constitutional provisions. Only political representation for Faroe Islanders and Greenlanders in the Danish parliament is constitutionally established. However, ordinary constitutional rights and freedoms are applied in these two jurisdictions. Primary protection is adopted in law and formally amended by law. In addition, whereas Denmark only recognises one minority language (German), Finland, Norway and Sweden recognise more minority languages under the Language Charter.

In relation to the formalised cooperation between the Nordic countries in the Nordic Council, the Faroe Islands, Greenland and the Åland Islands each act independently and are represented by their own delegations in that inter-governmental organisation. The three autonomous regions are referred to explicitly in several provisions of the cooperation agreement between the Nordic countries.[60]

References

Amatulli G (2015) The legal position of the Sami in the exploitation of Mineral Resources in Finland, Norway and Sweden. https://www.abo.fi/wp-content/uploads/2018/03/2015-Amatulli-The-legal-position-of-the-Sami-in-the-exploitation-of-mineral-resources.pdf. Accessed 16 July 2018

Björkholm M, Rosas A (1990) Ålandsöarnas demilitarisering och neutralisering. Åbo Akademi, Åbo

Danish Institute for International Studies (2007) Afvikling af Grønlands kolonistatus 1945-54. Danish Institute for International Studies, Copenhagen

Ministry of Justice (2013) Report of the Government on the application of language legislation. Helsinki. http://oikeusministerio.fi/en/index/basicprovisions/perusoikeudetjademokratia/kielilaki.html. Accessed 16 July 2018

Ravna Ø (2012) Legal protection of coastal Sámi culture and livelihood in Norway. Yearb Polar Law 4:261–278

Suksi M (2008) Land rights and real property in the Nordic countries: a tentative sketch of an argument with some Nordic examples. Eur Ethn, 3–4

Suksi M (2011) Sub-state governance through territorial autonomy. Springer, Heidelberg

[60] Cooperation Agreement signed on 23 March 1962 between Denmark, Finland, Iceland, Norway and Sweden (*Helsingforsaftalen*).

Suksi M (2012) European and Nordic Norms concerning public and private use of language in the horizontal dimension. In: Knudsen KJL, Petersen HP, Rógvi K (eds) Language policy challenges of the future. Novus forlag, Oslo, pp 131–153
Suksi M (2014a) Rätten att använda sitt eget språk. Brunstad E, Helland Gujord A, & Bugge E (red) Rom for språk – nye innsikter i språkleg mangflald. Novus forlag, Oslo, pp 33–70
Suksi M (2014b) Territorial autonomy: the Åland Islands in comparison with other sub-state entities. In: Kántor Z (ed) Territorial autonomies in Europe: solutions and challenges. NPKI & L'Harmattan, Budapest
Suksi M (2015) Non-territorial autonomy: the meaning of '(Non-)Territoriality'. In: Malloy T, Palermo F (eds) Minority accommodation through territorial and non-territorial autonomy. Oxford University Press, Oxford, pp 83–115

Promoting Gender Equality

Johanna Niemi

Abstract In the following the Nordic legal feminism is discussed. Nordic gender equality policy and law have been integrated with the welfare state, promoting general equality. All Nordic countries have ascribed to strategic equality policies, however, with somewhat different vigour. In all these countries gender equality laws have been assigned an active role in promoting equality and preventing discrimination. Lately, research in law and gender has turned to theory and gender and sex are seen as socially constructed through legal discourses and practices in all fields of law. The chapter argues that different feminist approaches are still relevant for the analysis of law.

1 Introduction

The Nordic countries always score highest in gender equality rankings. The foundations for gender equality are found in the history of these countries: Finnish women received the right to vote and to be elected in national elections as early as 1906, and in the other Nordic countries during the next decades. Apart from suffrage for white women in Australia in 1903 and the right to vote (but not to be elected) in New Zealand in 1893, Finnish women were the first in the world to achieve comprehensive electoral rights.

The number of female parliamentarians has been relatively high in the Nordic countries and Nordic women have broken the glass ceiling at the highest level in politics. In Denmark, Queen Margrethe II has reigned since 1972 and both Iceland and Finland have had female heads of state in the shape of Icelandic President Vigdis Finnbogadottir (1980–1996) and Finnish President Tarja Halonen (2000–2012). Norway enjoys a tradition of female prime ministers with Gro Harlem Bruntland, who served several terms between 1981 and 1996, and Erna Solberg

J. Niemi (✉)
Faculty of Law, University of Turku, Turku, Finland
e-mail: johanna.niemi@utu.fi

© Springer Nature Switzerland AG 2019

P. Letto-Vanamo et al. (eds.), *Nordic Law in European Context*,
Ius Gentium: Comparative Perspectives on Law and Justice 73,
https://doi.org/10.1007/978-3-030-03006-3_5

since 2013. Finland has also had two short-term female prime ministers in the shape of Anneli Jäätteenmäki and Mari Kiviniemi.

The Nordic people are both conscious and proud of their gender equality. However, some differences still exist among them in laws, policies and attitudes. Feminism has been a state policy in Sweden, especially in the 1990s; indeed, Sweden has promoted feminist values even in its foreign policy. In Norway we find a profile of promoting women's issues. In Finland, both politicians and the public take equality for granted, as something already achieved, so that feminist critique can meet fierce opposition.

In all Nordic countries, women's position has been advanced together with the development of the welfare state.[1] From the 1960s until the 1980s the welfare state project meant, among other things, a levelling of social stratification, a widening of access to higher education and rapid urbanization. All these changes favoured women, who accessed education en masse. Thus, the advancement of women has formed part of a more general policy towards welfare, well-being and social equality than a conscious gender policy. Equality has often been understood as a general policy goal, rather than a concrete right of individual women not to be discriminated against.

International commitments in the field of equality have provided important impulses to equality work and legislation. In particular, international and European legal instruments have promoted anti-discrimination laws and a shift towards a more individualistic approach to equality. The international Convention on the Elimination of All Forms of Discrimination against Women (CEDAW)[2] was important for the enactment of equality laws in the 1980s. Additionally, European Union law, in which legislation against sex discrimination evolved as part of the development of the internal market alongside the prohibition of discrimination on the basis of nationality, influenced Nordic equality laws even before Finland and Sweden joined the European Union in 1995.

In European Union law, anti-discrimination became a central principle in the Charter of Fundamental Rights (2000) and the Lisbon Treaty on European Union (2009). In 2000, after the Treaty of Amsterdam, the European Union strengthened its equality policy and anti-discrimination legislation on the grounds of race, religion, belief, disability, age and sexual orientation. In the Nordic countries, anti-discrimination laws have also incorporated these grounds of discrimination.[3]

This chapter discusses the main areas of law that are central from the point of view of gender. Besides equality law, anti-discrimination law concerning other grounds of discrimination is also important for the rights of women, because discrimination on multiple grounds often means that women are discriminated against both as women and as members of an ethnic group or because of their age, disability, or other status.

---

[1]Pylkkänen (2009) and Bailliet (2016).

[2]1979, UNTC I-20378.

[3]NIKK (2008) and Skjeie and Langvasbråten (2009).

In gender studies, different phases of gender politics and research have been classified into three waves of feminism. The wave metaphor has been used in somewhat different ways as the feminist movement has assumed somewhat different forms in different countries. However, broadly speaking we can distinguish liberal feminism, standpoint feminism and postmodern feminism.[4] In the Nordic context, the second wave was intertwined with the welfare state and often described as state feminism, as discussed in Sect. 3 of the chapter.

These phases or waves are not, however, distinct. Even if gender studies are today predominantly preoccupied with postmodern issues of construction of sex and gender, feminist claims for gender equality and governmental equality policies are still based on liberal and welfare state views on equality more generally. However, these claims today encompass other vulnerable groups and sex and sexual minorities in particular.

Today, we use the terms "law and gender" or "gender studies in law". By the term "gender" we mean gender as a social construction as opposed to a biological category. In a postmodern understanding, gender is not limited to the dichotomy of men and women but includes other possible gender identifications as well. In Scandinavian scholarship, the terms "women's studies" and "women and law" were frequently used in the 1990s. This has a connection with the idea of promoting women's rights. Feminist studies and feminist legal studies, the terms used in English-speaking countries in the 1980s and 1990s, have not gained popularity in the Nordic countries. Particularly in Finland, the word "feminist" is still often understood as pejorative, in contrast to Sweden, where everyone, including present and former prime ministers Fredrik Reinfelt and Göran Persson, have declared themselves to be feminists.

Actually, the term "feminism" possesses certain merits: Feminism is a wide concept, covering many different schools of feminist thought (which exist in abundance), and including postmodern pluralist thinking. The ideas that all feminists share are that gender equality constitutes an important social goal which we have not yet reached and that this state of affairs is in some way or other related to gendered power structures in society. When this definition is used, most Nordic people are feminists—notwithstanding their gender. This definition of feminism covers a wide range of research topics and a variety of methodological choices, including in the field of law. Usually gender research is also related to political feminism in that it aims at improving women's position and promoting equality.

Therefore, it is natural to see the present shift towards gender studies as a continuum of feminist studies. Gender studies also cover other manifestations of sex and gender, such as gay, lesbian, bisexual and transgender individuals, often covered by the term 'queer'. Queer studies is a theoretical term that involves wide implications for traditional feminist studies as well, as I shall show later in this article. In recent masculinity research the position of men and the male sex is also

[4]My terminology has been influenced by Smart (1991).

highlighted. Contemporary men's studies, or men and masculinity studies, share with feminism a critical analysis of the gender system.

2 Liberal Feminism and Gender Neutrality of Laws

Liberal feminism has striven for equal rights on the premise that persons with equal merits should enjoy similar entitlements. The liberal concept of equality is based on similarity: similarity in law and similarity in merits. If the liberal pursuit in law is understood as gender neutrality and as similar law irrespective of one's sex and gender, then equality is to a large extent a state that in the Nordic countries has already been achieved.

Besides universal suffrage, several other legal reforms in the late 19th and early 20th centuries gave women the same rights that men already enjoyed. Unmarried women of legal age were no longer under male guardianship as they had been before. Women gradually obtained access to the labour market, where industrialization created a demand for a cheap female work force. At first, unmarried women and widows were allowed to work, later followed by married women. Gradually they even obtained the right to keep and use the money they earned, instead of having to hand it over to their husbands. Women also obtained access to the civil service, for example in Finland in 1926.

Equal rights in marriage were granted in reform of the Marriage Act, for example in Finland in 1929.[5] The main principle in matrimonial property is that each spouse controls their own income and property during the marriage and on divorce the property is divided equally between them. Additionally, male privileges in the guardianship of children were abolished. The right for men and women to inherit on an equal footing was achieved by the late 19th century.

In labour law, special measures that protected women from heavy and hazardous working conditions have largely been abolished. These regulations were criticized by feminists because they restricted women's access to the labour market. For example, protection against night shifts kept women out of well-paid jobs in factories but never excluded them from low-paid jobs in hospitals. I have a personal recollection from the 1960s, when I could read newspapers for the first time. A single mother working in a metal foundry was interviewed and asked what she thought about the work. "At first I thought I could never do such a tough job but when I heard the wages, I changed my mind."

Pension ages long differed between women and men. Although clearly discriminatory, this was experienced in different ways. Some people thought that it was a privilege for women to retire earlier than men. However, many women found that their pension benefits remained very low, especially if their working years had

[5] Melby et al. (2000).

been interrupted by childbirth and childcare. Due to European Union law, retirement ages have been equalized as between men and women.

Today, most gender-specific laws have been abolished. Achieving this has not been a simple matter, however. As late as the early 1980s the Finnish Parliament was unable to agree on a woman's right to keep her own last name upon marriage, and the government had to withdraw a Bill to that effect. This law was finally passed in 1986, though, following ratification of the 1979 CEDAW Convention in 1986.

The Lutheran Christian Church has been the dominant religion in all Nordic countries. Today all Nordic Lutheran churches ordain women as priests. The Danish church was the first in the world to do so in 1948, followed by the Swedish church in 1958 and Norway in 1961. In Finland, the Church still works in close proximity to the state. Thus, when Finland ratified the CEDAW in 1985, the Church accepted that women can be ordained as priests. Still today some male priests find it difficult to work with women in Denmark as well as Finland.

Still a few sex-specific regulations remain, such as conscription in military service, which is mandatory for men in Finland and to some extent in Sweden and Norway but an option for women. Another example of a sex-specific regulation is maternity leave. However, parental leave is gender-neutral, even if used mostly by women. These exceptions may be symbolically important but by and large the liberal goal of gender-neutral laws and formally equal rights for all has been achieved.

3 State Feminism and Women's Law

Promotion of women's rights in the Nordic countries has formed an essential part of general welfare policies. General social, health and educational policies have enormously benefited women.[6] Of specific importance for women have been childcare policies, although these may in part have reinforced traditional gender roles.

Two issues of legal relevance are of key importance: the universal and individual nature of rights.[7] Basic social and educational rights belong universally to every individual, instead of being left to the discretion of families, employers or local communities. The educational system, starting with the introduction of compulsory basic education in the 1920s and encompassing free school meals in Finland and Sweden after the Second World War, has been the key to the social ladder for both men and women. Free university education and the expansion of the university

[6]Kantola (2014) and Kalliomaa-Puha (2000).

[7]See for example Esping-Andersen (1990).

system in the 1960s and 1970s gave women access to the highest levels of education, an opportunity that women have taken full advantage of. Today, over half of university graduates and half of new doctors are women. Equally, access to healthcare has benefited women.

Free prenatal care, which is combined with cash benefits after a baby is born, has secured the health of both mothers and babies. These reforms have formed part of the general welfare state project, instead of falling specifically under the category of women's rights. Social security contributions, both at the residual level and earned benefits, are organized as individual rights, not on a family basis. This has promoted women's roles as working mothers both in marriage and as single parents.

Nordic women have actively contributed to development of the welfare state. In addition to political participation at the highest levels, women have been active in formulating welfare policies as civil servants in the healthcare and social sector. Incorporation of women's interests in the welfare state project is known as state feminism. In the Nordic countries most feminists have seen the state as an ally for women and as a forum for realizing women-friendly policies, as opposed to more critical approaches towards the state in, for example, German and American feminism.[8] There has also been a tendency to see equality policy as an issue for social welfare, rather than one of rights. This is evident in the institutional setting of the European Union and for example in Finland equality policy has always been the responsibility of the Ministry of Social Affairs, thus underlining the connection of women's rights as a dimension of the welfare state project.

The proximity between the welfare state project and women's interests is also seen in research on women's rights in the 1970s and 1980s. In the 1980s, feminist legal scholarship started to gain ground when Professor Tove Stang Dahl in Oslo set up a research group and a research school in Women's Law with a research agenda of introducing women's perspective in legal analysis. The group mostly employed the strict legal dogmatic method in analyses of legal problems that women often encounter in their everyday lives, such as rights of a home-maker wife, and life crises, such as divorce. Stang Dahl's major works are entitled Women's Law I and II.[9] After Stang Dahl's early death, many Norwegian scholars continued this type of work.

The early studies on women's rights in the 1970s and 1980s often focused on labour law and social law.[10] Women's economic and social rights have been analysed in the triangle of three support systems: market (women's employment), state (welfare state) and family (Fig. 5.1). For example, in Denmark Ruth Nielsen and Kirsten Ketcher were interested in these issues.

Both in equality politics and in feminist research, including feminist legal research, typical questions concerned the possibility for women to combine work and family. Women's economic self-reliance was an unquestioned goal. Economic

[8]Elman (1996) and Holli (2003).

[9]Stang Dahl (1985a, b).

[10]Kalliomaa-Puha (2000).

Fig. 5.1 Triangle of three support systems

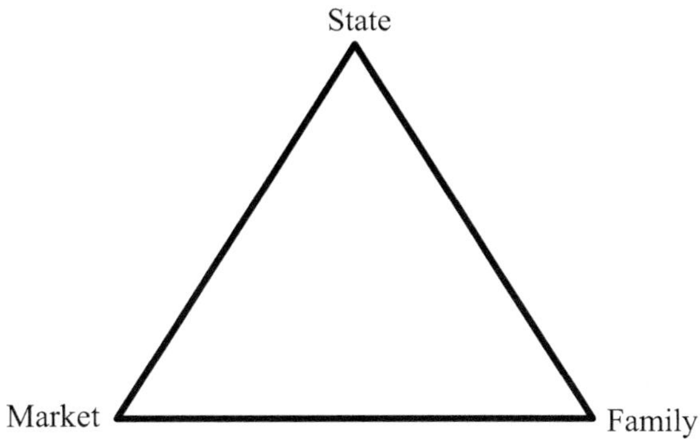

independence was seen as a key to women's emancipation. Issues about unequal pay for equal work and social support benefits, such as retirement benefit, which depend on the level of salaries and years in paid labour, have been discussed in equality politics and research.

The combination of work and childcare has interested feminist legal scholars in the Nordic countries, very often from the point of view of social security benefits and childcare. Women's rights to benefits, the possible discriminatory effects of regulation, and access to childcare have been typical areas of research. A goal of the research has been to depict and articulate in legal form situations that are typical for women and argue for interpretations and legal reforms that take women's interests into account.

One of the most important welfare state reforms for women has been the establishment of childcare systems in the 1970s and 1980s. All the Nordic countries have established childcare and early childhood education systems that enable women to work full-time. All Nordic countries provide a network of childcare centres, which are seven-to-five Kindergartens with a professional staff, accessible for children over the age of one year. All Nordic countries also make generous parental leave available during a child's first year. There are differences, however, and the Swedish and the Finnish system are compared next.

Both feminist equality politics and concern about falling birth rates have contributed to childcare reforms in Sweden. Childcare centres, *dagis*, are either run or subsidised by municipalities, provided at low cost to families and very popular among parents of children under school age. The right to parental leave is an individual right up to thirteen months, for both parents. Up to ten months (half of it to each parent) leave is supported at a level relative to the parent's income. A parent can allocate his or her share of paid leave to the other parent.

The real innovation about Swedish parental leave is its flexibility. The parents can agree between themselves and together with their employers the most suitable use of parental leave time. It is possible to take the traditional mode in which one parent stays at home with the baby for a certain number of months and then returns to full-time work. But it is also possible to agree on less conventional approaches to childcare. Some parents choose to work part-time, so that one of them cares for the baby in the mornings and the other in the afternoons, with both on parental leave from work for 50% or one for 40 and the other for 60%. One of them can be on parental leave on Mondays and Tuesdays and the other for the rest of the week. It is also possible to stretch out parental leave until the child is seven years old. This is an option if the parents work part-time anyway or if they are helped by relatives.

The flexibility of the Swedish parental leave system has helped to increase the fertility rate. Employers do not complain because in many cases flexibility is helpful for them as well. It is important, however, to make agreements on how parental leave is used well in advance.

In Finland, the question of a subjective right to day care turned out to be a paramount issue in feminist legal jurisprudence. In the late 1970s and 1980s, demand for municipal childcare facilities increased. Day care became a threshold for women's participation in the labour force when middle class women started to enrol their children in municipal day care centres, which had earlier mostly served single mothers. Law reforms in the 1980s gave a subjective right to day care for parents and children, with a duty placed on municipalities to provide it. The nature of this right was contested in the courts, which confirmed that it is a subjective right entailing entitlement to monetary compensation if the municipality is unable to provide day care for a child.

Parental leave has been gradually extended up to ten months. After the initial period, which is allocated to the mother, parents can share the leave but in practice women use well over 90% of parental leave. To incentivize fathers, a specific "father's month" that only a father can use has been introduced. Today a father's month amounts to fifty-four days excluding Sundays and can be used while the mother is on leave as well.

The costs of day care centres scared Finnish politicians, many of whom have strong family sentiments. To facilitate home care by the mother and to keep children out of municipal childcare, a home care allowance was introduced in the early 1990s. The home care allowance is available until a child is three years old. The state allowance is relatively low but many municipalities complement it with their own contributions.[11]

The consequence of these complementary systems is that the share of children in childcare centres and in early childhood education in Finland is much lower than in other Nordic countries.[12] Women with a university education return to work after parental leave when the child is one year old and use both municipal and private childcare centres and other private arrangements. The home care allowance is used almost exclusively by women of modest education and without a job to return to after three years at home.

Women's rights have been central in establishing a childcare system. The goal has been to ensure women the same opportunities as men in the labour market. The Swedish system has clearly promoted that goal. The share of men using parental

[11]Salmi (2000).

[12]Eydal and Rostgaard (2011) and Meagher and Szebehely (2012).

leave days is the highest in the world at well over twenty per cent. In Finland the system has had a perverted opposite effect for women of modest education. Another effect has been that all young women, irrespective of education, work much more on fixed-term job contracts than men of the same age. Only recently has discussion started on reform of the system but the proposals have so far been based on models in which one parent stays at home for a certain number of months. A flexibility that would better correspond to the post-modern labour market has not been put on the table.

4 Equality Law

Both gender-neutral legislation and the welfare state have promoted women's rights in many ways. Nevertheless, equality has not been achieved, so that differences in the respective positions of women and men persist in many areas of social and private life, to the detriment of women.[13] Pay gaps have diminished but women's salaries remain at 80–85% of those of men, which can only partly be explained by factors other than gender. When women and men with the same education and the same type of occupation are compared, the gender pay gap is roughly ten per cent. The gender pay gap increases when well-educated women and men are compared. At higher levels of the labour hierarchy we still find few women. Women tend to rise to a certain level but not to the highest levels, the so-called glass ceiling effect. The labour market is heavily segregated along gender lines. Women tend to work in healthcare and social services and in the public sector, while men work in manufacturing and private businesses. Young women work more often than men on fixed-term contracts. Women still bear the main responsibility for childcare and household work, both during and after marriage, even when both parents work full time. In political decision-making women do relatively well, but non-elected bodies tend to have more men than women.

These problems were acknowledged when ratification of CEDAW (1979) came on the political agenda. The Convention is based on a strong notion of material, real-life equality and requires active measures and policies by state governments and other actors to achieve equality. The Convention prohibits both direct and indirect discrimination, in law and in practice. It also obliges states to promulgate active measures and policies to ensure equality between the sexes and to promote women by guaranteeing them the exercise of their human rights on an equal footing with men.

[13]Nousiainen (2008).

The Convention contributed to the enactment of equality laws in the 1980s and to the setting up of equality bodies. These acts[14] introduced both anti-discrimination measures and measures to promote equality.[15] The purpose of equality laws is to promote the position of women, with the focus on working life. Private relationships, referring to family, friendship and religious worship, are excluded from the scope of equality laws.

These laws prohibit both direct and indirect discrimination. Indirect discrimination is defined along the same lines as in CEDAW and European Union anti-discrimination directives, meaning all measures and policies that de facto lead to differential treatment of the sexes. Sexual harassment is specifically mentioned as a form of unlawful discrimination.

Specific measures to promote equality are not considered discriminatory even if they include differential treatment of employees on the grounds of sex, at least for a while. This provision enables promotion of the underrepresented sex in access to employment, promotion and other situations. According to the case law of the European Court of Justice (ECJ), such positive action is possible if applicants have merits that are assessed at an almost equal level and if positive action follows a plan and is of intermediate duration.[16] Sometimes the Nordic countries have wanted to take more progressive steps, such as in Sweden's programme in the 1990s to increase the share of female professors at universities, which initially stood at below twenty per cent. In *Abrahamsson* et al. the ECJ confirmed that the sex of the applicant could not be decisive beyond the above mentioned specific conditions. In reality, affirmative action-type measures are hardly ever used in recruitment or promotion procedures in the Nordic countries.

The equality laws include other types of positive measures to promote equality that are not connected to individual rights. Since equality is both a fundamental, constitutional right and a legal principle according to equality laws, the authorities and employers should take it into account in their activities and promote equality.

In Finland an important tool is an equality plan, which each employer with over thirty employees is obliged to set up, as are educational institutions, too. According to surveys, many employers have made equality plans since the duty was upgraded in 2005. In practice, however, the planning process is not yet well-rooted in relationships between employers and employees. A specific issue debated in the legislative reform of 2005 concerned transparency in mapping pay differentials between the sexes.[17]

[14]Denmark: *Lov om ligestilling af kvinder og mænd* 2013 no 1678, Finland: *Laki naisten ja miesten välisestä tasa-arvosta/Lag om jämställdhet mellan kvinnor och män* 609/1986, Island: *Lög um jafna stöðu og jafnan rétt kvenna og karla* 10/2008, Norway: *Lov om likestilling mellom kjønnene* 1978 no 45, Sweden: *Diskrimineringslag* 2008:567.

[15]This development is seen as individualization of gender equality and its beneficial impact on women has been questioned. See Pylkkänen (2008).

[16]E.g. ECJ *Kalanke v Freie Hansestadt Bremen* (1995) C-450/93.

[17]Saari (2011) and Ikävalko (2016).

Another important tool is quotas to promote equal representation of the sexes in public and expert bodies. At least forty per cent of the members of appointed state and municipal bodies should be of each sex. At first, this rule was met with serious reservations in the municipalities. The argument was that it is impossible to find competent women for municipal boards dealing with, for example, public works. In practice, though, the municipalities have been successful in fulfilling their quotas with qualified women and men. However, in state government we can still find committees, boards and working groups that do not have the required quota of women. In Norway, quotas are also required on the boards of publicly traded companies.

In the other Nordic countries, discussions about quotas for company boards have been discussed, at times even heatedly. In Finland the Chamber of Commerce, representing business interests, has actively promoted voluntary appointment of women to the boards, in order to avoid binding legislation. The campaign has been successful and the share of female board members is close to thirty per cent.

Equality laws, equality policies by governments and feminist movements have been successful in many respects. The problems listed at the beginning of this chapter still exist but to a lesser extent than before active engagement in equality work.[18] Thus, equality policies are still needed. However, some aspects of discrimination have been slowly recognized as equality problems. One of these is violence against women.

5 Gender Difference and Violence Against Women

Both liberal and welfare state approaches to equality can be and have been criticized for setting men as the norm. The liberal take on equality argues that women have the right to equality if and when they have the same merits as men. The same criticism can be directed at equality legislation, which favours active policies to promote women's achievements at the same level with men. The goal is to achieve equality according to the standards of men, so that it is against the male standard that gender inequality is compared.

In cultural feminism of the 1980s, the sameness of the sexes was challenged and sexual difference was taken as the starting point. In legal studies, cultural feminism has not gained much popularity. Women's history, experiences and values have been visible in art, theatre and literature as well as in the historical, social and cultural sciences. However, gender difference is not easily adapted into legal standards. Rather, female lawyers and scholars have often noted that differential treatment is a double-edged sword. It may protect some women but it is easily directed against some of those whom it should have protected.

[18]About Nordic Legal research see Svensson et al. (2011).

In issues of violence it is difficult to maintain the position that sameness is the norm of equality. Violence is clearly gendered: while men and women are, roughly, equally often victimized by violence, the circumstances of victimization are gendered. While the most dangerous place for men is the street and, especially in Finland, the company of other intoxicated and socially marginalized men, the most dangerous place for women is the home. The perpetrators are in both cases predominantly men. Sexual violence is directed mostly towards women, along with children of both sexes. The perpetrators are, again, predominantly (adult) males.

Feminists have long been raising issues of violence against women. However, the state apparatus has been somewhat slow to take action. The ideology of equality was one of the factors that delayed the "detection" of domestic violence and other forms of violence against women.[19] Since the laws have been formally gender-neutral, reform proposals have often been rejected. Legal reform has proceeded at different speeds in the Nordic countries. While rape in marriage was made a crime in Swedish Penal Code reform in 1965, in Finland the same reform was only achieved in 1994. Petty assault, that is, minor violence with no physical damage, became subject to public prosecution in the early 1980s in most Nordic countries, though only in 2011 in Finland.

Serious research on prevalence and legal practices started in the Nordic countries in the 1990s. The results of prevalence studies have been sobering. A large and ambitious prevalence study was conducted at about the same time in Finland and Sweden in the late 1990s.[20] These studies showed that violence against women was far more prevalent than expected. Some 40% of women had experienced violence in some form since they turned 15; about 20% had experienced violence in an intimate partnership during their lifetime; and almost ten per cent during the previous year.

Compared with national studies in many other parts of the world and global studies by the WHO, these figures are not alarming, high as they may seem. However, a recent study by the European Union Fundamental Rights Agency (2014)[21] reported very high levels of violence against women in the Nordic members of the EU as compared to other Member States on almost any form of violence. The results may be partly explained by the research methodology and partly by social conditions.[22] It is possible that in a door-to-door survey Nordic women speak about domestic and sexual violence more freely than women in some other Member States. It is also possible that Nordic women who work and spend leisure time outside the home encounter more sexual harassment than women in countries where they are more controlled. Notwithstanding, there seems to be no reason to be deluded into believing the Nordic countries have no problem of violence against women.

---

[19]Elman (1996) and Nousiainen et al. (2001). From the perspective of children Eriksson et al. (2005).

[20]Lundgren et al. (2001) and Piispa and Heiskanen (1998).

[21]FRA (2014).

[22]Gracia and Merlo (2016).

In Sweden, a prevalence study in 2000[23] provoked heated discussion. Its methodology was criticized but the main response was concern. Sweden had already started a review of legislation on violence against women and the report on Women's Peace in 1995 proposed several amendments.[24] Two reforms appeared as the flagship of the reform package: the new crime of violating a woman's peace and a prohibition on buying sex. The first-mentioned reform means that repeated violence against a spouse or other close person leads, on conviction, to a penalty according to a higher sentencing scale than an isolated assault.[25] This reform is in line with an overall European reform trend of assessing violence between family members as more serious than violence in other contexts. The prohibition on buying sex was remarkable because only buying sex is an offence but not the behaviour of the seller, that is, the woman who is abused in prostitution. This reform was introduced later in Norway and Iceland (2009) and as a prohibition on abusing a person who has been subject to trafficking or procuring in Finland (2006).[26]

Structures that restrain effective responses to violence against women do not always involve clear and explicit legal provisions. The research project on Violence in the Shadow of Equality (1998–2004) undertook to analyse whether legislation and/or the reactions of the criminal justice system could be improved. The gendered features of law and legal practices could not, however, be straightforwardly seen. Therefore, the project started to analyse how violence was spoken about in legal texts. Law texts, preparatory works, court cases and police protocols were analysed as texts that construct central concepts of law and legally relevant practices, such as violence, gender, self-defence, consent, aggravated circumstances, and so on. In the eyes of the legal system, real violence involved violence between two males, whereas violence at home was often constructed as a disturbance, quarrel or dispute.[27] Violence could be downgraded or ignored, for example, in child custody cases, in rape cases and in cases involving domestic violence. In cases where a woman had killed her partner and tried to invoke self-defence, evidence of violence by the male partner was often dismissed.[28] The project concluded that legal texts, documents and practices are powerful discourses in constructing the concept of violence.

6 Gender as a Social Construction

Second wave feminism, which in this account is represented by state feminism, has been criticized for taking the woman in women's perspective for granted. Criticism has come from many fronts. Women from ethnic minorities have raised their voices

---

[23]Lundgren et al. (2001).

[24]Niemi-Kiesiläinen (2010).

[25]Nordborg and Niemi-Kiesiläinen (2001).

[26]Niemi (2010).

[27]Niemi-Kiesiläinen (2005).

[28]Ruuskanen (2001).

and asked "Ain't I a woman?", to quote the famous anti-slavery campaigner Sojouner Truth, as well as Third World women and lesbian women. The core of the criticism has been that white, middle class women have hijacked feminism and simply replaced white, middle class men with their own self-image.

The theoretical issue involved has been the concept of "woman". Liberal feminism, arguing for similar rights, emphasizes the universal similarity of human beings and thus the sameness of the sexes. The Nordic welfare state was also based on promoting similarity and the idea that equality meant the same rights for everyone. Second wave feminism acknowledged that women's position is not the same as men's and drew a distinction between sex, as biological and static sex, and gender, as the social organization of the roles of men and women. Welfare state proposals for change were often based on the belief that societal obstacles to equality could be removed and equality as sameness achieved.[29]

The idea of the sameness of the sexes has been questioned in many ways.[30] Research on violence against women, while arguing strongly that violence involves a social context, made clear beyond doubt the gendered and sexed nature of violence and its sexualized dimensions. But sex difference was a difficult issue for feminists as it has been historically used to marginalize women and their rights.

Thus, the idea of gender as socially constructed has been welcomed by feminist researchers. When gender is understood as constructed in social practices or, to use Judith Butler's theoretical concept,[31] as performed by different women and men, the differences among women are not an obstacle to theoretical understandings of gender. Gender theory has also opened up new opportunities for acknowledging women's agency in achieving change in gender roles and gendered patterns, without abandoning the understanding of gender as an existing fact and even as a societal structure.

At the same time it has become clear that the man/woman dichotomy is not sufficient to encompass gender differences in postmodern and multicultural societies. The study of gender, indeed the concept of gender itself, also has to cover gays and lesbians, bisexuals and those who have a transgender identity or who undergo sex correction. Alongside feminist studies, queer studies have questioned the binary gender structure using the concept of heteronormativity. Queer studies argue that societies are structured around the idea of two sexes and two gender roles, excluding other expressions of sexuality, gender identity and other forms of organizing private and social lives.

As feminist studies have turned into gender studies and become more theoretical,[32] the close connections between feminist studies and feminism as a political movement seem to have thinned out. This may be an illusion. Legal studies in

[29]Equality work as a requirement for women to change has been identified as an underlying structure in Nordic equality work. See Edström and Brunila (2016).

[30]Svensson et al. (2004).

[31]Butler (2006).

[32]Gunnarsson et al. (2007) and Gunnarsson and Svensson (2009).

particular are still relevant for feminist claims to equal rights and better protection. Legal arguments of non-discrimination and equality are frequently used, for example, to argue for gay and lesbian rights. Responding to intersecting categories or multiple discrimination still requires legal categories.[33] The standard comparison between men and women has lost its central role in anti-discrimination law but the concept of differential treatment on the basis of sex and gender is still central. Now differential treatment can be induced from the circumstances of the case. For example, discrimination on the basis of pregnancy no longer requires a non-pregnant comparator. Intersecting grounds of discrimination should not lead to confusion but to the understanding that legal practices also contribute to the construction of new categories.

7 Conclusion

We have seen enormous growth and development in gender research during recent decades. From liberal conceptions of formal equality and the simple idea of equality as sameness, we have moved to welfare state goals of promoting gender equality and women's position as part of the general policy of promoting social equality. Today, gender studies occupy a broad scope on gender, including gay, lesbian, bisexual and transgender rights. Yet gender studies, including men's studies or studies in masculinity, build firmly on the basis of feminist studies of the last century.

Besides presenting Nordic law on gender, the purpose of this chapter has been to show that gender research is relevant to the study of law. Liberal notions of equality remain important for the regulation of civil, criminal and distributive rights. Gender perspectives as an empirical and analytical approach are important in implementing rights and in monitoring how rights are realized. Finally, the emancipatory potential of law can only be understood when we start to see the legal system and legal discourses as constitutive of sex, gender and other identities.

References

Bailliet CM (2016) A Nordic approach to promoting women's rights within international law: internal v. external perspectives. Nord J Int Law 85(4):368–394. http://booksandjournals.brillonline.com/content/journals/10.1163/15718107-08504003. Accessed 13 July 2018

Butler J (2006) Gender trouble: feminism and the subversion of identity. Routledge Classics. Routledge, London

Edström C, Brunila K (2016) Troubling gender equality: revisiting gender equality work in the famous Nordic model countries. Educ Change 20(1):10–27

[33] Schiek and Chege (2009).

Elman RA (1996) Sexual subordination and state intervention: comparing Sweden and the United States. Berghahn Books, Providence (R.I.)
Eriksson M, Hester M, Keskinen S, Pringle K (eds) (2005) Tackling men's violence in families: Nordic issues and dilemmas. Polity Press, Bristol
Esping-Andersen G (1990) The three worlds of welfare capitalism. Polity Press, Cambridge
Eydal GB, Rostgaard T (2011) Gender equality revisited—changes in Nordic childcare policies in the 2000s. Soc Policy Adm 45(2):161–179
FRA (2014) Violence against women: An EU-wide survey. European Union Agency for Fundamental Rights. http://fra.europa.eu/sites/default/files/fra-2014-vaw-survey-main-results-apr14_en.pdf. Accessed 13 July 2018
Gracia E, Merlo J (2016) Intimate partner violence against women and the Nordic paradox. Soc Sci Med 157:27–30
Gunnarsson Å, Svensson E (2009) Genusrättsvetenskap. Lund, Studentlitteratur. http://linda.linneanet.fi/F/?func=direct&doc_number=005238663&local_base=fin01. Accessed 13 July 2018
Gunnarsson Å, Svensson E, Davies M (eds) (2007) Exploiting the limits of law: Swedish feminism and the challenge to pessimism. Ashgate, Aldershot
Holli A (2003) Discourse and politics for gender equality in late twentieth century Finland. Acta Politica 23. Department of Social Science, University of Helsinki
Ikävalko E (2016) Vaikenemisia Ja Vastarintaa: Valtasuhteet Ja Toiminnan Mahdollisuudet Oppilaitosten Tasa-Arvosuunnittelussa. University of Helsinki
Kalliomaa-Puha L (ed) (2000) Perspectives of equality: work, women and family in the Nordic Countries and EU. Nordisk ministerråd, Copenhagen
Kantola J (2014) The paradoxical gendered consequences of the EU policy on multiple discrimination: the Nordic case. Eur Integr Online Pap 18:1–19
Lundgren E, Heimer G, Westerstrand J, Kalliokoski A (2001) Slagen Dam. Mäns Våld Mot Kvinnor I Jämställda Sverige - En Omfångsundersökning. Fritzes, Umeå
Meagher G, Szebehely M (2012) Equality in the social service state: Nordic childcare models in comparative perspective. In: Kvist J, Fritzell J, Hvinden B, Kangar O (eds) Changing social equality: the nordic welfare model in the 21st century. Policy Press, Bristol, pp 89–118
Melby K, Pylkkänen A, Rosenbeck B, Carlsson-Wetterberg C (eds) (2000) The Nordic model of marriage and the welfare state. Nord, Copenhagen
Nordborg G, Niemi-Kiesiläinen J (2001) Women's peace: a criminal law reform in Sweden. In: Nousiainen K, Gunnarsson Å, Lundström K, Niemi-Kiesiläinen J (eds) The responsible selves. Women in Nordic legal culture. Ashgate, Aldershot, pp 353–373
Nordic Gender Institute (NIKK) (2008) Multidimensional discrimination policies in the Nordic Countries: an overview. Oslo. http://www.nikk.no/wp-content/uploads/NIKKpub2008_Flerdimensionel-ligestilling_Flerdimensional-diskrimineringspolitik.pdf. Accessed 13 July 2018
Niemi-Kiesiläinen J (2005) Sukupuoli ja rikosoikeuspolitiikka. Oikeus 3, pp 230–245. Available at http://www.utu.fi/fi/yksikot/law/tiedekunta/henkilosto/Sivut/niemi_johanna.aspx
Niemi-Kiesiläinen J (2010) Feminist policy against violence in Sweden. In: Bondeson U (ed) Law and morality. Förlaget Thomson, Copenhagen, pp 289–300
Niemi J (2010) What we talk about when we talk about buying sex. Violence Against Women 16(2):159–172
Nousiainen K (2008) Utility-based equality and disparate diversities: from a Finnish perspective. In: Schiek D, Chege V (eds) European Union non-discrimination law: comparative perspectives on multidimensional equality law. Routledge, London, pp 187–214
Nousiainen K, Gunnarsson Å, Lundström K, Niemi-Kiesiläinen J (eds) (2001) Responsible selves: women in the Nordic legal culture. Ashgate, Aldershot
Piispa M, Heiskanen M (1998) Faith, hope and battering. StatFin, Helsinki
Pylkkänen A (2009) Trapped in equality: women as legal persons in the modernisation of Finnish law. Finnish Literature Society, Helsinki
Pylkkänen A (2008) Transformation of the Nordic model: from welfare politics to gendered rights. Can J Women Law 19(2):335–354

Ruuskanen M (2001) 'The good battered woman': a silenced defendant. In: Nousiainen K, Gunnarsson Å, KLundström K, Niemi-Kiesiläinen J (eds) The responsible selves. Women in the Nordic legal culture. Ashgate, pp 311–330

Saari M (2011) Työllä Tasa-Arvoon – Tasa-Arvosuunnittelu Ja Samapalkkaisuuden Edistäminen Vakuutusalan Työpaikoilla. Helsinki, Vakuutusväen Liitto VvL ry

Salmi M (2000) Analyzing the Finnish home care allowance: challenges to research and problems of interpretation. In: Kalliomaa-Puha L (ed) Perspectives of equality. Nordic Council of Ministers, Copenhagen

Schiek D, Chege V (2009) European Union non-discrimination law: comparative perspectives on multidimensional equality law. Routledge-Cavendish, London

Skjeie H, Langvasbråten T (2009) Intersectionality in practice? Int Fem J Polit 11(4):513–529

Smart C (1991) Feminism and the power of law. Routledge, London

Stang Dahl T (ed) (1985a) Kvinnerett: 1. Universitetsforlaget, Oslo

Stang Dahl T (ed) (1985b) Kvinnerett: 2. Universitetsforlaget, Oslo

Stang Dahl T (1987) Women's Law: an introduction to feminist jurisprudence. Oslo, Universitetsforlaget

Svensson E, Pylkkänen A, Niemi-Kiesiläinen J (eds) (2004) Nordic equality at a crossroads: feminist legal studies coping with difference. Ashgate, Aldershot

Svensson E et al (2011) På vei: kjønn og rett i Norden. Göteborg, Makadam. Available at http://linda.linneanet.fi/F/?func=direct&doc_number=006021816&local_base=fin01

Marriage and Family Relations

Ingrid Lund-Andersen and Annette Kronborg

Abstract This chapter describes and analyses the developments in Nordic family law, the law of succession and the legal relationship between children and parents. There is a long tradition of trying to harmonize family law, and cooperation in this field was especially intense when new legislation on marriage was being drafted at the beginning of the twentieth century. By contrast, the regulation of property relations between cohabitants has taken place without any Nordic cooperation and with very different solutions. Therefore, it is interesting that harmonization has led to almost identical regulation of same-sex relations, although the tempo has differed.

1 Introduction

In the field of family law, cooperation between the Nordic Countries has been intensive for nearly a century, dating back to the early 1900s, a period of major reforms in Denmark, Norway and Sweden. The purpose was to achieve complete harmonization of family law. As a corollary, in the 1910s and 1920s these same three Nordic countries introduced new progressive marriage acts on contracting and dissolving marriage and on property relations based on solidarity and equal rights as well as on self-determination concerning property between spouses at almost the same time.[1] In the following years, similar laws were also enacted in Finland and

[1]The Swedish Marriage Act in 1920, the Danish Act on the Legal Effects of Marriage in 1925, and the Norwegian Marriage Act in 1927. Current marriage acts are Denmark: *Ægteskabsloven* 2017 no 548, Finland: *Avioliittolaki/Äktenskapslag*, 234/1929, Iceland: *Hjúskaparlög* 14/1993, Norway: *Lov om ekteskap* 1991 no 47, Sweden: *Äktenskapsbalk* 1987:230.

I. Lund-Andersen (✉)
Faculty of Law, University of Copenhagen, Copenhagen, Denmark
e-mail: ingrid.lund-andersen@jur.ku.dk

A. Kronborg
Department of Law, University of Southern Denmark, Odense, Denmark
e-mail: ank@sam.sdu.dk

© Springer Nature Switzerland AG 2019

P. Letto-Vanamo et al. (eds.), *Nordic Law in European Context*,
Ius Gentium: Comparative Perspectives on Law and Justice 73,
https://doi.org/10.1007/978-3-030-03006-3_6

Iceland. However, the law of succession has not been similarly included in Nordic legal cooperation.

From a European perspective, deferred community of property is one of five different property regimes applied by the jurisdictions represented in the Commission on European Family Law (CEFL).[2] An important outcome of common Nordic legislation was the introduction of this system in all the Nordic countries.

Through the 1900s and in the early 2000s all Nordic countries met great challenges in terms of how to modernize their marriage acts, how to regulate the legal status of same-sex couples and how to regulate unmarried cohabitation. Additionally, the succession acts and various acts concerning the relation between parents and children have posed challenges. The central dilemmas have been how to balance the interests of the community versus individualism, solidarity versus self-realization and to determine whether rules should be mandatory or optional.

Some important common features characterize the development of Nordic family law. Among these, it should be stressed that the concept of marriage today is basically secular. A couple may quite easily get married, whether before the civil authorities or in church by a minister, while a marriage can be dissolved without much formality if the parties are incompatible and the marriage does not work. Marriage is seen as a contract. In line with increasing ease to obtain a divorce, in 2013 Denmark introduced rules on immediate divorce if both spouses agree.

Another feature to take into consideration is that compared to other European countries women in great numbers have come into the labour market and got their own money. A consequence of this has been reforms to the law on economic relations between spouses, including ways to reduce the extent of community of property. Spousal maintenance after divorce is no longer common: maintenance will be imposed only if a serious difference exists as to the economic situation between the spouses after divorce or other compelling reasons and even then normally only for a few years. Furthermore, it is important to note, that the Nordic countries are welfare states: In principle, social benefits are paid to everyone who cannot support themselves.

Neither in the law of succession law nor in regulation of the relationship between parents and children has similar close Nordic cooperation occurred as is the case in relation to family law. Nevertheless, some obvious similarities exist in the way these questions are handled in the Nordic countries. With regard to inheritance, the position of the family has gradually weakened (apart from Finland). In a country like Denmark, the increasingly strong position of the spouse has operated to the detriment of the testator's children. Indeed, generally the tendency has been to increase testators' right to dispose of their belongings. As to parental rights, an improvement is evident in unmarried parents' rights, especially the rights of an unmarried father.

[2]CEFL is a private academic organization that represents 26 European countries or regions including Norway, Russia and Switzerland outside the EU. See Boele-Woelki et al. (2013).

2 Family Law

2.1 Changing Regimes of Marriage and Divorce

Over the last century, Nordic cooperation in the field of family law has developed over several phases.[3] The period 1910–1931 was characterized by close cooperation, leading to major reforms. The following decade saw less cooperation and minor reforms, whereas the next thirty years from around 1968 to the end of the century were dominated by intense debates on broad issues of family and social policy. Current cooperation, however, is mainly in the hands of university professors specialising in family law.

As long ago as 1872, at the first Nordic Lawyers Meeting in Copenhagen, property rights of spouses were discussed. However, the debate did not immediately result in any initiative at the political level. Only in 1910, based on an invitation from the Swedish Government, was a conference held in Stockholm with the aim of discussing the most appropriate common Scandinavian legislation in the field of family law. The topics selected were separation and divorce, property rights between spouses and resolution of international private law conflicts of law in these areas. A three-member committee was then appointed in Denmark, Sweden and Norway in order to prepare new legislation.

In 1913, recommendations were made in each of the three countries to prepare legislation on the right to separation on the grounds of incompatibility and to divorce after a certain period of separation, thereby acknowledging that a marriage was not to be preserved at any price. Legislation on dissolution of marriage was introduced in Sweden, Norway and Denmark in the years between 1915 and 1922. The basis for the new default rules on community property in the 1920s was the principle of legal equality between husband and wife. Consideration as to the value of housework by housewives was an argument against separate property. The Nordic perspective was manifested by the fact of consensus on the governing principles, even if the legal solution to particular questions could vary slightly. In 1931 Denmark, Finland, Iceland, Norway and Sweden signed a convention on interregional (Nordic) private law provisions on marriage, adoption and guardianship.[4]

After a long period without changes in the basic acts, there followed a period (1955–1967) of minor reform with only partial harmonization. In 1954 at the Nordic Lawyers' Meeting, a revision of legislation on matrimonial property was discussed. A year later, the Nordic Council adopted a resolution recommending that the Nordic governments should consider the need for revision of laws on spousal property rights. The final extent of revision varied between the countries. Among

---

[3]This section is partly based on the following articles: Danielsen and Lødrup (1988), Lund-Andersen (2007) and Lødrup (2008). See also Bradley (1996) and Sörgjerd (2012).

[4]The Convention of February 6, 1931 between Denmark, Finland, Iceland, Norway and Sweden with Private International Law provisions on marriage, adoption and legal guardianship.

other things, rules on separation and divorce were changed to facilitate dissolution of marriage.

The youth revolt in 1968 had an influence on the family, while new family forms appeared. Family law was one of the subjects that became suddenly politically interesting. In Sweden, the Social Democrats had long enjoyed a firm hold on the Government, and the desire for radical reform was strong. The Swedish attitude was that no time should be lost in discussions within the Nordic framework, nor was there felt to be a need for Nordic legal unanimity. In 1969, the Swedish Minister of Justice outlined guidelines for the newly established Committee on Family Law. The guidelines formulated the famous Swedish "neutrality policy". These stated that marriage should retain its central place within family law, but at the same time, the law should not create unnecessary difficulties for those who decided to build a family without marrying.[5] The message was that legislation should as far as possible be neutral with respect to different forms of cohabitation and various moral conceptions.

In all the Nordic countries committees were appointed to revise the marriage laws, and for the first time politicians were appointed as members. The general attitude was that the debate in one's own country mattered most. Hence, Nordic cooperation was weaker and harmonization was only sporadic. In 1987, Sweden introduced the first legislation on cohabitation, the Cohabitation Act, which regulated the division of property as between unmarried cohabitees. The legislation was an expression of the political decision to maintain neutrality between different forms of family structure. None of the other Nordic countries has chosen a legislative solution that corresponds to the Swedish Cohabitation Act,[6] whereas a solution similar to the Danish Act on Registered Partnership[7] of 1989 for same-sex partners was adopted in the other Nordic countries over the next twelve years.

In 1998, the Nordic Council of Ministers established a project group to undertake a comparative study of Nordic family law. The aim was to assess the possibilities for harmonizing laws and the benefits of doing so. A group of Nordic law professors were asked to describe, clarify and analyze the requirements for establishing a valid marriage, divorce, maintenance, matrimonial property, the relationship between parents and children, and the law of succession as well as to discuss issues suitable for harmonization. The result of this work has been a series of books[8] on family law and the law of succession in all five Nordic countries. These books identify important differences. Further proposals were made for uniform rules within each sector. The books have been very useful for lawyers, judges and other legal practitioners but it is more doubtful to what extent the professors'

[5]The directives are reprinted in the report of the Swedish Committee on Family Law: SOU 1972:4: 57. See also Antokolskaia (2006).

[6]*Sambolag* 2003:376.

[7]*Lov om registreret partnerskab* 1989 no 372.

[8]Agell (2003), Lødrup (2003), Lødrup et al. (2003) and Danielsen (2003).

proposals have influenced legal policy. Later, an academic Nordic working group on the legal situation of unmarried cohabitees was also founded.[9]

A series of working groups among Nordic family law professors may be seen as a partial return to the older model of collaboration with a focus on more intense collaboration and greater harmonization. It also characterizes current co-operation that politicians are no longer members of family law committees. Instead, representatives of special interest groups and professional experts are often appointed. Usually the reports include brief descriptions of the legal position in several of the other Nordic countries.

2.2 *Property Relations Between Spouses*

Under the Nordic marriage acts, deferred community of property is the default position. As a starting point, all of a spouse's possessions form part of communal property, of which each of the parties can retain a half when the marriage is dissolved by death, separation or divorce. The community includes both property which the spouses owned at the time of their marriage and property acquired by them during their marriage. If an asset is to be held by one of the spouses as separate property, a special agreement is needed.[10] The concept of deferred community of property has no bearing upon which spouse deals with specific assets, nor does it concern a creditor's right to satisfy their claim from the matrimonial assets. The spouses are thus economically independent individuals with respect to the law of property in spite of their marriage, and regardless of whether they have agreed to enjoy separate property or deferred community of property. This means that although an asset forms part of the communal property, the spouse who acquired it also owns that asset.

These rules are supplemented by rules on unequal distribution if the marriage has been short-lived (normally less than five years) just as rights are increasingly not included in the division of communal property e.g. personal rights and some pension rights. Since 1991 the 'uneven distribution rule' in the Norwegian Marriage Act provides that the value of assets that can be traced back to having been owned by a spouse at the start of the marriage, or later acquired by inheritance or gift from persons other than a spouse, are not shared on termination of marriage. Thus, the general rule in Norway now is that only assets acquired during the marriage are divided equally.

Norwegian and Swedish case law has introduced two different kinds of co-ownership in family relationships, which can be seen as supplements to deferred community of property. In 1975, the Norwegian Supreme Court acknowledged that

---

[9]See Asland et al. (2014), Asland et al. (2015).

[10]See more about the Nordic property regimes (apart from Iceland) at: www.ceflonline.net/country-reports.

indirect contributions in the form of childcare and housework are relevant factors in determining the ownership of specific assets, the so-called "housewife ruling".[11] According to the Court's decision, a wife who stays at home and cares for small children can become the co-owner of a house purchased by her husband during the marriage using solely his income earned during the marriage. The house in question was acquired during the marriage and the husband held the title. Especially interesting is the opinion of one of the judges that to deny a woman's work in the home as a contribution towards acquiring a common home would be contrary to today's sense of justice. Further, indirect contributions in the form of bigger payments than the spouse's share of living expenses have also been acknowledged.[12]

In Swedish case law, a principle of concealed covert co-ownership of property ("covert property") has been developed with respect to property to which only one of the spouses holds title but which has been acquired for the spouses' joint use, provided the spouses can be deemed to have intended the property to be owned by them jointly and that the other spouse also made some financial contribution to the acquisition.[13]

In all the Nordic countries, contracts of marriage settlement on separate property can be made. Additionally, a donor or testator (in a will) can determine that a gift or inheritance should be separate property. A marital agreement on separate property can apply to all the property or to the specific property of one spouse. For example, the spouses can agree that a family farm will be separate property or that both spouses' assets are to be separate property. Today, interest in limiting communal property is much greater than in the early 1900s. There is considerable freedom to vary the content of a marriage settlement, especially in Danish and Norwegian law. For example, in these two countries the spouses may agree that there should be separate property in the case of divorce, but not if one of the spouses dies (introduced in Norway in 1937 and Denmark in 1990). The Finnish Supreme Court also recognized this kind of agreement in a judgment of 2000.[14]

In Denmark, a spouse may be ordered by the court to give part of their separate property to the other spouse in order to ensure that the second spouse does not suffer grave financial hardship. Such a decision may only be made if warranted by the spouses' property relations, the duration of the marriage or other relevant circumstances. If one spouse has contributed to the other spouse's separate property, either indirectly by savings during the marriage or by direct efforts in the spouse's business enterprise, this will favour payment being ordered by the court. Housework can also be taken into consideration. If a spouse needs money to establish a suitable home, this may also be grounds for payment. The other Nordic

---

[11]Norsk Retstidende 1975, p. 220.

[12]See Sverdrup (2008).

[13]See the judgments in Nytt juridisk arkiv 1980.705, 1981.693 and 1982.589. See also Jäntera-Jareborg et al. (2008).

[14]KKO 2000:100.

countries have other ways to mitigate the effects of separate property, in particular by determining that an unreasonable agreement on separate property is invalid.

Development is characterised by a softening of the rules on separate property, particularly the many opportunities to vary the rules by agreement and to award compensation or set aside a marital agreement. It has also been necessary to supplement the Nordic principle of deferred community of property with discretionary uneven distribution rules, most extensively in Norway. Thus, the borderline between the two basic types of property, deferred community and separate property, is becoming increasingly blurred.

Because of continuing changes in family structures, the extension of welfare systems and the fact that both husbands and wives are often active in the labour market, a Danish committee between 2009 and 2014 had to consider whether the existing basis of deferred community of property should be maintained or whether rules should be introduced whereby assets brought into the marriage and inheritance and gifts received before or during the marriage should be kept out of the community of property. In January 2015, the committee published its report on property relations between spouses.[15] The committee split into a majority and two minorities, so that the report contained three different proposals for new rules on property division, namely either a stepwise sharing of the spouses' assets so that they are equally divided after seven years (the majority) or an equal sharing limited to assets acquired by the spouses during marriage. A third proposal was sharing based on discretion. As no political agreement was reached on any of the three proposals, in 2017 a bill on spouses' economic relations was proposed with no change to the Danish rules on division of community property. A new Act was adopted on May 23, 2017 with effect from 1 January 2018.[16]

2.3 Same-Sex Relations

In 1989, Denmark was the first country to allow two persons of the same sex to enter into a registered partnership.[17] The main reason for introducing the Registered Partnership Act[18] was to make a political statement: only by giving homosexual couples almost the same legal status as married couples was a step towards full social recognition possible.[19]

[15]Report No. 2015:1552.

[16]*Lov om ægtefællers økonomiske forhold* 2017 no 548.

[17]For more detail on same-sex relations, see Lund-Andersen (2012, 2017).

[18]*Partnerskabsloven* 2005 no 938.

[19]See Villaverde (2013). The legislation was used as an instrument to change attitudes. This aspect was strongly emphasized by the Danish Association of Gays and Lesbians during a discussion prior to adoption of the Act. The role and influence of this association was decisive, and the Act has changed general views towards homosexuality in Denmark, including towards same-sex couples who do not register their partnership.

Similar registered partnership acts followed in the other Nordic countries: Norway[20] in 1993; Sweden[21] in 1994; Iceland[22] in 1996; and Finland[23]in 2001. None of the registered partnership acts had opened the door to heterosexual couples. Subsequently, all exceptions concerning children were repealed by amendments to the registered partnership acts apart from Finland. The Finnish rules allowed adoption of a stepchild provided that the child was adopted from abroad, but joint adoption was not allowed for registered partners.

Since 2009, Denmark has been overtaken by developments in Norway, Sweden and Iceland, as those three countries introduced the same concept of gender-neutral marriage in 2009, 2009 and 2010 respectively. After a lengthy debate in the Norwegian Parliament, an amendment to the Marriage Act was enacted on 17 June 2008 by 84 votes to 41. This gives same-sex couples the formal right to marry on the same basis as heterosexuals. Previously registered partners can have their partnerships converted into marriage. The amended Marriage Act entered into force on 1 January 2009. In Sweden, gender-neutral marriage was adopted by 261 votes to 16, and the new rules of the Marriage Act came into effect in May 2009. In 2010, the Icelandic Parliament unanimously passed a bill on gender-neutral marriage.[24] In June 2012, the Danish parliament passed a bill on same-sex marriage by 85 votes to 24. The Act came into force in June 2012. After years of discussion in Finland, an act allowing gender-neutral marriage came into effect from March 2017.

2.4 Property Relations Between Unmarried Cohabitees

It is assumed that the most prevalent form of family living for couples under the age of 30 is unmarried cohabitation, while the relative occurrence of non-married couples falls with rising age. The number of unmarried couples in the Nordic countries amounts to 20–30% of all cohabiting couples (married, in a registered partnership and unmarried).[25]

Declining marriage rates in the Nordic countries have given rise to a dramatic increase in the number of children born outside marriage; this amounts to 40–65%,

[20]*Partnerskapsloven* 1993 no 40.

[21]*Lag* (1994:1117*) om registrerat partnerskap.*

[22]*Lög um staðfesta samvist* 87/1996.

[23]*Laki rekisteröidystä parisuhteesta/Lag om registrerat partnerskap* 950/2001.

[24]The Act came into effect immediately. On the same day, the Icelandic Prime Minister, Jóhanna Sigurðardóttir, married her female partner. The couple had entered into a registered partnership in 2002, and now they transformed their partnership into a marriage.

[25]See more on family formation trends in the Nordic countries in Asland et al. (2015), pp. 3–10.

with the highest number in Iceland. The majority of children who are born to unmarried parents grow up with their father and mother in an unmarried cohabiting family. Their family life is in most respects no different to families in which the parents are married.

In contrast to the legal situation for same-sex couples, the division of property between unmarried cohabitees on termination of cohabitation is different in all five Nordic countries. One important difference is whether or not special family law rules have been introduced for unmarried cohabitees.

For many years, Sweden was the only Nordic country with special legislation on financial circumstances upon termination of cohabitation. The act dates from 1987 and deals with the parties' joint dwelling as well as with household goods acquired for joint use during the period of cohabitation.[26] If a relationship ends, the net value of these assets is shared, regardless of which party is the owner. Further, a cohabitee can take possession of the assets of the other cohabitee based on an assessment of the parties' needs. Thus, with regard to domestic assets cohabitees are treated in the same way as married partners with deferred community property.

In 2011, Finland introduced overall legislation dealing with the financial division of the parties' possessions upon dissolution of cohabitation[27] with a presumption of joint ownership of movable assets. Additionally, a rule was introduced addressing compensation in the event of unjust enrichment. The Norwegian Household Community Act[28] of 1991 covers various kinds of association between individuals who live together, the majority being those who live together as couples. The Act does not regulate division of property, but entitles a member of a household—under certain conditions—to take possession of the household residence and the household goods.

Due to lack of legislation concerning division of cohabitation property, it has been the courts that have assessed whether a cohabitee can be granted compensation or reimbursement They have done so on the basis of the doctrine of unjust enrichment, restitution and reasonable expectations, based on property law principles, subject to new interpretations and incorporating family law considerations. In addition, special principles of co-ownership have been developed through case law in Norway and Sweden both for spouses and for cohabitees.[29] In particular, Danish and Icelandic case law on compensation gives limited protection to the weaker party.

[26]The Act was revised in 2003; see the Swedish Cohabitation Act, *Sambolag* 2003:376.

[27]Act on the Dissolution of the Household of Cohabiting Partners, *Laki avopuolisoiden yhteistalouden purkamisesta/Lag om upplösning av sambors gemensamma hushåll* 26/2011.

[28]*Lov om rett til felles bolig og innbo når husstandsfellesskap opphører* 1991 no 45.

[29]See more on Sweden's concealed right of co-ownership and Norway's co-ownership by contributing to acquisition ("housewife co-ownership") in Asland et al. (2015), pp. 66–75.

3 The Legal Relationship Between Children and Parents

3.1 Legal Parenthood

The legal parent-child relationship in the Nordic countries is characterized by societal development in the late 20th Century, liberating it from marriage as the institution defining the relationship. Today, this field of law is an independent part of family law replacing its previous position in (primarily) matrimonial law. The breadwinner-housewife model was replaced by a new democratic model of parenthood based on equality. This law may still be characterized as private law but is closely related to public law based on the Nordic welfare regimes and public interest in child welfare. The political challenge today is to develop the relation between private and public law based on the best interests of the child. The ethics of liberated family patterns as described above—encompassing cohabitees and same-sex marriage—are framed by the right of all family members to family life as codified in ECHR Article 8 and children's human rights as defined in the UN Convention on the Rights of the Child. The connection between marriage and parenthood has become more fluent.[30]

A shared characteristic of Nordic law is the public duty to establish legal parenthood at the time of birth. If no father is registered at the time of birth, the state will initiate proceedings to establish paternity. The initiative is thus not left with the parties involved. When the mother is married to a man, his paternity is presumed (*pater est quem nuptiae demonstrant*). More importantly, when the mother is not married she must address the question of establishing the legal paternity of the father (or possibly the legal co-mother). Legal paternity is a prejudicial matter which has many legal effects such as maintenance, parental responsibility and mutual inheritance rights. Adoption has identical legal effects. Children cannot have more than one or two legal parents but the parents may be of the same sex.

Whereas regulation of legal paternity early on reflected the obligation of an unmarried father to contribute to child maintenance (rather than the state), present regulation reflects a political balancing act where the law substantively mirrors either biological fatherhood or the decision of the mother and the social father (or co-mother) which in turn may overrule biological fatherhood. Procedurally, paternity follows from marriage, the father's (or co-mother's) acknowledgement in agreement with the mother, or a court order. Acknowledgements and court orders are both decisions on paternity covered by a Nordic conflict of law act of 1980.

If a child is naturally conceived, the biological father is obliged to become the legal father. This fact may be established by a court, typically based on a DNA test. The biological father may have the right to establish paternity without the consent of the mother. However, the biological father's right is not absolute or without time limit: his right to pursue his legal status differs among the Nordic countries. The father has the strongest position in Norway, where there is no legal limitation on the

[30]For a Nordic comparison of parenthood, see Asland et al. (2015), pp. 212–215.

biological father's right to pursue the biological truth until the child is three years old. Thus, the legal paternity of the biological father may be established despite the mother's arrangement with another possible partner.

Assisted reproduction is regulated as the interplay between the establishment of parentage in private law, and access to fertility treatment in both the public as well as the private health system. In all the Nordic countries, a woman who gives birth to a child is the child's legal mother (*mater semper certa est*). In recent decades, developments in fertility treatment have been rapid, with political and ethical discussions relating to ongoing legal reforms about which treatment and legal arrangements should be allowed, or—in other words—defining the legal "limits of parentage". It may seem that family law and health law are becoming entangled.

The authorization of treatment in health law is transformed into legal parentage. In respect of fertility treatment, Denmark and Iceland may be viewed as the "most liberal" (at least from a parental perspective) as they continue to allow parents the choice between anonymous or non-anonymous sperm donation. Denmark is also the host country of the largest sperm bank in the world.[31] Norway may be viewed as taking a less liberal approach by not allowing single women to receive fertility treatment, although allowing same-sex lesbian couples treatment like the other Nordic countries.[32]

3.2 *Child Maintenance*

Legal parents are obliged to support their children. Parents living together with their children thus fulfil their duties of maintenance. A parent who does not fulfil his/her obligation in this way is obliged to pay child support to the other parent (the primary caregiver). If the parents do not agree on the amount of support, the primary caregiver may apply to the family law authorities. The duty is legally connected to legal parenthood and therefore includes all legal parents independent of marital status and irrespective of establishment of new relationships. It also includes parents without contact with their children, even if it is the child that does not wish to have contact. Agreements between parents about non-payment of child support are not binding. The obligation to maintain is a continuing obligation towards minor children and the amount is subject to alteration during the period of payment.[33] The duty ceases when the child reaches 18 years, though with exceptions in relation to children receiving education.[34]

---

[31]dk.cryosinternational.com.

[32]For a comparison of the development of national fertility treatment based on national history in Denmark, Sweden and Norway, see Kronborg (2016).

[33]Calculating the amount in the Nordic countries is based on different systems; either a standard sum where percentages may be added if the income of the responsible parent is high (Denmark and Iceland); or a model based on the costs of raising a child (Sweden, Finland, Norway).

[34]For a Nordic view from a Finnish perspective, see Kangas (2015).

Despite differences in the Nordic countries' relationship with the EU, they are covered by the same conflict of law rules concerning maintenance obligations covering jurisdiction and recognition originating from the EU: Finland and Sweden as full members, Denmark by a parallel EU agreement, and Norway and Iceland based on the "Lugano Convention" with almost identical content. The private law obligation to support children interplays with complex rules of public law on public maintenance obligations.[35]

3.3 Parental Responsibility

The preferred legal arrangement in the Nordic countries is joint parental responsibility of the legal parents, either because the parents are or have been married, or in Norway, Denmark and Iceland due to co-habitation or by agreement. The making of such an agreement is facilitated in different ways, for example, in connection with establishment of paternity, but common in all the Nordic countries. Parents with joint parental responsibility are expected to agree on all issues relating to raising a child but they may only obtain a court decision in relation to specific issues such as concerning the child's residence. Further, court decisions on contact are available to parents with or without joint parental responsibilities if they do not agree on the matter, possibly after attending counselling or mediation. A common feature in the Nordic countries is the absence of general access for disputes such as concerning medical treatment or choice of school to be decided by a competent authority.[36]

A common arrangement in Nordic families is shared residence, defined as an arrangement where the child lives with each parent, typically alternating with one week at one parent's house and the following week at the other parent's house. On the one hand, this arrangement has been viewed as an ideal arrangement mirroring equality between the parents and legitimation of the developing counselling and mediation regimes. On the other hand, it has created a need to legally define the category of children that are better off with only one holder of parental responsibility and limited or no contact with the other parent.[37]

---

[35]The dominant Nordic feature is that a certain basic amount of support that a parent must pay may be covered, upon request, by the public authorities if the debtor parent does not meet their obligation. The amount is then collected by the public authorities from the debtor parent. In addition to this public guarantee of private support for the child, all Nordic countries provide public financial support for all children, though this may vary according to financial circumstances and the targeting of, for example, single parents.

[36]Jeppesen de Boer (2008), p. 78, footnote 221.

[37]For a Nordic comparison of parental responsibility, see Fridriksdottir (2016).

All the Nordic countries are parties to The Hague[38] Convention on Child Abduction.[39] The definition of child abduction relates to violation of custody rights and covers parents in the Nordic countries with joint parental responsibility. Sweden and Finland are also members of a EU regulation on parental responsibility[40] operating with a more efficient "quick-return mechanism" between the member states but respecting The Hague Convention in relation to the other Nordic countries. Except for Iceland, all the Nordic countries are members of The Hague Convention on conflict of laws.[41]

The competent family law authority addresses the issue of a defined conflict (parental responsibility, residence and contact) between the parents, and there is no obligation to supervise whether a decision based on the best interests of the child continues to be so. This differs from the public law understanding of the situation as covered by child welfare law, where the parents are not "in control" of the case as in family law. The public authorities are involved in the family as defined from a more holistic child welfare perspective. Family law is designed to uphold individual rights, whereas child welfare law is designed to address the needs of potentially all children. While child welfare may be viewed as having substantive content in both legal fields, the division between private and public law remains a factor influencing how child welfare is addressed.

3.4 *Parental Leave*

The Nordic countries were among the pioneers in developing paid maternity leave. All the Nordic countries' parental leave programmes provide parents with an earnings-based wage replacement when they take leave. In the 1970s and 1980s they were among the first countries to develop schemes of paid parental leave that provided both parents with the opportunity to choose how they would divide the leave period between them.[42]

A political focus has been to what extent the state should encourage the father to take leave. The question is whether dual care should be the consequence of a dual-earner family with the father's quota of parental leave based on the "use it, or lose it" principle. While in Norway, Sweden and Iceland the development has been towards equal "use it, or lose it" quotas for both parents, with Norway as the

[38]See the homepage of The Hague Conference on Private International Law: https://www.hcch.net/.

[39]Convention of 25 October 1980 on the Civil Aspects of International Child Abduction.

[40]Council Regulation (EC) No. 2201/2003 of 27 November 2003 concerning jurisdiction and the recognition and enforcement of judgments in matrimonial matters and matters of parental responsibility, repealing Regulation (EC) No. 1347/2000.

[41]Convention of 19 October 1996 on Jurisdiction, Applicable Law, Recognition, Enforcement and Co-operation in Respect of Parental Responsibility and Measures for the Protection of Children.

[42]Eydal et al. (2015), p. 170.

pioneer, Finland was the last country to fix the entitlement of fathers as a quota.[43] Denmark is the only Nordic country that does not provide fathers with a quota—except for two weeks leave in connection with the birth of a child—which may suggest that gender equality is less supported by the state.[44] A previous father's quota was abolished in 2002, the argument being the parents' freedom to make their own choice instead of state coercion limiting the parents' freedom of choice. Nevertheless, agreements between employers and trade unions in various labour market areas have included a father's quota, thereby reinstating it.[45]

4 The Law of Succession

Achieving harmonization was not the aim within the field of law of succession in the same way as with regard to marriage laws.[46] An initiative towards reform of the law of succession was taken in 1953 at a meeting of the Nordic Ministers of Justice. In the following years, reform committees were appointed in Denmark, Norway, Sweden and Iceland.[47] Reforms were undertaken in all the Nordic countries.[48] There is a considerable spread in years and legislative work was carried out without any specific thought about legislative harmonization.

Denmark in 2008 was the first country to introduce a new Inheritance Act with a rather radical revision based on several years of committee work. In Norway, a report on a new inheritance law was published in 2014. A new Act will probably be introduced soon. The mandate of the Norwegian Succession Committee appointed in 2011 illustrates the main challenges today in relation to Nordic inheritance laws. The committee should assess whether the inheritance rights of blood relatives should be limited in favour of the surviving spouse, including a closer look at a spouse's minimum basic portion. In view of Nordic legal cooperation, the committee should also consider whether the rules on undivided possession of the estate should be simplified, consider the children's intestacy rights and look into the legal position of cohabitees.

As to the right of inheritance by blood relatives, the rules are broadly the same in all the Nordic countries. Regulation expresses the so-called *per stirpes* rule, where each of the deceased's children forms a branch. In this way, the portion to be

[43]Eydal et al. (2015), p. 178.

[44]Eydal et al. (2015), p. 177.

[45]Borchorst (2006).

[46]The description of developments in Nordic inheritance laws is partly based on Lødrup (2003) and on NOU 2014:1.

[47]Finland participated as an observer in further cooperation at a Nordic level.

[48]In 1958, the Swedish Inheritance Act, *Successionsordning* (1810:0926); in 1962, the Icelandic Inheritance Act, *Erfðalög* 1962 no 8; in 1963, the Danish Inheritance Act, *Arveloven* 2007 no 515; in 1965 the Finnish Inheritance Act, *Perintökaari/Ärvdabalk* 40/1965 and in 1972, the Norwegian Inheritance Act, Lov om arv m.m. 1972 no 5.

inherited by a dead child is inherited by their children equally, and so on. As long as beneficiaries exist within the first class, more distant relatives have no right to inherit. One difference between the Nordic countries is that cousins enjoy inheritance rights in Norway, whereas they do not inherit in the other Nordic countries. The Norwegian Succession Committee has not proposed any changes in this respect. In most European countries the right of inheritance extends further than in the Nordic countries.

The trend today seems to be more freedom in disposing by will of the estate and strengthening the surviving spouse's rights. The position of the surviving spouse depends on whether the deceased has other heirs in the first class. In the Danish Succession Act of 2008, the spouse's inheritance share increased from 1/3 to 1/2 in competition with the deceased's children. The Norwegian Succession Law Committee proposes correspondingly that the spouse's share be increased from 1/4 to 1/2 in competition with the deceased's children. In Iceland, the spouse's share is 1/3. In Sweden, the surviving spouse's position is even stronger since he or she takes the whole estate of the deceased with a free right of disposal, while the first issue of the deceased inherits only on the death of the surviving spouse. This right does not apply with respect to children from previous relationships. The legal situation in Finland differs from the other countries, with more emphasis on inheritance to the wider family. The surviving spouse has no inheritance rights, provided the deceased leaves heirs in the first hereditary class. However, the surviving spouse can use the dwelling and household goods both in relation to common children and to children from previous relationships.

In Denmark and Norway, the spouse is entitled to undivided possession of the estate under certain conditions. In Denmark, this right is reserved only if there are children in common or other issue of the first class—a child from previous relationships has to give his or her consent—and community property. In Norway there is also a requirement of common children, but the right to undivided possession may in some cases apply to both community property and to separate property.

In none of the Nordic countries are spouses and cohabitees equated in inheritance law.[49] However, during recent years the legal position of surviving cohabitees has been strengthened in Norway, Denmark and Finland. The Danish Inheritance Act of 2008 entitles cohabitees to decide by will that they inherit from each other in full or in part, as if they were spouses with separate property. The parties must either have, have had or be expecting a child together, or must have lived together in a marriage-like relationship for the last two years. In Norway (since 2009) a surviving cohabitee has a limited right to inheritance by intestate succession and a right to undivided possession of certain types of asset. The rules cover the same group of cohabitees as in the Danish Inheritance Act, apart from a requirement of at least five years of living together. Lastly, in 2011, legal rules were introduced in Finland which entitle a surviving cohabitee to claim support from the estate on certain terms and to apply for compensation e.g. through contributions to the shared

[49]For more detail, see Asland et al. (2015), pp. 66–75.

household. In Sweden, the Cohabitation Act of 1987 guarantees a surviving cohabitee half of the net value of the dwelling and household goods acquired for joint use. Secondly, a cohabitee is entitled to a kind of minimum inheritance right that is half of the amount of spouses. Icelandic inheritance legislation does not protect a surviving cohabitee.

5 Conclusion

Nordic cooperation within the field of family law since the 1970s has taken a new turn and it is not—as was the case at the beginning of the 19th century—seen as a goal in itself to achieve harmonization. Legislation has moved with different spreads among each of these countries and the courts have chosen different directions in this field. Some important basic principles are still common and the Nordic countries seem to be moving in the same direction. However, a Nordic lawyer dealing with questions of family law in another country than their own and even more within the field of the law of succession would be well advised to look for the many differences among the details from one Nordic country to another instead of assuming that the law will be the same.

References

Agell A (2003) Nordisk äktenskapsrätt. Nord, Copenhagen, p 2
Antokolskaia M (2006) Harmonisation of family law in Europe: a historical perspective. Intersentia, Antwerp
Asland J, Brattström M, Lind G, Lund-Andersen I, Singer A, Sverdrup T (2014) Nordisk samboerrett. Gyldendal, Oslo
Asland J, Brattström M, Lind G, Lund-Andersen I, Singer A, Sverdrup T (2015) Nordic cohabitation law. Intersentia, Antwerp
Boele-Woelki K et al (2013) Principles of European family law regarding property relations between spouses. Intersentia, Antwerp
Borchorst A (2006) The public-private split rearticulated: abolishment of the Danish daddy leave. In: Ellingsæter AL, Leira A (eds) Politicing parenthood: gender relations in a Scandinavian welfare state design. The Polity Press, London, pp 101–120
Bradley D (1996) Family law and political culture: Scandinavian laws in comparative perspective. Sweet & Maxwell, London
Danielsen S, Lødrup P (1988) Det nordiske arbejde på familierettens område. Tidsskrift for Rettsvitenskap, pp 565–585
Danielsen S (2003) Nordisk Børnerett II. Nord, Copenhagen, p 14
Eydal GB et al (2015) Trends in parental leave in the Nordic countries: has the forward march of gender equality halted? Community Work Family 18(2):167–181
Fridriksdottir H (2016) Nordic family law: new framework—new fatherhoods. In: Eydal GB, Rostgaard T (eds) Fatherhood in the Nordic welfare states: comparing care policies and practice. Policy Press, pp 53–78

Jeppesen de Boer CG (2008) Joint parental authority: a comparative legal study on the continuation of joint parental authority after divorce and the breakup of a relationship in Dutch and Danish law and the CEFL principles. Intersentia, Utrecht

Jäntera-Jareborg M, Brattström M, Walleng K (2008) Swedish report on property relations between spouses. http://ceflonline.net/wp-content/uploads/Sweden-Property.pdf. Accessed 29 May 2018

Kangas U (2015) Familie- och kvarlåtenskapsrättens grunder. Talentum, Helsinki

Kronborg A (2016) Family formation in Scandinavia: a comparative study in family law. Utrecht Law Rev 12(2):81–93. https://www.utrechtlawreview.org/articles/abstract/10.18352/ulr.345/

Lund-Andersen I (2007) Approximation of Nordic family law within the framework of Nordic cooperation. In: Antokolskaia M (ed) Convergence and divergence of family law in Europe. Intersentia, Antwerp, pp 51–61

Lund-Andersen I (2012) The Nordic countries: same direction—different speeds. In: Boele-Woelki K, Fuchs A (eds) Legal recognition of same-sex relations in Europe: national, cross-border and European perspectives. Intersentia, Cambridge, pp 3–18

Lund-Andersen I (2017) Northern Europe: same-sex relations and family law. In: Boele-Woelki K, Fuchs A (eds) Same-sex relationships and beyond: gender matters in the EU. Intersentia, Antwerp

Lødrup P (2003) Nordisk arverett. Nord, Copenhagen, p 3

Lødrup P, Agell A, Singer A (2003) Nordisk børneret I. Nord, Copenhagen, p 3

Lødrup P (2008) The reharmonisation of Nordic family law. In: Boele-Woelki K, Sverdrup T (eds) European challenges in contemporary family law. Intersentia, Antwerp, pp 17–26

Retsvirkningslovsudvalget (2015) Ægtefællers økonomiske forhold. Betænkning 1552. Rosendahls

Sverdrup T (2008) Norwegian report on property relations between spouses. http://ceflonline.net/wp-content/uploads/Norway-Property.pdf. Accessed 29 May 2018

Sörgjerd C (2012) Reconstructing marriage—the legal status of relationships in a changing society. Intersentia, Antwerp

Villaverde JML (2013) Legal recognition of same-sex couples in Denmark: from the first debates to the enactment of the registered partnership Act of 1989. In: Petersen H, Villaverde JML, Lund-Andersen I (eds) Contemporary gender relations and changes in legal cultures. DJØF Publishing, Copenhagen, pp 147–164

Contracting with a Social Dimension

Johan Bärlund and Peter Moegelvang-Hansen

Abstract The Nordic countries show great similarities in contract law. The countries have no civil code, while important parts of private law have been regulated by individual acts. In the first half of the 20th century, the countries succeeded in harmonizing central parts of contract law through the Nordic Contract Acts. After the 1980s, both CISG and EU law have influenced Nordic contract law. The most important general principles are the principle of freedom of contract, the principle of legitimate expectations, the principle of loyalty and the principle of protecting the weaker party. The social dimension of Nordic contract law has gained particular emphasis through the idea of social civil law in consumer law and in the regulation of debt adjusting.

1 Introduction

1.1 Nordic Contract Law

It is often said that in the area of contract, Nordic law forms a legal family of its own, positioned between the civil law families and the common law family.[1] Like the common law, Nordic law principles on civil obligations are unwritten and based on case law supplemented by a variety of fragmentary statutes dealing mostly with rather specific questions. On the other hand, legal scholarship of the civil law countries, primarily of Germany, has heavily influenced the development of the general legal concepts and principles of Nordic law. Nevertheless, perhaps due to

[1]Zweigert and Kötz (1998), p. 277.

J. Bärlund (✉)
Faculty of Law, University of Helsinki, Helsinki, Finland
e-mail: johan.barlund@helsinki.fi

P. Moegelvang-Hansen
Law Department, Copenhagen Business School, Copenhagen, Denmark
e-mail: pmh.jur@cbs.dk

© Springer Nature Switzerland AG 2019

P. Letto-Vanamo et al. (eds.), *Nordic Law in European Context*,
Ius Gentium: Comparative Perspectives on Law and Justice 73,
https://doi.org/10.1007/978-3-030-03006-3_7

the lack of civil codes, common sense and pragmatism rather than conceptual thinking is a characteristic feature of Nordic jurisprudence and legal reasoning in contract law, too.[2]

For historical reasons, Nordic contract law is also one of the most homogeneous disciplines of the Nordic countries' national legal orders. During the first half of the 20th century, several important harmonization projects in contract law were concluded, among them the first Sale of Goods Act (1905–1922)[3] and the Contracts Act (1915–1936).[4] At first sight, the contract laws of the Nordic countries appear incredibly similar. However, a detailed comparison will often disclose significant differences.[5]

An attempt in the 1980s aiming at joint Nordic modernisation of sale of goods legislation was a partial success in that it resulted in new legislation in all the Nordic countries except Denmark, which still adheres to the original joint Nordic Act of 1906.

Although Nordic legal cooperation since the Second World War cannot boast of similar monumental achievements, a common legal tradition and legislative mindset have continued to influence legal development in the Nordic countries. As is illustrated by examples mentioned later, new legislative ideas and innovations to the legal infrastructure implemented by one Nordic country have often inspired similar legal solutions in the other Nordic countries.

1.2 EU Impacts

Since the late 1980s, Nordic legislative cooperation concerning the law of obligations has focused mainly on technical implementation of European Union (EU) consumer protection directives. Generally, the Nordic countries meticulously implement EU legal requirements correctly without taking further steps than necessary. Furthermore, the general trend seems to be rather defensive in that EU-based provisions are to the widest possible extent turned into supplements to existing

---

[2]See Chap. 1, Andersen and Runesson (2015), pp. 15–17; Lando et al. (2016), pp. 18–24; Zweigert and Kötz (1998), pp. 284–285.

[3]Denmark: *Købeloven* 2014 no 140, Finland: *Kauppalaki/Köplag* 355/1987, Iceland: *Lög um lausafjárkaup* 50/2000, Norway: *Lov om kjøp* 1988 no 27, Sweden: *Köplag* 1990:931.

[4]Denmark: *Aftaleloven* 2016 nr 193, Finland: *Laki varallisuusoikeudellisista oikeustoimista/Lag om rättshandlingar på förmögenhetsrättens område* 228/1929, Iceland: *Lög um samningsgerð, umboð og ógilda löggerninga* 7/1936, Norway: *Lov om avslutning av avtaler, om fuldmagt og om ugyldige viljeserklæringer* 1918 no 4, Sweden: *Lag* (1915:218) *om avtal och andra rättshandlingar på förmögenhetsrättens område.*

[5]For a detailed account of Nordic cooperation, see Andersen and Runesson (2015), pp. 17–23 and Chap. 1 above.

national rules so that the latter are kept in force to the widest possible extent.[6] There seems to have been no attempt to take more offensive joint Nordic action aimed at influencing European legal development in a direction closer to Nordic legislative traditions and thinking. One important factor may be the differences characterising the affiliation of the various Nordic countries to the EU.[7]

The differences between the legal traditions in the Nordic countries and in the EU have become apparent in decisions by the Court of Justice of the European Union (CJEU), which occasionally cause surprise among Nordic lawyers. For instance, Nordic implementation of the consumer protection directives has sometimes highlighted the significantly different roles played by the *travaux préparatoires* according to the Nordic tradition and in EU jurisprudence. The importance attached to the explanations and statements by political decision makers during the legislative process when Nordic courts interpret the law has no counterpart in the EU.

In the case of *Commission v. Sweden*,[8] the Commission claimed that Sweden had failed to implement the Unfair Contract Terms Directive[9] by not including a (non-binding) indicative list of contract terms (found in the annex of the Directive) in the implementation act. The list was reproduced in its entirety in the preparatory work for the Swedish act implementing the Directive but, according to the Commission, this was not enough. However, the CJEU decided the case in favour of Sweden, referring to the fact that according to 'a legal tradition that is well established in Sweden and common to the Nordic countries, preparatory work constitutes an important aid to interpreting legislation' and 'that such preparatory work may easily be consulted'. Denmark and Finland had implemented the Directive in the same way as Sweden and both intervened in the case in support of Sweden.

In another case, *Skov and Bilka*,[10] the Danish Government based its interpretation of the Product Liability Directive partly on a statement in the Council minutes from the meeting that adopted the Directive. The CJEU held that the statement had no relevance under EU law: 'it must be recalled that, where a statement recorded in Council minutes is not referred to in the wording of a provision of secondary legislation, it cannot be used for the purpose of interpreting that provision'.[11]

---

[6]See Andersen and Runesson (2015), pp. 22–23.

[7]See Chap. 1 for details.

[8]Case C-478/99, *Commission v. Sweden* [2002] ECR I-4147.

[9]Council Directive 93/13/EEC of 5 April 1993 on unfair terms in consumer contracts.

[10]Case C-402/03 [2006] ECR I-199.

[11]Para. 42 of the judgment.

1.3 CISG

When the Nordic countries joined the United Nations Convention on Contracts for the International Sale of Goods (CISG) in the late 1980s, they invoked the so-called 'neighbouring country' reservation in CISG Article 94 concerning countries with '*the same or closely related legal rules on matters governed by this Convention*'. The reservation has the effect that Nordic national sale of goods legislation, applicable according to the general rules on the conflict of laws, applies to inter-Nordic sale contracts. Ironically enough, however, as mentioned above, Nordic sale of goods legislation is no longer joint since the old joint act from 1906 is still in force only in Denmark whereas the other Nordic countries have modernized their national sales law and adjusted it to the CISG.

Originally, none of the Nordic countries (except Iceland) joined the CISG Part II on formation of contract but opted out according to CISG Article 92. This was because they preferred to maintain the joint Nordic Contracts Act as far as possible in international sales contracts as well. The Nordic countries have recently repealed this reservation.[12]

2 General Principles

2.1 Rules and Principles

Nordic contract law is one of the fields of law where great emphasis has been placed on the development of general doctrines (in German: *Allgemeine Lehren*, in Swedish: *allmänna läror*). An important part of the general doctrines are general principles of law. When considering the concept of a general principle of law, the distinction between legal rules and legal principles is a good place to start. In short, a legal rule is a norm that can be characterized as an all-or-nothing norm, i.e. it is either applied or not. On the other hand, a legal principle will be applied to a greater or lesser extent and is considered to have a dimension of weight.[13] The goal is often to find the optimal application of the principle. In this chapter, the focus will lie on general principles of contract law that can be categorized as legal principles. Broad rules applicable to different sub-branches of contract law, such as the rule that the right to rescind a contract requires a fundamental breach of contract, are not legal principles as they are not applied to a greater or lesser extent. The right to rescind is of an all-or-nothing character: a party either has the right or does not have the right to rescind a contract.

---

[12]See Kleineman (2014).

[13]Alexy (1985), p. 16. See also Bärlund (2015), pp. 85–90, for a more detailed discussion on the difference between rules and principles. The Restatement of Nordic Contract Law 2016 Chap. 1: 'General principles' is based on a broader concept of 'principle' than the one applied here.

In the Nordic doctrine of sources of law, we find legal principles to be strongly binding, weakly binding or permitted legal sources depending on their manifestation in the legal order. If a legal principle is laid down in legislation, it is of course a strongly binding legal source. A useful example to mention is the principle of loyalty in the Finnish Employment Contracts Act[14] Ch. 3 Sec. 1. According to this provision, employees 'shall avoid everything that conflicts with the actions reasonably required of employees in their position'. A legal principle can also be included in the *travaux préparatoires* or be mentioned in a precedent of the supreme court. Here, general principles are weakly binding due to the status of the sources of the principle, as the principle enjoys so-called institutional support, being included in the *travaux préparatoires* or in a precedent.

A good example of argumentation in the Finnish Supreme Court regarding general principles of law is found in case 2008:91. In this case, the Supreme Court states that the beginning of contract negotiations will give rise to a duty of loyalty between the parties, a duty that compels one party to act so that the other party does not err on the essential conditions or the significance of the agreement. A principle that is found only in legal literature will gain the status of a permitted legal source in legal discourse provided that it also has acceptance in the "legal auditorium" (i.e. in legal practice).[15]

2.2 Freedom of Contract

One of the cornerstone principles of Nordic contract law is the principle of freedom of contract. The principle forms an important part of the notion of private autonomy. Although the principle of freedom of contract is important in Nordic contract law, in many situations that freedom is significantly limited. The most important ground for limiting the principle of freedom of contract is when socio-political circumstances require limitations on the parties' possibility to freely arrange their mutual relationship through a contract. The functioning of free competition needs a different set of norms in order to balance this harsh mechanism with other interests in society. As the Italian scholar Alessandro Somma puts it: 'Freedom of contract had to be combined with mainly indirect state interventions aimed at conditioning individual behaviour as needed to avoid market failures or to promote social cohesion.'[16] However, restriction of the principle of freedom of contract is needed not only on social grounds, but also in order to enhance smoothly functioning trade.

Important exceptions to the principle of freedom of contract all involve situations where the counterpart to the contract is considered to have a duty to contract. The need for compulsory contracting in modern Nordic society is increasing for

[14]*Työsopimuslaki/Arbetsavtalslag* 55/2001.

[15]Aarnio (2011), pp. 162–163.

[16]Somma (2013), p. 110.

several reasons, i.e. during times of economic depression,[17] or when consumers are compelled to use developing technologies to acquire necessity goods and services. The virtual marketplace requires e.g. that the consumer can access modern banking services.[18] At the same time, the scope of compulsory contracting is increasing as the principle of freedom of contract is correspondingly losing its importance.

Clear restrictions on the principle of freedom of contract can more generally be seen as an impact of the ideal of the Nordic welfare state in private law. As long as the Nordic countries still have the competence to regulate important fields of contract law, there are possibilities, on a national basis, to restrict the harsh functioning of the principle of freedom of contract. In relations between consumers and businesses, compulsory contracting is even stricter, meaning that business can deny a contract only if acceptable grounds exist to do so. In this respect, the principle of freedom of contract is restricted by a duty to refrain from discriminating on the grounds of social or personal characteristics.[19] Compulsory contracting can follow not only from a legal or factual monopoly of a business, or if the object of the contract is necessity goods and services,[20] several other situations involve compulsory contracting, for instance in Nordic labour and insurance law. Actually, the scope of compulsory contracting has clearly grown during recent years.[21]

2.3 *Legitimate Expectations*

Another important legal principle is the principle of legitimate expectations, which could be described as the interest of exchanges of goods and services in society. The tendency towards rules that take into account legitimate expectations is certainly based on the growing mass production of goods and services and the use of standard contracts. It has been pointed out that the mass character of contracting motivates an even stronger emphasis on the question of what legitimate expectations are.[22]

Already during the first half of the 20th century, Nordic scholars expressed their doubts about the intent paradigm as the sole explanation for why contracts are binding. Factual intent was set aside and, instead, the binding force of the contract was built on one party's confidence in the other party's declaration of intent. Although legitimate expectations play a central role in commercial contracts, the principle is also common in consumer contracts. In Denmark, the Supreme Court

[17]Nybergh (2004), p. 297.

[18]Nybergh (2014).

[19]Nielsen (2010), p. 382.

[20]See e.g. Giertsen (2014), p. 37 and Andersen (2013), p. 232.

[21]Adlercreutz and Gorton (2016), p. 83–85.

[22]Häyhä (1996) passim stresses the mass character of contracting, meaning standardization of the activity of contracting.

has established e.g. that a window display of goods with a price tag is a legally binding offer and not just an invitation to treat.[23] In combination with retailers' obligation to indicate the price of products, this is seen as an example of compulsory contracting.[24]

However, according to the Danish Supreme Court judgment, the display was in itself a legally binding offer, meaning that the retailer had already irrevocably obligated itself. Thus, Nordic contract law is based on the so-called 'promise or offer theory' (in Danish: *løfteteori*), which entails that contractual obligations arise from the promise given by each of the parties. Thus, the offer binds the offeror temporarily from the moment the offeree becomes aware of the offer and definitively if the offer is accepted by the offeree, who is not bound to accept the offer.[25]

2.4 Loyalty

A closely related principle to the principle of legitimate expectations is the principle of loyalty. This principle is strongly based on the fundamental belief that a contract is an instrument for cooperation between the contracting parties, and that a party to a contract is also obliged to take into account the other party's interests.[26] This deviates from the thinking that a contract settles contradictions between the parties. During the last ten years, the loyalty principle has garnered increasing interest from a Nordic academic point of view, as several doctoral theses have been written on the topic.[27]

It is said that the principle is 'a cornerstone of contract law' in both Finland and Norway.[28] In two cases from the Finnish Supreme court, 2007:72 and 2008:92, the Supreme Court imposed upon a bank the duty to act loyally towards a limited liability company. In Finland the claim is that although manifesting the principle of loyalty in a general clause in a piece of legislation causes some difficulty, no reason exists to restrict its scope of application.[29]

In Sweden, the position on the principle of loyalty has strengthened due to lively discussion.[30] The principle is seen as something rather new and difficult to grasp in particular cases.[31] Interestingly, discussion about the position of loyalty has not yet

[23]Ugeskrift for Retsvæsen (UfR)1985.877.

[24]Forbrugerstyrelsen Juridisk Årbog (1991), p. 13.

[25]See Lando et al. (2016), p. 92.

[26]Taxell (1997), p. 45.

[27]Munukka (2015).

[28]Munukka (2007), p. 461.

[29]Taxell (1997), p. 66.

[30]E.g. Holm (2004) and Munukka (2007).

[31]Ramberg and Ramberg (2016), p. 36. Cfr. Lindskog (2015), p. 326 who seems to stress the principle of freedom of contract in commercial relations to the maximum according to the principles of pure competition.

reached topical Danish legal literature. Still, the duty to act loyally is said to concern most contractual relations.[32] Having said this, the impression is, however, that some scepticism exists towards the role of the loyalty principle in Nordic law. It has been said that the principle does not pervade Nordic contract law 'to the same extent that the principle of good faith pervades other European legal systems.'[33]

2.5 *Protecting the Weaker Party*

The principle of protecting the weaker party is widely recognized in Finnish law. The principle is one of the cornerstones of Nordic consumer contract law and it finds its manifestation in all special regulation, not only influenced by the vast body of EU norms, but also stemming from national consumer legislation with its roots in the 1970s. Beyond consumer relations, the principle has gained a rather strong position in Finnish law.

In 2010, in a judgment between two businesses, the Finnish Supreme Court referred explicitly to the principle of protecting the weaker party.[34] The dispute involved a big oil company and a small gas station dealer, whose business had the form of a limited partnership. According to the contract, the oil company's right of termination was restricted. The oil company had terminated the contract in 2004 after setting a termination period of one year, compared to the half-year-period laid down in the contract, and referring to grounds that did not precisely fit the wording of the contract. The Supreme Court stated that the limited partnership was the weaker party in the contractual relationship, so that the wording of the termination clause could not be interpreted extensively. The fact that one of the parties was clearly subordinated to the other party thus had a clear impact on the interpretation of the contract.

In fact, basic Finnish textbooks on contract law contain references to the principle of protecting the weaker party as a general principle that is of importance for all sorts of contractual relations. It is said that the aim of protecting the weaker party has 'a visible impact on … contract law' in Finland. There is even a claim that protection of small businesses is possible without any specific legislation, because of general principles that provide for protection of the weaker party.[35]

The situation is apparently different in the other Nordic countries. In consumer relations, the principle is of course recognized, but traces of the principle are scarce beyond consumer contracts. In Danish, Icelandic, Norwegian and Swedish court

[32]Gomard (2016), pp. 64–66 and Andersen (2013), p. 458. Compare with Andersen and Lookofsky (2015), p. 29 and 71. According to Lando et al. (2016), p. 81, the scope of application of the principle of loyalty is not clear.

[33]Lando et al. (2016), p. 86.

[34]Finnish Supreme Court case 2010:69.

[35]Halila and Hemmo (2008), p. 6 and 8.

cases and legal textbooks, the terminology of the principle of protecting the weaker party is not used, although some references can be found to situations where differences in the relative strength of the parties should be taken into account.[36]

2.6 *Principle of Fairness as Balance*

The principle of fairness as balance is the last general principle discussed here. This principle is the most important legal principle behind the general rule in the Nordic Contract Acts (see Section 36) in that it allows the courts to adjust individual contracts, or other juridical acts, to avoid unreasonableness.[37] However, the idea of the requirement of balance in contracts is not unique to Finnish law, but is perhaps not clearly articulated.[38] The requirement of balance is also discussed in both Danish and Norwegian legal literature.[39]

After having discussed some of the most important general legal principles of contract law, the question arises as to what the role of general principles of contract law is. More seldom, general legal principles can give clear answers on how to solve so-called hard cases. Instead, they are a way to operationalize values that are important in Nordic societies so that they can better form part of legal discourse.

3 Social Civil Law

As already mentioned, legal scholarship in Finland during recent decades has stressed the role of general doctrines. Actually, one could state that in Finland a slightly stronger emphasis is placed on legal literature as a source of law compared to other Nordic countries. Therefore, it is not surprising that one of the innovations of Nordic, but especially Finnish, contract law is so-called *social civil law*, espoused by Finnish legal scholar Thomas Wilhelmsson.[40] The theory of social

---

[36]See for instance Danish Supreme Court decision UfR 1988, p 1042 using Sec. 36 of the Contracts Act (see subchapter 4.2 below) to set aside as unreasonably long a contract period in a contract between an oil company and a fuel oil dealer.

[37]The possibility to adjust contracts according to the Nordic Contracts Act Sec. 36 is also mentioned in Restatement of Nordic Contract Law 2016, pp. 86–88. The principle of fairness as balance is even elevated to the leading principle of modern contract law theory in one thesis in Finland, see Pöyhönen (1988).

[38]Taxell (1997), p. 65 counts the principle of fairness as balance as one of the main general principles of law, besides the principle of loyalty.

[39]See Andersen (2013), p. 462–472 and Giertsen (2014), p. 12.

[40]Wilhelmsson first introduced the theory of social civil law in the Swedish language in 1987, Wilhelmsson (1987). For a non-Nordic, international audience the theory was presented in English in 1992. However, it is important to notice that Nordic legal scholars have not unanimously accepted the theory of social civil law. Especially in Swedish law, opposition against the theory

civil law is a good example of how traditional ways of perceiving principles of contract law can be questioned. If new legal material contains legal rules with identical content that was formerly perceived as exemptions, then it is possible to consider these former exemptions as the new main rules, if there are enough of these new rules.

The starting point for Thomas Wilhelmsson was that the ideology of the Nordic welfare state must also be taken seriously when determining the content of contract law. Wilhelmsson described how legal roles evolved from very general and abstract notions, such as debtors, creditors, buyers, sellers, lessors, lessees and so on, into more specific legal roles within each of the general roles. This development occurred during the 1960s and 1970s, when a parallel set of legal norms was created for relations between consumers and business enterprises. As for sale of goods, there were different kinds of sales from then on: a consumer buying goods from a business enterprise was legally different from a business enterprise buying goods from another enterprise or a private person buying goods from another private person. Different legal sets are thus used depending on what sort of purchases we are dealing with.

The last phase of development contained an even more specific differentiation between legal roles. The personal characteristics of the party were given more importance. According to Wilhelmsson, both ability-oriented legal roles and need-oriented roles could be found in the legislation of the late 1980s when the theory of social civil law was elaborated, where need-oriented roles in particular were given important legal status in the theory of *social force majeure*.[41]

The major general principle of social contract law is the principle of protecting the weaker party. Wilhelmsson distinguishes three kinds of weaker-party roles[42]: (1) Formal weaker-party roles, where the individuals are fully interchangeable and where protection is based regardless of the bargaining power of the individual in the formal role, e.g. the insured as a party to an insurance contract can be described as in the formal weaker party role; (2) Function-related weaker-party role, where the function of the party in a specific case will be decisive regarding the applicable rules regardless of the bargaining power of the individual, e.g. application of consumer protection provisions does not depend on the strength or weakness of the individual consumer; (3) Person-related weaker-party roles, where individual characteristics, especially due to specific social occurrences such as illness, unemployment, and housing problems are of great importance when deciding on

---

has been strong, see e.g. Sandgren (1993), pp. 157–196. Also noteworthy is that in Sweden the term social civil law is used to describe fields of law where the social dimension is strong, as in labour law and family law. In Sweden, an institute at the University of Stockholm is called the *Institutet för social civilrätt*, but in English the term Institute of Social Private Law is used. According to the Institute's homepage, the focus is nowadays on labour law, see http://www.juridicum.su.se/social_civilratt/index_english.htm.

[41]Wilhelmsson (1992), pp. 89–90 and 93–100.

[42]Wilhelmsson (1992), p. 88–100.

the level of protection, e.g. the rules on social *force majeure* will be applicable only when all the specific qualifications of the rules are fulfilled.

The theory of social civil law is a good example of a strong emphasis on general doctrines in Finnish legal thinking since the late 1970s. The core area of the theory is consumer law, although the same arguments used in theory can be applied to other situations.[43] As already noted, an important part of social civil law is the idea of social *force majeure*. As the notion 'social *force majeure*' indicates, a situation must exist where a party to a contract is unable to perform due to a social occurrence.

The prerequisites for applying the rules of social *force majeure* are fourfold: Firstly, the party who has the duty to perform is affected by a personal, social occurrence, such as illness, unemployment, marital problems, and the like. Secondly, these social occurrences must give cause to delays in the debtor's payments. A causal link must exist between the social occurrence and the delayed payment.[44] The delay in payment can be either physical, i.e. the debtor is unable to make payments needed due to e.g. illness, or based on difficulties in obtaining enough money for payment.[45]

The third prerequisite for the theory of social *force majeure* is that the social occurrence is unforeseeable. This means that surgery which has been planned beforehand is not an unforeseeable occurrence for the debtor and therefore, does not constitute social *force majeure*. Fourthly and lastly, the debtor must be innocent of fault regarding the social occurrence. Often, a debtor cannot be blamed for falling ill or being sacked. If, on the other hand, unemployment is due to the debtor's negligence, e.g. if the debtor neglected their working duties, the debtor cannot claim that they suffered a social occurrence that would count as social *force majeure*.[46]

The general effect of the rules of social *force majeure* is that a consumer's breach of contract does not lead to the same sanctions as without social *force majeure*: sanctions are mitigated.[47]

Finnish law contains many examples of social *force majeure*. The classic example is the Nordic acts on hire purchase agreements, which were drafted in close cooperation between the Nordic countries in the 1960s. According to the Finnish Act[48] Section 2, the seller is not entitled to claim sanctions if this would be unjust considering that delay in payment was due to financial difficulties caused by the buyer's illness or unemployment or some other special reason for which the buyer was not primarily at fault. Nowadays, only the Finnish Act has a clear social *force majeure* provision.

---

[43]Wilhelmsson (1992), p. 193.

[44]Wilhelmsson (1992), pp. 197–203.

[45]Bärlund (1990), p. 80.

[46]Wilhelmsson (1992), pp. 204–206.

[47]Wilhelmsson (1992), pp. 206–216.

[48]*Laki osamaksukaupasta/Lag om avbetalningsköp* 91/1966.

Already in 1986, the provisions on consumer credit in Chap. 7 of the Finnish Consumer Protection Act[49] contained a social *force majeure* provision. The current provision, Ch. 7 Sec. 34, is from 2010. According to this provision, a creditor is not entitled to remedies due to a consumer's late payment 'because of the consumer's illness, unemployment or other comparable reason not attributable to him or her, except where this would be manifestly unfair to the creditor with respect to time overdue and other circumstances.'

Another good example of social *force majeure* is found in the Finnish Interest Act[50] (633/1982). Section 11 allows adjustments of interest for late payment, if 'payment is delayed due to financial difficulties that the debtor has suffered because of illness, unemployment or other special reason which is primarily not attributable to the debtor himself or herself'.[51] A more recent example of social *force majeure* is found in the Finnish Code of the Information Society.[52] According to Section 115 of the Code a tele operator is not allowed to close or restrict the communication services of a consumer in specific cases. One situation prevails if the consumer shows that the reason for the late payment is illness, unemployment or some other reason comparable to these, which is not attributable to the consumer's fault, and the overdue fee is paid within a month from the request for payment.

Almost 30 years after publication of the theory of social civil law, one can state that the theory is well established only in Finland. However, the legislator in Denmark, Iceland, Norway and Sweden has not included the rules of social *force majeure* in new consumer legislation. The dividing line can also be seen in Nordic legal literature.

4 Consumer Protection

4.1 Sweden as the Forerunner

Legislation protecting 'weak' contractual parties is by no means a new phenomenon. Even prior to the consumer movement of the 1960s, legislation in this matter was in force in the Nordic countries concerning, for instance, insurance,[53] hire purchase, housing, and employment contracts. This legislation contained mandatory rules safeguarding a relatively well-defined minimum protection of the typically weak contract party, defined by his or her formal legal role as the

[49]*Kuluttajansuojalaki/Konsumentskyddslag* 38/1978.

[50]*Korkolaki/Räntelag* 633/1982.

[51]The Swedish Interest Act, *Räntelag* 1975:635, contains a similar provision in Sec. 8.

[52]*Laki sähköisen viestinnän palveluista/Lag om tjänster inom elektronisk kommunikation* 917/2014.

[53]The Insurance Contracts Act of 1930 was joint Nordic. It is still in force in Denmark, whereas the other Nordic countries have modernized their legislation in the area.

insured/buyer/tenant/employee, irrespective of whether the party in question acted within or outside their business.[54]

One of the achievements of the consumer movement was the introduction of the legal concept of 'consumer',[55] something that facilitated legislative initiatives 'tailor-made' to protect private customers *vis-à-vis* business. This started around 1970 and resulted in Nordic consumer protection legislation, which, despite important differences, generally tends to mutual accord.[56] In the development of a coherent legal protection system, Sweden was the forerunner that inspired the other Nordic countries. Around 1970, Sweden established the basic institutional arrangements, the institution of Consumer Ombudsman and the Consumer Complaint Board system, which have had a considerable impact on consumer protection law in the Nordic countries.[57] Both institutional arrangements (funded by the public purse) have contributed not only to enhancing and clarifying the substantive law protecting consumers but also to the further development of consumer protection law.

Similarly to many other European countries, mandatory rules protecting individual consumers in various forms of contract are important components of Nordic consumer protection law. Since the beginning of the 1970s, all Nordic countries have introduced mandatory consumer protection legislation concerning sale of goods to consumers, door-to-door sales and distance contracts, consumer credit, package travel, interest on late payments, and so on.[58] Much of the legislation has later been adjusted in order to harmonise it with EU directives which, in spite of the general trend in recent years towards total/full harmonisation, to some extent (still) leave room for the member states to lay down more extensive protection rules.

This is the case, for example, as mentioned below, with the general rule in the Nordic Contract Acts Section 36 as compared with the Unfair Contract Terms Directive.[59] Other examples can be found in the Danish Act on Consumer Contracts,[60] which goes further than the Consumer Rights Directive,[61] containing a general prohibition against unsolicited communication in person or by telephone with a consumer at his or her residence or workplace or another place to which there

---

[54]I.e. a 'formal weaker party role'. See above in subchapter 3 about the different kinds of 'weaker party roles' according to Thomas Wilhelmsson.

[55]I.e. a 'function related weaker party role', see preceding footnote.

[56]Bernitz (1979), p. 14 and Wilhelmsson (1989), p. 35.

[57]Iceland has no Consumer Ombudsman institution, but similar tasks are carried out by the Consumer Agency. In 2005, the Consumer Spokesman was established in order to advocate consumer interests not only in general but also towards the public authorities and the legislator. The Consumer Spokesman has an office in connection with the Consumer Agency.

[58]In Finland, nearly all consumer protection provisions are found in a single act, *Kuluttajansuojalaki/Konsumentskyddslag* 38/1978. The other Nordic countries stick to the tradition of fragmented legislation.

[59]Council Directive 93/13/EEC of 5 April 1993 on unfair terms in consumer contracts.

[60]*Lov om forbrugeraftaler* 2013 no 1457.

[61]Directive (2011/83/EU) on consumer rights.

is no public access, with a view to obtaining, immediately or subsequently, an offer or acceptance of an offer to conclude a contract. A promise made by a consumer in connection with such unsolicited communication is not binding. Furthermore, Section 25 of the Danish act protects consumers against terms in contracts concerning the continuing delivery of goods or services for an indefinite period by giving the consumer a general right to terminate the contract by one month's notice after five months have passed since conclusion of the contract.

4.2 Adjusting Contracts

The general and relatively precise mandatory protection rules in the consumer contract acts mentioned above are supplemented by the general rule in the Nordic Contracts Acts Section 36 allowing the courts to adjust individual contracts or other juridical acts to avoid unreasonableness. This rule offers a contract party protection adjusted to the particular circumstances of the individual case when the need arises to avoid unreasonable results that cannot be achieved by means of interpretation or other rules of contract law.

According to Section 36 the courts can, in whole or in part, disregard an agreement if it would be unreasonable or contrary to the principles of fair conduct to enforce it. The decision can rely not only on the circumstances surrounding formation of the contract, but also on its content and on subsequent circumstances. The clause applies to contracts in general, including both business-to-consumer and business-to-business contracts.[62] The operation of Section 36 is considered to be flexible enough to allow such differences to be taken into account to the extent appropriate in view of the facts of the individual case, and also to allow a distinction to be drawn between more or less vulnerable consumers.

In a consumer contract context, the clause also serves a supplemental function to the rather precise mandatory protection rules embedded in the acts mentioned above. This is because, in appropriate individual cases by broad analogy, it facilitates an expansion of consumer protection to types of contracts that do not fall within the scope of mandatory protection provisions.[63] It protects Nordic consumers to a wider extent than Directive 93/13/EEC on unfair contract terms in consumer contracts.

Thus, all types of contract terms fall within the scope of the clause, i.e. including individually negotiated terms; the main subject matter of the contract and the remuneration, are not excluded.[64] The criterion of the section is '*unreasonable or contrary to principles of fair conduct*' without the qualifications mentioned in

---

[62]Thus, Sec. 36 is an example of a 'person-related weaker party role' See above on the different kinds of 'weaker party roles' according to Thomas Wilhelmsson.

[63]For instance in service contracts that are not within the scope of the mandatory protection acts.

[64]This is in contrast to the EU Directive (93/13/EEC) on unfair contract terms.

Article 3 of the Directive (i.e. contrary to the requirement of good faith and a significant imbalance). Furthermore, in contrast to Article 4(1) of the Directive, subsequent facts can also be taken into account in favour of the consumer (but not to the detriment of the consumer).

4.3 Consumer Protection Bodies

The Nordic consumer complaint board system offers individual consumers easy, relatively quick and inexpensive dispute resolution in cases concerning complaints about goods or services. The public consumer complaint boards are independent public bodies. They consist of a chairperson (typically, a professional judge) and consumer and business representatives. The board procedure is optional for the consumer but mandatory for the business party. The procedure is written. A decision by the board does not prevent the parties from bringing the matter before the courts.

At the same time, the collective interests of consumers are protected through preventive control exercised by the Consumer Ombudsman, (in Iceland the Consumer Authority) a public authority. The Consumer Ombudsman is an independent public servant with the task of monitoring business marketing practices and the fairness of contract terms in consumer contracts and to protect the collective consumer interest through good and reasonable business practices in the market. The Consumer Ombudsman acts both as a 'watchdog' and as an enforcer of legislation. The intervention of the Consumer Ombudsman is governed by a general principle of negotiation, according to which the Ombudsman will endeavour by negotiation to induce business to act in accordance with the principles of good marketing practices, as well as other provisions of acts regulating marketing practices, including contract terms. The Consumer Ombudsman also has standing to sue for injunctions.

Whereas individual protection concerns the fairness of contract terms in a given concrete dispute between individual parties, preventive control in the collective interest of consumers is proactive and has a potentially wider impact in that it concerns the use of a contract term in future contracts of a certain type. The difference entails that assessment according to the rules on preventive control focuses on the expected typical effects of the contract term in question. This is confronted with the expected typical effects if contracts were instead "filled out" with the statutory and non-statutory default rules of general contract law, which are generally assumed to express what is a fair balancing of the parties' interests in typical situations.[65]

As noted, the Nordic model of consumer protection is characterised by being a relatively coherent protection system for the solution of legal problems of

[65]Wilhelmsson (2008), pp. 176–182; Andersen and Madsen (2012), pp. 237–239.

consumers, with a basic institutional arrangement that both gives individual consumers relatively easy 'access to justice' and enables public intervention in the collective consumer interest. Furthermore, the construction of the protection system to some extent allows an interplay between, and a co-ordination of, individual and collective protection elements.

The following example is illustrative of this interplay and coordination: A car owner acknowledged that he was obliged to pay a parking fee but refused to pay a reminder fee of 100 DKK (approximately 13 euro), which was authorised by the act on interest on late payments. The case went to the Danish Supreme Court, which in 2010 decided the case in favour of the car owner.[66] The Supreme Court stated that, according to general rules, the parking fee was not due until the claim had reached the car owner and held that placing the paying-in-slip under the windscreen wiper of the car did not in itself mean that the slip had reached the car owner. After unsuccessful negotiation with the parking company, the Consumer Ombudsman sued for an injunction claiming that the company had violated 'good marketing practices'. The Court agreed with the Consumer Ombudsman and issued an injunction prohibiting the car parking company from sending out claims for a reminder fee unless the company was able to prove that the paying-in-slip had reached the car owner. In addition, the decision had the effect of a mandatory injunction obliging the parking company to repay the reminder fee to all car owners from whom it had claimed the fee since the date of the Supreme Court judgment, with the exception of car owners who had directly or indirectly recognised that they had received the paying-in-slip.[67]

5 Debt Adjustment

Although enforcement procedures to collect debts have during the last century been characterized by greater humanity and a certain social understanding, until recently this trend had no effect on the rules of substantive law concerning maintenance of legal claims. Thus, it is a well-established maxim in Nordic law, as well as the law of many other European countries, that the existence of debt does not depend on the debtor's financial situation.

However, in 1984, Danish legislation introduced a new debtor-oriented remedy: adjustment of debt.[68] The aim of the debt adjustment scheme was to mitigate the harmful social effects of permanent indebtedness by enabling over-burdened private individuals to initiate a new type of insolvency proceedings. These proceedings

[66]UfR 2010, p 1534. The Danish Car Owners Organization acted on behalf of the car owner in the proceedings.

[67]UfR 2013, p 1181.

[68]Danish Act 1984 no 187 amending the Bankruptcy Act. The rules have been adjusted a couple of times, most significantly by Act 2005 no 365.

now involve a court order to the effect that the debtor be released from their personal liability for (all or) part of the debt, without the prior consent of (any of) their creditors, and that payment of remaining debts be rescheduled.

The development was inspired by the discharge provisions in English and American bankruptcy law. In the 1980s, rules to this effect were unknown outside the common law countries. However, in the wake of the Danish rules, the other Nordic countries subsequently introduced legislation to the same effect.[69]

Under the Nordic debt adjustment systems, the debtor must prove that he or she is unable, and within the foreseeable future has no prospect of being able, to fulfil his or her obligations. The important point is whether the debtor's payment of the debt (in full) appears futile, seen in light of his or her present and future ability to pay. It is a matter of establishing how much is at the debtor's disposal after reasonable costs towards rent, heating, electricity, food, clothing, and the like are paid and other maintenance obligations are met. In order to decide which expenses are to be considered reasonable, the financial situation of the other members of the household must be taken into account, because it must be established to what extent it is necessary for the debtor to contribute to the reasonable costs of living in the household. The decisive factor is whether a high degree of probability exists that the debtor will never be able to pay all their debts in full.

According to the Finnish system, 'social *force majeure*' may also fulfil the financial requirement for debt adjustment. This is in line with the theory of social civil law discussed above. Thus, according to the Finnish act, the financial requirements are met if insolvency is caused by an essential decline in the ability of the debtor to pay, owing to illness, inability to work, unemployment or other change of circumstances not primarily the fault of the debtor. Alternatively, debt adjustment may be granted if otherwise there is a good reason for the adjustment in view of the proportion of the debts and other liabilities of the debtor to their ability to pay, and the debtor cannot reasonably improve their ability to pay so as to be able to service the debt.

In addition to the financial requirement, the acts lay down a number of criteria intended to safeguard general readiness to pay and other considerations which, from a general point of view, call for the traditional rule that the existence of debts incurred in a legal manner is independent of the debtor's financial situation. The acts list a number of relevant factors, e.g. debt incurred by criminal acts, fraudulent behaviour, financial arrangements to the detriment of creditors, and if there is reason to believe that, in case of debt adjustment, the debtor will not comply with the schedule for payment of the adjusted debt.

A debt adjustment order in all cases has the effect of either reducing (unsecured) debt to a manageable size or eliminating all the personal debts of the debtor in

[69]Finland: *Laki yksityishenkilön velkajärjestelystä/Lag om skuldsanering för privatpersoner* 57/1993 (as amended most recently by Act 2014/1123), Iceland: *Lög um greiðsluaðlögun einstaklinga* 101/2010, Norway: *Lov om frivillig og tvungen gjeldsordning for privatpersoner* 1992 no 99 (amended most recently by Act no 53 of 22 June 2018), Sweden, *Skuldsaneringslag* 1994:334, replaced most recently by Act 2016:675.

question. As a rule of thumb, debt is reduced to an amount that the debtor can pay over a period of five years. The percentage reduction is based on a forecast of the debtor's expected income and cost of living over the period in question. Normally, writing-down the debt is combined with a payment plan for the remaining debt. One of the aims of debt adjustment is to 'normalise' the debt situation of the debtor. This indicates the need for a longer settlement period than the rule of thumb of five years, if the debtor would otherwise be in a better position than others in an otherwise identical situation, e.g. the repayment period for debt adjustment in connection with student loans is based on the fact that student loans are normally repaid over a relatively long period, counting from completion of studies.

The release of the debtor from debt written off by a debt adjustment order is unconditional, in the sense that the debtor's performance of the payment plan is not an absolute condition for release. The bankruptcy court may annul a debt adjustment order at the request of a creditor if the debtor grossly neglects their obligations under the plan, or if the debtor has acted fraudulently during the case.

References

Aarnio A (2011) Essays on the doctrinal study of law. Springer, Dordrecht

Adlercreutz A, Gorton L (2016) Avtalsrätt I. Juristförlaget I Lund, Lund

Alexy R (1985) Rechtsregeln und Rechtsprinzipien. In: MacCormick N, Panou S, Lombardi Vallauri L (eds) Conditions of validity and cognition in modern legal thought. ARSP Archiv für Rechts- und Sozialphilosophie Beiheft, Stuttgart, pp 13–29

Andersen MB (2013) Grundlæggende aftaleret. Gjellerup, Copenhagen

Andersen MB, Lookofsky J (2015) Lærebog i obligationsret I. Karnov Group, Copenhagen

Andersen LL, Madsen PB (eds) (2012) Aftaler og mellemmænd. Karnov Group, Copenhagen

Andersen MB, Runesson E (2015) An overview of Nordic contract law. In: Håstad T (ed) The Nordic contracts act—essays in celebration of its one hundredth anniversary. DJØF Publishing, Copenhagen

Årbog J (1991) Juridisk Årbog Forbrugerstyrelsen 1991. Forbrugerstyrelsen, Copenhagen

Bärlund J (1990) Sociala prestationshinder i konsumentavtal, Näk-rapport 1990:6. Nordisk Ministerråd, Copenhagen

Bärlund J (2015) Protection of the weaker party in B2B relations in Nordic contract law. In: Håstad T (ed) The Nordic contracts act—essays in celebration of its one hundredth anniversary. DJØF Publishing, Copenhagen, pp 83–106

Bernitz U (1979) Konsumentret i Norden. Nordisk Embedsmandskomité, Stockholm

Giertsen J (2014) Avtaler. Universitetsforlaget, Oslo

Gomard B (2016) Obligationsret Del 1. Jurist- og Økonomforbundets Forlag, Gråsten

Halila H, Hemmo M (2008) Sopimustyypit. Talentum, Helsinki

Häyhä J (1996) Sopimus, laki ja vakuutustoiminta. Suomalainen Lakimiesyhdistys, Helsinki

Holm A (2004) Den avtalsgrundade lojalitetsplikten – en allmän rättsprincip. Linköpings universitet, Linköping

Kleineman J (2014) The new Nordic approach to CISG part ii: pragmatism wins the day? In: Lookofsky J, Andersen MB (eds) The CISG convention and domestic contract law. Harmony, cross-inspiration or discord? Djøf Publishing, Copenhagen, pp 21–33

Lando O, Holle M, Håstad T et al (eds) (2016) Restatement of Nordic law. Djøf Publishing, Copenhagen

Lindskog S (2015) Jämkning i kommersiella avtalsförhållanden. In: Andersen MB, Bärlund J, Flodgren B, Giertsen J (eds) Aftaleloven 100 år – Baggrund, status, udfordringer fremtid. DJØF Publishing, Copenhagen, pp 305–327

Munukka J (2007) Kontraktuell lojalitetsplikt. Jure förlag, Stockholm

Munukka J (2015) The contractual duty of loyalty: good faith in the performance and enforcement of contracts. In: Håstad T (ed) The Nordic contracts act—essays in celebration of its one hundredth anniversary. DJØF Publishing, Copenhagen, pp 203–215

Nielsen R (2010) Civilretlige diskriminationsforbud. Jurist- og Økonomforbundets Forlag, Århus

Nybergh F (2004) Rätten till tjänster i informations- och kreditsamhället – En rättsdogmatisk undersökning om tillgången till infrastrukturen för handeln, särskilt banktjänster. Suomalainen Lakimiesyhdistys, Helsinki

Nybergh F (2014) Access to long-term banking services in the Nordic states. In: Nogler L, Reifner U (eds) Life time contracts—social long-term contracts in labour, tenancy and consumer credit law. Eleven International Publishing, The Hague, pp 495–530

Pöyhönen J (1988) Sopimusoikeuden järjestelmä ja sopimusten sovittelu. Suomalainen Lakimiesyhdistys, Helsinki

Ramberg J, Ramberg C (2016) Allmän avtalsrätt. Wolters Kluwer, Stockholm

Sandgren C (1993) A social law of contract? Scand Stud Law 37:157–196

Somma A (2013) Private law as biopolitics: ordoliberalism, social market economy, and the public dimension of contract. Law Contemp Prob 76:105–116

Taxell LE (1997) Avtalsrätt: Bekgrund – sammanfattning – utblick. Juristförlaget, Stockholm

Wilhelmsson T (1987) Social civilrätt – Om behovsorienterade element I kontraktsrättens allmänna läror. Juristförbundets förlag, Helsingfors

Wilhelmsson T (1989) Konsumentskyddet i Finland. Almän del. Juristförbundets förlag, Helsingfors

Wilhelmsson T (1992) Critical studies in private law—a treatise on need-rational principles in modern law. Kluwer Academic Publishers, Dordrecht

Wilhelmsson T (2008) Standardavtal och oskäliga avtalsvillkor. Talentum, Tampere

Zweigert K, Kötz H (1998) An introduction to comparative law. Oxford University Press, Oxford

Property and Its Limits

Patrik Lindskoug

Abstract There is no national comprehensive code or specific legislation which regulates property law matters as a whole in any of the Nordic countries. Some issues are regulated by statutory law, others by customary law, court decisions or general principles. Furthermore, the is no common (Nordic) legal definition of property, and many differences exist between the Nordic countries. Still, it is important to underline that the most significant right to property, ownership, is protected in all Nordic countries by constitutional law.

1 Nordic Property Law?

As already mentioned in Chap. 1, there is no such thing as Nordic law. That statement goes for property law in the Nordic countries as well. Even so, the sister states, with certain reservations, do share some basic features in terms of how property law is regulated. In this chapter, the fundamental structure of property and its regulation will be presented.[1]

First of all, it should be noticed that there is no national comprehensive code or specific legislation which regulates property law matters as a whole in any of the Nordic countries. Instead, these matters are dealt with in a markedly fragmented way. Some issues are covered by specific statutes, others by customary law or general principles; an approach which may seem somewhat odd for those studying Nordic law from a foreign perspective. Obviously, court decisions constitute the most important source of law in situations not covered by statutes. The courts' work with construing and adapting the governing property law has had a vast influence on the development of this topic.

[1]The author wishes to thank Dr. Teemu Juutilainen, University of Helsinki, for comments.

P. Lindskoug (✉)
Law Department, Copenhagen Business School, Copenhagen, Denmark
e-mail: pli.jur@cbs.dk

© Springer Nature Switzerland AG 2019

P. Letto-Vanamo et al. (eds.), *Nordic Law in European Context*,
Ius Gentium: Comparative Perspectives on Law and Justice 73,
https://doi.org/10.1007/978-3-030-03006-3_8

Furthermore, there is no common definition of property law as such in the Nordic countries. From an international point of view, this is rather unusual even though property law in many ways is defined differently in different countries. While some countries have a definition based on the objects affected (for example German law, which operates with a definition covering only tangible assets such as land and movables), the Nordic countries to a large extent base their characterization on the rights that are to be covered by the concept of property law, a fact which extends the understanding of property law, besides land and movables, to receivables and intellectual property rights. Hence, the lack of comprehensive legislation and common definitions does not prevent legislation in the Nordic countries from approaching this section of law in a (basically) common way.

In this context, it is essential to underline that the most significant right to property, namely ownership, is respected in the Nordic countries; a fact that is clarified in constitutional law, of which more below. The owner of property enjoys some powers in relation to other persons. Thus, for example, the owner has the right to possess property and enjoy any yield it may bring, the right to damages if someone causes its destruction or by other means interferes with the property so as to cause hindrance from enjoying it, as well as the right to recover the property if possession is lost through theft or some similar illicit act. Any such right falls under the concept of a static property right (or static third-party protection); as an owner, you have the right to decide over what is yours. As a complement to the static property right, the scope of a dynamic property right (or dynamic third-party protection) concerns rights against a third party when the property is fully or partly transferred from the owner to another person.

Whenever property, or a specific right in property, is sold, hired, pledged, left in someone's custody and so forth, the risk arises of conflict, not only between the parties but also between one of the parties to the contract and a third person. A situation concerning a conflict between a purchaser and the seller's creditors in the case of the latter's insolvency—or vice versa—as well as a dispute between a *bona fide* purchaser and a previous owner will not only make the dynamic property right topical, but will also reveal a major difference between the Nordic countries and most other jurisdictions. While in many other legal families, questions regarding property law aspects in situations such as those described will be dealt with from an ownership point of view, the Nordic approach—sometimes referred to as a functional approach[2]—is not that concerned with ownership per se.

Indeed, the concept of ownership as such is not even defined in the national legislation of any of the Nordic countries.[3] And while in many foreign jurisdictions the major question regarding property law conflicts such as those described would be "who is the owner of?", the major question in the functional approach-oriented Nordic property law is "who has the better right to?" the object in question.

[2]Lilja (2011).

[3]Even so, several Nordic statutes refer to "ownership", but in each case the purport and effect of the ownership mentioned is obvious.

Furthermore, the answer to the question who has the better right varies and is quite independent of what other jurisdictions would typically regard as ownership. Instead, any conflict over property will be resolved by certain rules adopted for and applicable to the specific situation, while rules used for solving one type of conflict do not necessarily have any bearing on resolving another conflict type. As a result of this method, the Nordic approach has also been characterized as an "issue-by-issue approach", where every question will be resolved "on its own merits in each situation".[4]

Conflict classification is thus more important in the Nordic countries than actual ownership per se; once the conflict has been identified and categorized, the applicable rules governing the actual category of conflicts will be applied. The drawback of this method is a somewhat widespread and fragmented pattern of legal solutions which falls within the dynamic property right field.

This Nordic way of thinking has historical roots and was originally adapted to solve specific problems in Denmark during the 19th century. Danish law professor Julius Lassen is said to be the first to have introduced the solutions in an article from 1890.[5] Nevertheless it is his countryman, law professor Carl Torp, who is most often connected with the non-dogmatic reasoning that characterizes the Nordic approach.[6] The arguments presented by him at the Nordic lawyers' meeting in 1902 have been recognized and since then followed by several other prominent Nordic legal scholars.[7]

Yet another important aspect of Nordic property law lies in the categorization of property as such. For almost all aspects of private law a distinction is drawn between real (immovable) property on one side and movable property on the other. To a large extent, questions of rights in real property are regulated by particular rules and principles. The outline of a presentation such as the present one on a fragmented and un-harmonized area of law can be structured in a number of ways, but in order to create an overview that reflects the property law rules in the Nordic countries, it is useful to stick to three major areas concerning aspects of property rights: 1. constitutional property protection, 2. regulation of real property and 3. regulation of movables.[8]

[4]Håstad (2006a, b), p. 39.

[5]Lassen (1890), p. 619.

[6]Torp (1902).

[7]See, for instance, in Denmark Ross (1935) and Vinding Kruse (1951); in Norway Brækhus and Hærem (1964); in Sweden Håstad (2004).

[8]For further studies in Scandinavian property law, see inter alia Björne (2007), Brækhus and Hærem (1964), Elmer and Skovby (1999), Lilja (2011), Falkanger and Falkanger (2013), Hansen Jensen (2007), Håstad (2004), Hessler (1973), Martinson (2012), Millqvist (2015), Mortensen (2008), Pöyhöne (2002), Ross (1957), Sandstedt (2013), Tepora (2009), and Vinding Kruse (1924).

2 Constitutional Protection of Property Rights

While most other property law rules have the purpose of regulating relationships between private parties (and sometimes that party's relation with a particular public institution), a person's property rights are also guaranteed by a country's constitution. Even though their age varies, the content is similar:

The Constitutional Act of Denmark, Section 73, Subsection 1: The right of property shall be inviolable. No person shall be ordered to surrender his property except when required in the public interest. It shall be done only as provided by statute and against full compensation.

The Constitution of Finland, Section 15—Protection of property: The property of everyone is protected. Provisions on the expropriation of property, for public needs and against full compensation, are laid down by an Act.

The Constitution of the Republic of Iceland, Article 72: The right of private ownership shall be inviolate. No one may be obliged to surrender his property unless required by public interests. Such a measure shall be provided for by law, and full compensation shall be paid. The right of foreign parties to own real property interests or shares in business enterprises in Iceland may be limited by law.

The Norwegian Constitution, Article 105: If the welfare of the state requires that any person shall surrender their movable or immovable property for public use, they shall receive full compensation from the Treasury.

The Swedish Constitutional Act (The Instrument of Government), Chap. 2, Art. 15: The property of every individual shall be so guaranteed that no one may be compelled by expropriation or other such disposition to surrender property to public institutions or to a private subject, or tolerate restriction by public institutions of the use of land or buildings, other than where necessary to satisfy pressing public interests.

Constitutional protection governs all kinds of property and, as observable from these texts, protection concerns a single person's or a company's right not to be deprived of their possessions unless a certain interest calls for it (a topic that will be further dealt with below). Hence, the protection laid down in these articles is consistent with the first Protocol to the Convention for the Protection of Human Rights and Fundamental Freedoms (EHCR). The assured right of property can be said to protect an individual's or a company's financial interests since any proceedings where public interest leads to loss of a property right must be subject to conditions provided for by law where the party affected is guaranteed compensation for forfeiture.[9]

[9]For situations where the right of property may come into conflict with other rights and interests from a Danish point of view, see Hansen Jensen (2007), p. 123. For the same, from a Swedish point of view, see Åhman (2000), p. 307.

3 Real Property

3.1 Introduction

Real property consists, above all, of *land*. The definitions of real property within the Nordic countries are somewhat vague and varying. Norway and Sweden both have definitions clarified in specific acts, where, for example, the Swedish Land Code states that "Real property is Land. This is subdivided into property units".[10] The other countries do not have any statutory definitions as such, but this does not impede the factual circumstance that the concept of real property is basically considered as land as well. The area of land establishing a property unit is fundamentally nothing other than a piece of ground that is normally delimited horizontally or, in all the Nordic countries but Finland, both vertically and horizontally. Such a three-dimensional property unit makes it possible to qualify a flat in a building as a real property unit of its own (compare *condominium*, *commonhold* or *Wohnungseigentum* in other jurisdictions). However, it must be stressed that this qualification is subject to a specific registration procedure in the four Nordic countries where this form of real property exists.

Defined as real property and considered as included in property units are also some specific fixtures, such as buildings, fences, and other facilities constructed with a property unit for permanent use. Furthermore, a building includes fixtures and other things with which it has been provided by the owner. Accordingly, an object normally regarded as a moveable—for example a stove or a washing machine—can in some situations be categorized as real property as soon as it is included in a building.

Any modern country needs to provide legal rules regarding the disposition of its territory. The Nordic rules on real property are of both a private law and a public law nature. The parts addressing private relations, whether established in statutes or not, include aspects such as sale and tenancy as well as how property may be used as security for credit. They also concern issues regarding rights to property. Rules of a public law nature involve aspects such as creation and identification of property units, different kinds of property registration and taxation of real property. Yet other public laws deal with different kinds of public interest in land, from infrastructure and environmental issues to community rights to privately-owned land.

3.2 Acquisition of Real Property

Private acquisition of real property is primarily achieved through normal property dispositions, i.e. through purchase, exchange or gift. A comparison between the Nordic countries shows that such acquisitions are regulated differently. While Finland and Sweden in their respective codes regarding land and real estate have statutory

[10] *Jordabalk* (1970:994).

requirements as to form, primarily written form,[11] the Norwegian Act includes a provision which states that an agreement regarding sale of real property may be either oral or written, but must be put in writing if one of the parties so requires.[12]

Denmark, on the other hand, has neither such requirements nor any written statutes at all regarding the sale of real property, so that acquisition of real property in Denmark is legally based on principles emanating from case law and comments in the literature. The Sale of Goods Act, which is normally used for handling contractual obligations either directly (as in the case of goods and tangibles) or by analogy, will only "apply to all contracts of sale other than contracts for the sale of immovable property."[13] Hence, rules concerning rights and obligations for the vendor and the purchaser must be extracted from other principles, although arguably these principles may to a large extent be "inspired" by the Sale of Goods Act as being the major law of obligations in Danish law.

From a practical point of view, this legislative difference does not lead to major dissimilarities between the countries as such. The main idea of a formal requirement in connection with formation of a contract in the Finnish and Swedish Acts is to establish a reliable foundation for the registration procedure, which in turn is necessary for two other aspects: publicity for protection against third party claims and enabling the property to be used as security for credit. Any contract not complying with the formal requirements is invalid,[14] which means that—in contrast to the principal rule in Nordic contract acts—neither an offer nor an acceptance is binding unless the requirement of written form is fulfilled. If a buyer in Denmark or Norway wants to achieve the same protection and status, registration of their acquisition is actually necessary as well. Registration can only be completed if it is based on a written contract and hence acquisitions of real property are mostly in writing in these two countries as well.

When two parties enter into a contract for the sale of real property, questions may arise regarding the condition of the property. The main rule is that the seller must ensure that the property conforms to what follows from the agreement. Any deviation from that, or from what the buyer could have justifiably anticipated at the time of the purchase, entitles the purchaser to make a deduction from the price or, in some cases, to cancel the purchase. The buyer may also be entitled to compensation by way of damages if the defect or loss is due to the negligence of the seller, or if the property deviated from what the seller must be deemed to have promised at the time of the purchase.

That being said, these rights of the purchaser are restricted to a certain level of *caveat emptor*. Hence, deviations that the purchaser ought to have discovered in the

[11]According to the Finnish Code of Real Estate, *Maakaari/Jordabalk* 540/1995, acquisition of real property can also be concluded by electronic means. The parties will then employ electronic documents following as a systemized structure regulated in the code.

[12]*Lov om jord* 1995 no 23.

[13]*Købeloven* 2003 no 237.

[14]Thus, an agreed purchase price different from the one stated in the purchase document is void and will replaced by the written one.

course of examining the property which were motivated by the state of the property unit, the normal state of comparable properties and other circumstances appearing at the time of the purchase may not be claimed to be defects.

3.3 Real Property as Security for Credit

In the Nordic countries, no other property is as important as real property in terms of credit security. Both industry and households to a large extent raise money by mortgaging real property. The explanation is, primarily, that the economic stability of real property in the Nordic countries (even though financial crises have shown that this stability is not completely resilient),[15] in combination with trustworthy registration systems institute a level of security high enough for creditors to trust in the value of this kind of property.

Commonly in the Nordic countries, the mortgagee is entitled to payment when the revenues from an executive sale of the property are distributed. To ensure that right, the mortgage must be formally processed: a procedure that includes registration of the mortgage certificate. The procedural system varies between the Nordic countries, though. In Finland and Sweden, any registered owner of real property who wants to grant a mortgage lien on the property as security for a claim must first obtain a mortgage certificate of a certain sum of money from the land registration authority.

The issue of a mortgage certificate is combined with registration in the mortgage certificate register under certain provisions. In Sweden, the certificate is issued either as a written mortgage certificate or as a digital mortgage certificate, whereas under Finnish law only digital certificates are issued from 1 June 2017. The right of mortgage lien as such is established when the property owner surrenders the mortgage certificate as security for a claim. In the case of a digital mortgage certificate, it will be deemed to have been delivered to the creditor when the creditor was registered as holder of the mortgage certificate in the Mortgage Certificates Register.

In Denmark and Norway, where no legal requirement exists to register the acquisition of real property per se, most buyers register their acquisition nonetheless, since this is the only way to protect their acquisition against the seller's creditors or, in the case of a double disposition by the seller, another purchaser. In order to use real property as credit security in Denmark, as well as in Norway, there is no need to obtain an official mortgage certificate as is the case in Finland and Sweden. Instead, the real property owner may create their own mortgage document. This can be structured in different ways, and one of the most widely used categories is the *mortgage registered to the owner*. This is a mortgage issued by the owner of a property to himself; a document that can, when registered, subsequently be used as security for credit.

---

[15] At least not in Sweden, where the crises in the property market at the beginning of the 1990s and again in the late 2000s have demonstrated that real property may not always be considered as completely reliable.

In Norway, and formerly in Denmark, the mortgage document must be surrendered to the creditor, who afterwards has to register it according to the Land Registration Act in order to establish a mortgage lien.[16] Since 2009, the registration process in Denmark has been completely digitalized, though. This means that the whole procedure, from issuing the mortgage document to registration of the same document, can only be done by electronic means, following the regulations in the Danish Registration Act.[17]

3.4 Expropriation

In the Nordic countries, forced dispossession of the title to real property, the right of use or of a right of easement to it, is limited to situations where the public interest requires it. With reference to national constitutional laws, and as described above, expropriation (i.e. not an executive sale) can only be performed by statute and against compensation.

The basis for expropriation can be found in a number of reasons concerning aspects such as the construction of roads, railways, harbours, military or other public installations, or otherwise when it serves progress, such as ensuring implementation of an urban development in accordance with realization of a municipal, regional or national plan. While Iceland, Finland and Sweden all have specific expropriation acts governing typical situations and purposes where expropriation is permissible,[18] Denmark and Norway have a large number of laws concerning specific purposes where expropriation may take place, such as those above-mentioned.

A feature common to the Nordic countries is that a certain balance must be considered and weighed in expropriation cases. The gain of the public interest must outweigh the disadvantages of the private losses of those whose property rights are expropriated. From this it follows that if a purpose can be achieved appropriately by the use of alternative methods, expropriation will not be permitted. Compensation may be regulated by law, as in the existing expropriation acts, or delegated to a certain authority, as is the case in Denmark, where compensation is usually determined by a special commissioner. Interestingly, Denmark has no legislation on the principles of setting compensation, which is mainly based on practice. Basically, there may be no compensation beyond commercial value, such as removal costs on the loss of homes or losses relating to business disposal. Likewise with "sentimental loss": nothing will be replaced.

---

[16]*Lov om tinglysing* 1935 no 2.

[17]*Tinglysningsloven* 1986 no 622.

[18]These acts do not cover all situations, though, but are to be applied unless otherwise enacted elsewhere.

3.5 *Everyman's Right*

The concept of everyman's right (the right of public access, freedom to roam) covers the right for the public to access open land and nature, even though it may be owned by somebody else. The scope of the right is somewhat imprecise, and is based on an old common Nordic tradition. Nevertheless, the right as it is known today cannot be understood as one and the same since it has developed differently in each of the Nordic countries. Denmark has the most restrictive set of rules; free access to certain land areas was abolished in the 19th century and it is now disputed whether there is such a thing as everyman's right in Denmark at all. According to the Danish rules, one may, during daytime, wander through private ways or paths as long as they are not blocked by the landowner, but after sunset admission is not allowed. In certain zones, though, access is always legitimate, such as the coastline and some public forests where it is even permitted to erect a tent and stay overnight outside the areas of registered camping places.

In Iceland, Finland, Norway, and Sweden, everyman's right is still quite extensive, allowing everybody to move freely in the countryside. The phenomenon is also guaranteed by law, even though it must be described as a somewhat vague regulation in all four countries. In Norway, the content of everyman's right is to some extent more clarified in the Outdoor Life Act.[19] In Finland and Sweden, the concept is less regulated and is mostly based on tradition. In any case, certain provisions can in both countries be found in various sources. In Finland, the most important ones are declared in the Penal Code[20] and in the Environment Protection Act.[21]

In Sweden, everyman's right is vaguely guaranteed in constitutional law.[22] Since there is no definition of everyman's right per se, the concept is often referred to as defined by negative terms and is, as for example in Sweden, practically limited by the rules of the Penal Code regulating the offence of "taking an unlawful path".[23] The wrongdoing herein lies in entering a curtilage or a planted area, which thus cannot be done by reference to the Swedish everyman's right. Besides that, everybody is allowed to benefit from nature by hiking, biking, camping, fishing, picking berries and mushrooms as long as there is no risk of damage.

The right is so extensive that it applies even if the landowner has marked the area with a fence, "private property" signs or similar demarcation measures. In spite of the vague concept and wide-ranging understanding of the concept of everyman's right, certain implicit limitations restrict the freedom to roam. Beside the rules mentioned in the penal codes, limitations are based on an implied responsibility

---

[19]*Lov om friluftslivet* 1957 no 16.

[20]*Rikoslaki/Strafflag* 39/1889.

[21]*Luonnonsuojelulaki/Naturvårdslag* 1096/1996.

[22]More relevant is the fairly vague mentioning of everyman's right in the Environment Code, *Miljöbalk* (1998:808).

[23]A similar provision can be found in the Finnish Penal Code.

placed on the visitor. In Finland, where everyman's right is quite extensive, certain delimitation rules can be found in different statutes, such as the Rescue Act, the Waste Act and the Off Road Traffic Act.

All in all, the fundamental principle to show consideration is regularly presented as "don't disturb—don't destroy". In accordance with this statement, everyman's right does not allow anyone to disturb those who live in the visited area by crossing over or occupying someone's home grounds or to interfere with the landowner's activities. Furthermore, nobody is allowed to damage nature by taking twigs, branches or bark from growing plants or trees, or to hike, ride or cycle where the ground is soft or fragile or otherwise at risk of being damaged. Needless to say, there is no access for motorized vehicles on bare ground in the terrain. Camping is allowed for a night or two, but not where farming is carried out and not close to a residence unless one has the landowner's consent to stay there.

In Sweden and Norway, building a fire is permitted as long as there is no risk of uncontrolled spread. Afterwards, the fire must be thoroughly extinguished and no trace of the fire may be left in the form of a fireplace or similar. In Finland, a permit from the landowner is required to build a fire, unless it is built on an area of water covered with ice. Rubbish or litter may not be left in nature. As to fishing and hunting, none of these are covered by everyman's right. Thus, both activities require specific licences. Angling and fishing with certain other kinds of hand equipment is nonetheless normally allowed along the coasts in Finland and Sweden, as well as in the largest lakes. In Norway some fishing is free, but several fishing regulations, national as well as local, must be observed.

A more problematic part of everyman's right is when the rights of individuals are exploited by professionals. For over a hundred years, discussion has focused on whether everyman's right may include commercial or otherwise organized activities, such as letting hired berry pickers carry out their work for berry and fruit companies, business-related ride or tour activities, organized ski tracking or competitive events and so forth. At any rate, for the time being the law does not distinguish between private and commercial activities.

Finally, it must be stressed that everyman's right is an ambiguous phenomenon, based on old traditions and common behaviour. For that reason, it is almost impossible to determine the exact scope of the right. Any visitor who wants to enjoy the freedom to roam is advised to investigate the principles established in the country in question and consider that the right is balanced on a responsibility to act and behave in a solicitous way; "don't disturb—don't destroy".[24]

[24]For further studies in the Scandinavian concept of everyman's right, see inter alia Bengtsson (2004), Nordisk Ministerråd (1997), Nuuja and Viitanen (2007), and Reusch (2012).

4 Movables

4.1 Introduction

As mentioned above, the Nordic countries apply a functional approach to questions concerning property law matters. However, this does not mean that the rules and principles operate in the same way in every state. Quite the opposite, they are in many aspects different from each other, a fact that becomes particularly obvious when studying property law aspects of movables. Only with some few exceptions, no major attempt has been made to harmonize the legal rules; the basic structure of each national property law simply differs too much from the others.

Even trying to portray the thoughts and solutions regarding all the different conflict types within only one of the Nordic countries would be an assignment far too extensive for this chapter, not to mention an attempt to describe all the various solutions in all the different Nordic countries. Therefore, the following is restricted to describing how the functional approach is structured regarding contracts of sale and contracts for credit security in movables. The description will for obvious reasons highlight the characteristic aspects only, while certain details must be omitted.

4.2 Purchaser's Protection Against Seller's Creditors

As already noted, some jurisdictions provide rules for defining a certain moment when title is supposed to be transferred from one party to another, the result of which connotes all aspects of ownership, such as the right to dispose of the property, use it for credit security and enjoy protection against the seller's creditors.

This kind of *unitary approach* (see below) to the transfer of title is uncalled for in the Nordic countries. Instead, the functional approach entails a possibility to identify the party who has the better right to the object in any specific conflict situation where the question arises; each situation has to be dealt with on its own merits in the given situation according to the issue-by-issue approach mentioned above. In any case, the question of what it takes for a buyer to be protected against claims by the seller's creditors touches upon a topic where the differences between the legal solutions of each the Nordic countries differ the most. The following scenario might serve as an example:

> On 1 February A purchases a movable from B. It is agreed that A will pay the price the same day. It is also agreed that the object will remain in the custody of B until 1 April. B is declared bankrupt on 1 March.

In a case like this, both A and the bankruptcy estate will have an interest in the movable, and hence, the question is to whom it must be surrendered. Common for the Nordic countries, and according to the functional approach, is that the question of ownership as such is to a large extent irrelevant. Consequently—and in contrast, for example, to continental jurisdictions—the solution to a third-party conflict like this does not stem from the idea of identifying one of the parties as "owner", nor is the transfer of ownership of prime importance. The major issue instead is to decide whether the bankruptcy estate or A has the better right to the movable in question.

In order to further clarify this, a starting point could be taken in the bankruptcy legislation of any of the Nordic countries. Even though insolvency law is not harmonized, each of these acts declares that all property belonging to the debtor at the time of the decision on bankruptcy belongs to the bankruptcy estate—a rule that is not atypical; the same applies to bankruptcy acts in most other jurisdictions as well. However, the question to be answered concerns how to decide whether the property belongs to the buyer, party A, or if it belongs to the bankruptcy estate. Or —to put the question into Nordic legal terminology—whether the purchaser or the bankruptcy estate has the better right to the movable in question.

As indicated above, the answer to this question varies between the Nordic countries, a fact that elucidates that we are now moving beyond the common application of the functional approach. A distinct dividing line can be drawn between Sweden and the other Nordic countries, especially in relation to Denmark. In Sweden, the very opposite of the abovementioned unitary approach becomes most obvious because what is sometimes defined as the "split" approach could be said to be applied. According to this approach, originally derived from Roman law, a requirement of *traditio* (delivery) exists to let the title pass to the buyer. This principle applies in Swedish law as well and consequently the buyer, A, will only be protected if the movable involved has been delivered to A; but if the movable remains with the seller, the bankruptcy estate will be considered to have the better right to it.

It ought to be mentioned, though, that the *traditio* principle in Swedish law is little related with the ancient principle of Roman law and may not even be connected with any split approach principle based on a relationship between the contract providing for transfer of the title and the real transfer of title as such. Instead, the requirement of *traditio* in the Swedish legal system is based on a historical inclination to avoid fraudulent transactions.

Nevertheless, it is acknowledged that some genuine transactions require that the seller possesses the goods on behalf of the buyer on a *constitutum possessorium* basis. In order to gain protection against the seller's creditors in these cases, a buyer under Swedish law needs to have the transaction published in a newspaper and the acquisition registered according to a formal procedure laid down in a special act with historical roots from 1835. Be that as it may, in 2002 new rules were adopted for Swedish consumer sales in order to grant consumers protection against the seller's creditors at the time of the contract, but only as long as the object of the transaction is individualized in a way that clarifies that it is reserved for the consumer.

The *traditio* principle is also considered as the governing principle in Norwegian law, established as such due to two cases more than a hundred years old.[25] Even so, a certain doctrine of interest derived from these two cases, and devised by Norwegian law professor Sjur Brækhus, has inaugurated a *constitutum possessorium* exception from the *traditio* principle.[26] According to this doctrine, a buyer will be protected against the creditors of the seller even though the goods remain in the seller's possession *if* the two of them have entered into an agreement clarifying that the chosen solution is in the interest of the buyer. Nevertheless, the same goes for situations where it is clear that the goods remain with the seller for other reasons assignable to the buyer's interest, such as additional work on the goods or while awaiting transport to the buyer. Hence, the *traditio* principle is not applied in the same thorough and systematic way in Norway as it is in Sweden.

In the other Nordic countries, the *traditio* principle does not apply in connection with the acquisition of goods but plays a certain role in connection with other matters, such as security over movables. Instead, the buyer gains protection against the creditors of the seller even at the time of contract if the goods are individualised. This rule, not to be found in any particular statutes, is based on the premise that after being bound by an enforceable contract, the seller no longer has power to dispose of the goods. In such cases, the goods are no longer considered as belonging to the seller and, since the creditors only have entire disposal of property that actually belongs to the seller, the buyer is protected against the creditors and may separate the goods from the bankruptcy estate. However, if the buyer has not yet performed his/her obligation, i.e. payment, the bankruptcy estate can choose whether or not to enter into the contract.

This latter-described principle could easily be confused with *the transfer-of-title approach*, sometimes referred to as the *unitary approach*.[27] According to this approach, applied in, for example, France and to some extent England, a buyer acquires ownership at the moment of consensus, no matter whether the goods have been delivered or whether payment of the purchase price has taken place. This comparison is not appropriate, though. The idea of the unitary approach is based on the conception of ownership as the important and decisive factor when determining to whom the goods should be given. Yet again, it must be stressed that neither ownership nor transfer of title is of particular importance in the Nordic functional approach-oriented system.[28]

Thus, except for Sweden and to some extent Norway, the Nordic countries only use the method explained above in order to clarify whether the buyer or the seller's creditors have the better right to the goods in this very specific situation. And, as earlier mentioned, the chosen solution does not prejudice any other issue where the question of a better right may arise. This specific order will only apply as long as

[25]Norsk Retstidende 1910.231 and 1912.263.

[26]Brækhus and Hærem (1964), p. 513.

[27]Lilja (2011), p. 13; von Bar and Drobnig (2004), p. 316.

[28]Compare Göransson (1985), Håstad (2009), and Olsson (1954).

the goods are not considered to belong to the seller. However, should the seller still have some power over the goods in question after being bound by the contract and even after the buyer has paid for the goods, then the creditors will be seen as having the best right. This could, for example, be the case if the goods are not identified and agreed on; if the seller still has the right to choose which of a number of unascertained items he or she is to deliver to the buyer, the latter has only a claim on the seller and will thereby not be seen as having the better right to the object. While discussions have taken place in both Denmark and Finland regarding the requirements as to what extent the goods in question must be identified and agreed on, Icelandic law seems to acknowledge the right of the buyer if the latter can prove his or her acquisition.

Finally it ought to be mentioned that in all the Nordic countries it is a crime to use property which one has possession of but does not lawfully own, at least without consent from the owner, no matter whether it is a case of *constitutum possessorium* or a situation where, for example, a rented chattel is not returned as agreed.

4.3 Credit Security in Movables

Movables can be used as security for credit in different ways in the Nordic countries. A seller may make a reservation of title, a method that is well established in all five countries, and especially in relation to consumer instalment sales regulated in certain acts, where the focus is placed on consumer protection. But in other cases, too, the legislation of the Nordic countries not only recognizes that chattels may be used as credit security, but they also have legal provisions clarifying that such movables may be withheld and sold. The creditor is then entitled to payment from the proceeds. In the case of a judgment execution or bankruptcy, similar priority rights can also be found in a specific preferential rights act (as in Sweden) or simply as a part of bankruptcy or credit security legislation.

The structure of credit security rules has historical roots and is primarily based on solutions of a mortgage or pledge character.[29] While credit security in real property in all the Nordic countries is strongly connected with a registration system, the legal order for credit security in movables is more diverse. Nevertheless, they all share the feature that some kind of perfection is required in order to protect the creditor as a pledgee or mortgagee. One kind of perfection is completed by transfer of possession, i.e. by handing over the goods to the creditor in order to deprive the debtor of the right to dispose of the goods.

[29]The use of English terminology is somewhat risky; the nature of the Nordic solutions does not match the corresponding common law expressions pledge, mortgage, pawn and lien. Hence the need to raise a warning flag for the occurrence of some *false friends*. In order to achieve a passably consistent terminology, the glossary included in Kieninger (2004) has been used as a guideline.

This pledge method is acknowledged in all the Nordic countries. As for Sweden, the *traditio* principle again manifests itself. A pledge will only be accepted if the movable is handed over to the pledgee, although exceptions apply for certain property, such as shares, vessels and aircraft, where perfection may be completed by specific registration procedures. Thereafter the goods must remain in the pledgee's possession in order to qualify as credit security. If the goods are not originally possessed by the pledger but by a third party, a pledge can be given by notice to the third party explaining that the goods have been given in pledge. These rules are similar in Finland. In Denmark and Norway, perfection may be achieved by registration—a process that also enables the debtor to keep the pledged movables in his or her possession.

As for creation of security rights in personal property other than chattels, promissory notes and receivables should especially be mentioned. Thanks to Nordic cooperation as mentioned in the introductory chapter, the Nordic countries have harmonized their rules through the Promissory Notes Acts. According to this legislation, negotiable promissory notes can be given in pledge by transfer of possession. As to other money claims, non-negotiable ones (receivables) can be pledged by notifying the debtor of the pledging debtor.

In all the Nordic countries, security in receivables can also be given through an enterprise mortgage (see below). As for Denmark and Norway, business enterprises can also give security in receivables in a third—alternative—way, namely by establishing a certain document that grants security in every money claim that the debtor has or will acquire in the future. Perfection in these cases is achieved by registration of the relevant document. This latter alternative cannot, for obvious reasons, co-exist with an enterprise mortgage that includes receivables or, more correctly, which does not exclude receivables. Consequently, the debtor must choose one of the two options. Furthermore, it will only encompass money claims arising from the sale of goods and services.

As indicated above, business enterprises can also establish credit security rights by an enterprise mortgage. This gives the creditor security in some of the debtor's changing assets. The basic concept of the enterprise mortgage is similar to the 'floating charge' in common law and exists in all the Nordic countries; the security is 'floating' since the assets of the debtor may be used in ordinary business transactions. Even so, a closer comparison reveals noteworthy divergences between how they are regulated in individual national legislation. When property has been sold, the security right, as a principal rule, no longer includes property concerned by the sale, though certain exceptions to this rule exist.

In Denmark and Norway, an enterprise mortgage can be established on the basis of a document produced by the debtor, a document which must afterwards be registered by the creditor. As for Sweden, the system is closely related to the method of security in real property, as to which see above. Hence, the debtor must obtain a mortgage certificate from a public authority for a certain sum of money, and afterwards surrender the certificate to the creditor as security for the claim or, if the certificate is digital, have it registered. In Finland, the structure is closer to the mortgage systems for certain means of transport such as vessels, aircraft and certain land-based vehicles. These systems involve the use of promissory notes (typically, bearer bonds) as mortgage instruments.

5 Conclusion

This chapter has illuminated some property law aspects in the Nordic countries with the intention of clarifying that a common fundamental theoretical approach exists to property law issues, but at the same time that certain diversities affect the practicalities of property law legislation and solutions with regard to actual cases. The differences between the Nordic countries have many faces. Even so, a certain relationship connecting the approaches chosen in Finland and Sweden on the one side, as well as another relationship connecting Denmark and Norway on the other —with Iceland somewhere in between—appears when studying the structure of national approaches to this field.

More importantly for the future, rather than becoming stuck in old traditions, is the question whether the Nordic legal systems are moving towards more harmonization with each other or towards a more European approach where full EU membership will perhaps be a more decisive factor regarding the legal structure to come within this field of law. However, for the time being continuous national development appears, most of all, to be a significant element when trying to foresee the future of Nordic property law.

References

Åhman K (2000) Egendomsskyddet: äganderätten enligt artikel 1 första tilläggsprotokollet till den europeiska konventionen om de mänskliga fri- och rättigheterna. Iustus, Uppsala

Bengtsson B (2004) Allemansrätten – vad säger lagen? Naturvårdsverket, Solna

Björne L (2007) Realism och skandinavisk realism - Den nordiska rättsvetenskapens historia IV, Rättshistoriskt bibliotek 62. Institutet för rättshistorisk forskning, Stockholm

Brækhus S, Hærem A (1964) Norsk tingsrett. Universitetsforlaget, Oslo

Elmer M, Skovby L (1999) Ejendomsretten 1. Jurist- og Økonomforbundets Forlag, Copenhagen

Lilja M (2011) National report on the transfer of movables in Sweden. In: Faber W, Luger B (eds) National reports on the transfer of movables in Europe, vol 5: Sweden, Norway and Denmark, Finland, Spain. Munich, Sellier European Law Publishers, pp 1–204

Falkanger T, Falkanger AT (2013) Tingsrett. Universitetsforlaget, Oslo

Göransson U (1985) Traditionsprincipen. Iustus, Uppsala

Hansen Jensen M (2007) The protection of property rights under the Danish constitution. In: Wahlgren P (ed) Scandinavian studies in law, vol 52. Stockholm Institute for Scandinavian Law, Stockholm, pp 123–131

Håstad T (2004) Sakrätt avseende lös egendom (supplement 2004). Norstedts Juridik, Stockholm

Håstad T (2006a) General aspects of transfer and creation of property rights including security rights. In: Ulrich D, Snijders HJ, Zippro E (eds) Divergences of property law, an obstacle to the internal market. Sellier European law publishers, München, pp 37–44

Håstad T (2006b) Property rights regarding movables. In: Bogdan M (ed) Swedish law in the new millennium. Norstedts Juridik, Stockholm, pp 411–427
Håstad T (2009) Derivative acquisition of ownership of goods. Eur Rev Private Law 17(4):725–741
Hessler H (1973) Allmän sakrätt. Om det fömögenhetsrättsliga tredjemansskyddets principer., Stockholm, Norstedts
Kieninger E (ed) (2004) Security rights in movable property in European private law. Cambridge University Press, Cambridge
Lassen J (1890) Nogle bemærkninger om Proformaverk og Omgaaelse. Ugeskrift for Retsvæsen, Copenhagen. 1890.609
Martinson C (2012) Ejendomsrettens overgang – Norden kontra verden. In: Förhandlingarna vid Det 39:e nordiska juristmötet i Stockholm 18–19 augusti 2011. Stockholm, Den svenska styrelsen, pp 821–843
Millqvist G (2015) Sakrättens grunder. Norstedts Juridik, Stockholm
Mortensen P (2008) Indledning til tingsretten. Thomson Reuters, Copenhagen
Nordisk Ministerråd (1997) Allemansrätten i Norden: TemaNord, p 501. Nordisk Ministerråd, Copenhagen
Nuuja K, Viitanen K (2007) Finnish legislation on land-use restrictions and compensation. Wash Univ Glob Stud Law Rev 049. http://openscholarship.wustl.edu/law_globalstudies/vol6/iss1/4. Accessed 15 May 2018
Olsson C (1954) Om köpares borgenärsskydd vid köp av lös egendom. Söderström, Helsinki
Pöyhöne J (ed) (2002) An introduction to Finnish law. Kauppakaari, Helsinki
Reusch M (2012) Allemannsretten - Friluftslivets retsgrunnlag. Flux Forlag, Oslo
Ross A (1935) Ejendomsret og ejendomsovergang. Levin og Munksgaard, Copenhagen
Ross A (1957) Tû-Tû. In: Borum OA, Illum K (eds) Festskrift till Henry Ussing. Nyt Nordisk Forlag, Copenhagen, pp. 468–484
Sandstedt J (2013) Sakrätten, Norden och europeiseringen – nordisk funktionalism möter kontinental substantialism. Jure, Stockholm
Tepora J (2009) Inledning till grunderna för sakrätten. Juridiska fakulteten vid Helsingfors universitet, Helsinki
Torp C (1902) Hvilke grundsætninger bør være afgørende for Spørgsmaalet om Ejendomsovergangen ved Køb og Salg af individuelt bestemte løsøregenstande, og hvorvidt egner sig dette Forhold til positiv Lovordning? Förhandlingarna på det tionde nordiska Juristmötet 1902, bilaga VI. Stockholm
Vinding Kruse F (1951) Ejendomsretten I-III. Gad, Copenhagen
Vinding Kruse F (1924) Ejendomsrettens Overgang. Tidskrift for Rettsvitenskap 315–436
von Bar C, Drobnig U (2004) The interaction of contract law and tort and property law in Europe: a comparative study. Sellier European Law Publishers, München

Labour Market and Collective Agreements

Jens Kristiansen

Abstract The Nordic countries share a number of common features in the labour market compared with other European countries, among others a preference for collective agreements stipulating wages and working conditions. In recent years, the Nordic model has faced different challenges in interaction with regulation and case-law from the European Union. One of the major challenges is low-wage competition resulting from EU rules on free movement of services and posting of workers. Furthermore, employment legislation has become more common and the courts have gained a more prominent position vis-á-vis the social partners' due to implementation and enforcement of EU obligations.

1 Introduction

In labour-law contexts,[1] it is common to talk about "a Nordic agreement-based model" vis-à-vis "a continental law-based model".[2] Doing so stresses the fact that in dealing with labour the Nordic countries share a number of common features compared with other European countries.[3]

Among the common features of the Nordic countries we may highlight a high level of organization both by employees and employers as well as the fact that collective agreements play an important role in the national labour law systems. The fact that collective agreements normally stipulate wages and working conditions systematically in a specific sector means that legislation plays a more limited role in industrial relations and for employment conditions than in most other European

[1]This chapter is based on Kristiansen (2015). See also The International Encyclopaedia for Labour Law and Industrial Relations http://www.kluwerlawonline.com/toc.php?pubcode=IELL.
[2]In Hasselbalch (2002), p. 12 referred to as *the Nordic model*.
[3]The author wishes to thank Prof. Ulla Liukkunen, University of Helsinki.

J. Kristiansen (✉)
Faculty of Law, University of Copenhagen, Copenhagen, Denmark
e-mail: Jens.Kristiansen@jur.ku.dk

© Springer Nature Switzerland AG 2019

P. Letto-Vanamo et al. (eds.), *Nordic Law in European Context*,
Ius Gentium: Comparative Perspectives on Law and Justice 73,
https://doi.org/10.1007/978-3-030-03006-3_9

countries. There is also a long tradition of tripartite drafting of labour-market legislation between the government and the social partners.

A peculiarity of the Nordic collective-agreement systems—compared with other European countries—is that the agreements bind both the parties themselves and their members. The peace obligation, which is linked to collective agreements, applies to both the parties to the agreements (the organisations) and the members of parties concluding collective agreements. Finland is an exception, since Finnish employees are not subject to any collective peace obligation; only the organisations have the obligation. At the same time, employers bound by agreements must comply with the agreed wages and working conditions for all employees working in the sector concerned.

Conversely, the Nordic countries use different mechanisms to extend such agreements to cover employers outside the employer organisations. In Denmark and Sweden, it is up to the trade unions to make agreements ("accession agreements") with employers outside the employer organisations. This involves a broad right to take industrial action, including sympathy action, against single employers in support of accession to a collective agreement. In Finland and Iceland, nationwide collective agreements are extended either automatically or through a public body to be applied to all employers and wage-earners within a given industry. In Norway, trade unions are allowed to take industrial action as in Denmark and Sweden, but a mechanism has been introduced to make (selected parts of) collective agreements generally applicable with the aim of ensuring that foreign wage-earners enjoy equal wage and working conditions and of preventing social dumping in the Norwegian labour market.

Generally a substantial difference exists among the Nordic countries as to the role played by labour-market legislation in regard to other working conditions. While Denmark and Iceland are still largely characterised by collective agreements, legislation plays a bigger role in Sweden and a prominent role in Finland and Norway. Variations are also evident in the level of protection in a number of areas, e.g. with regard to an employer's right to terminate employees. Employers are freer to terminate employees in Denmark and Iceland than in, especially, Norway and Sweden, where a terminated employee may also remain on the job if the employee questions the objectivity of the termination before the court.

The social partners play a key role in settling industrial disputes in all the Nordic countries. Most disputes are settled before specific Labour Courts. In Sweden, the Labour Court enjoys competence within the entire labour law system, including disputes arising from employment legislation, while in the other Nordic countries competence is linked to disputes concerning or arising from a collective agreement. Both the Labour courts and the ordinary courts of law are characterised by considerable loyalty towards the political and economic compromises expressed through collective agreements and labour market legislation. In terms of interpreting collective agreements, the courts attach great importance to the intent of the parties of the contract. Likewise, labour-law legislation is interpreted with strong consideration for the intentions of the legislator (the *travaux préparatoires*). This Nordic tradition is not merely an expression of loyalty towards the social partners and the legislator; it also aims at protecting the right of wage-earners and employers to take an approach based on trust in agreed or adopted rules.

In recent years, the Nordic model has been challenged by European Union (EU) regulation and case-law from the Court of Justice of the European Union (CJEU) and the European Court of Human Rights (ECtHR). The following sections will highlight some of the unique features of the Nordic model and the challenges that the model faces in interaction with European regulation and case-law.

2 Free Movement and Low-Wage Competition

2.1 Foreign Collective Agreements

Denmark, Finland and Sweden are members of the EU, while The European Free Trade Association (EFTA) countries Iceland and Norway participate in the Single Market via the European Economic Area (EEA) Agreement between the EU and EFTA. Consequently, Iceland and Norway are to all intents and purposes bound by the same EU rules in the labour market as Denmark, Finland and Sweden. The EU Commission and the CJEU can control and enforce EU legislation vis-à-vis the EU Member States, while they do not have such competence vis-à-vis EFTA countries. Consequently, there are two parallel enforcement mechanisms, but the EFTA Court must wherever possible interpret the rules in accordance with the case law of the CJEU.

The EU rules on free movement do not aim to harmonise the legal systems, including the labour market systems, of the Member States. The primary purpose of the rules is to enable employees and employers free access to the (labour) market(s) of all Member States. The Nordic countries are among the "high-wage countries". Relocation of workplaces by Nordic companies to other parts of the EU (and globally) has not given rise to any significant trade-union or political conflict. Nordic trade unions generally accept that companies relocate activities to other countries. The primary disagreements arising from such relocations have concerned situations in which—after relocation—companies continue to carry on their activities in a Nordic country but using a foreign collective agreement. This was the issue which in 2007 resulted in the Judgment (C-438/05, *Viking*) of the European Court of Justice (CJEU) in a conflict between a Finnish trade union and a Finnish ship owner that wanted to reflag a ship with the primary purpose of replacing a Finnish collective agreement with an Estonian agreement on a route between Finland and Estonia.

The use of foreign "low wage-earner" labour by Nordic companies has been more controversial than the relocation of (parts of) the company to "low-wage countries". This applies in particular to posted workers who are not covered by the principles of equal payment and treatment, which applies according to the EU rules on free movement of workers.

2.2 The Right to Take Industrial Action as a Pivotal Force

When implementing the Posting of Workers Directive, both Denmark and Sweden refrained from instructing foreign service-providers to maintain a certain minimum wage. It was broadly agreed that it should be left up to the social partners to ensure that posted workers work under decent wage and working conditions. The largely identical implementation of the Directive in the two countries suffered a serious blow through a CJEU Judgment (C-341/05, *Laval*). Both countries chose to maintain the original starting point in a new statutory framework, but with the social partners in a somewhat different role.

The background for the *Laval* judgment was action taken by Swedish trade unions against a Latvian construction company (Laval un Partneri), which had posted a number of construction workers to its Swedish subsidiary as part of a construction project. The company refused to accede to the normal construction agreement in the Swedish labour market and guarantee the posted workers an hourly wage of minimum SEK 145 (EUR 15.25). The Swedish Labour Court asked the CJEU for a preliminary ruling on the right to take industrial action vis-à-vis the right to free exchange of services.

Formally, the *Laval* judgment was about Swedish industrial action practices, but it also questioned Denmark's—almost corresponding—practices. Unlike Sweden, the Danish social partners chose to find a common solution to the challenge brought about by the *Laval* judgment. A new rule on the right to take industrial action was included in the Danish Posting of Workers Act[4]; this proposal was adopted, without amendment, by a broad political majority of political parties. This new provision differs from the Swedish one because it links the minimum wage to collective agreements concluded by the most representative parties in the Danish labour market. The biggest difference, however, lies in the fact that this rule—unlike the Swedish rule—does not eliminate the right to take industrial action even if the foreign service-provider already pays wages that are in accordance with the minimum wage laid down in a collective agreement.

2.3 Generally Applicable Collective Agreements

As opposed to Denmark and Sweden, in Finland the Act of Posting Workers[5] orders foreign service-providers to apply the minimum wages laid down in generally applicable collective agreements. Setting the minimum wage thus depends on the specific, generally applicable agreement.

Like Finland, Iceland has also ordered foreign service-providers to comply with minimum wages in generally applicable collective agreements. The Icelandic

[4]*Udstationeringsloven* 2017 no 366.

[5]*Työsopimuslaki/Arbetsavtalslag* 55/2001.

Posting of Workers Act[6] has given rise to criticism from the EFTA Surveillance Authority, one point being that the Act specifies a duty of full pay during illness and occupational accidents and the obligation to arrange insurance, such as accident insurance. A judgment (E-12/10, *Iceland*) went against the Icelandic state, quoting a breach of the EEA Agreement. According to the EFTA Court, full pay during illness and accident could not be deemed to form an element of minimum wages in the sense of the Posting of Workers Directive. This judgment led to an amendment to the Posting of Workers Act. The provision on compulsory accident insurance was cancelled and replaced by a requirement that, in the case of absence due to illness or occupational accident, the labour market wage (instead of a full wage) is to be paid.

According to the Working Environment Act, which implements the Posting of Workers Directive, a foreign service provider must comply with the wage and working conditions of collective agreements which have become generally applicable pursuant to the 1993 Act. The 1993 Act also allows trade unions extended access to use blockades ("boycotts") against foreign service-providers in keeping with the rules of the Boycott Act in relation to domestic employers.

The arrangement of making selected parts of agreements generally applicable in especially exposed industries has been the subject of a landmark court case, which ended up before both the EFTA Court and the Norwegian Supreme Court. An employers' association (NI skipsverft) questioned the generalisation of the collective agreement, which ordered all employers in the industry to respect collective agreement rules on the minimum wage, a working week of 37.5 h, overtime rates of 50 and 100%, an out-of-town supplement of 20%, as well as covering the costs of travel, board and lodging. The provisions that had been made generally applicable also covered foreign service-providers who posted employees to Norway, but the employers' association felt that this violated EEA law, including the Posting of Workers Directive. The EFTA Court found that the supplement would also have to be assessed on the basis of Article 36 of the EEA Agreement and asked indirect questions as to whether compliance with requirements was ensured, but left the question to the submitting court. A similar reasoning was used in regard to the provision on covering the costs of travel, board and lodging.

In its judgment of 5 March 2013 (*STX Norway Offshore*), the Supreme Court questioned whether the elements that formed a minimum wage in the sense of the Directive should also be tested in light of Article 36 of the EEA Agreement on the right to free exchange of services. The Supreme Court found it difficult to reconcile the view of the EFTA Court with the case law of the European Court of Justice, but did not address this question, since the Court found that the out-of-town supplement was in any event compatible with Article 36, as it gives posted wage-earners an objective advantage. Furthermore, the Supreme Court found that a number of weighty reasons exist for demanding that the employer pays for a wage-earner's costs of travel, board and lodging. If the wage-earner were to pay these costs

[6]Icelandic Posting of Workers Act, *Lög um vinnumarkaðsaðgerðir* 13/1997.

personally, this would in reality led to a markedly lower minimum wage. Consequently, these costs would in any event reflect the fundamental principles of law in accordance with Article 3(10) of the Directive. The Supreme Court also attached importance to the fact that the Norwegian wage-bargaining model has long traditions and forms part of the fabric of Norwegian society. Since the other conditions that had been made generally applicable were also in line with the Posting of Workers Directive, the Court found in favour of the state. The judgment is controversial, since it counters the EFTA Court's interpretation of the Posting of Workers Directive and Article 36 of the EEA Agreement.

3 Freedom of Association

Freedom of association is a cornerstone of the Nordic labour market model due to the importance of the social partners. According to Article 11(1) of The European Convention on Human Rights (ECHR), all persons are entitled to establish and join associations, including trade unions, with the aim of protecting their interests. However, the European Court of Human Rights (ECtHR) has also stated that this provision includes a (more controversial) right not to join a trade union. The case-law of the ECtHR on the right not to join a trade union has broadly been concerned with cases from the Nordic countries.

In a judgment of 30 June 1993 (*Sigurjonsson*), the ECtHR found against Iceland where Iceland had cancelled a taxicab owner's licence because he left the association of which he had to be a member in order to obtain a licence, according to the law. The Icelandic Supreme Court had deemed the obligation to be a member of this association to be compatible with both the Icelandic Constitution and the ECHR. The judgment gave rise to much debate; however, Icelandic law was amended to match the judgment.

In a judgment from 11 January 2006 (*Sørensen and Rasmussen*), the ECtHR found against Denmark for not granting two wage-earners the necessary legal protection against mandatory membership of an organisation. Unlike the Icelandic case, the Danish breach of the Convention did not consist of membership of an organisation ordered by the state, but in Denmark having permitted overly extensive mandatory membership of organisations in connection with collective agreements. While a bill to prohibit closed-shop arrangements had just been rejected following a hectic political debate, the new judgment quickly led to an amendment of the Freedom of Association Act in the spring of 2006 without much political struggle. With the new Act, closed-shop arrangements and preferential arrangements became invalid, and employers were ordered not to attach any weight to membership of a given organisation when engaging and dismissing employees.

The ECtHR has traditionally held the view that Article 11 of the European Convention on Human Rights does not include a right to bargain collectively or to take industrial action. Particularly in Denmark and Norway, the question is of a highly sensitive nature due to the fact that both countries have a long-standing practice of intervention in ongoing industrial conflicts that threaten significant societal interests. Several governmental interventions in Danish and Norwegian industrial conflicts have prompted criticism from ILO committees.

In a judgment in 1997 (NRT 1997/580), the Norwegian Supreme Court rejected the claim that an intervention should violate freedom of association. The trade union appealed the judgment to the ECtHR, which in a decision on 27 June 2002 (*Federation of Offshore Workers' Trade Unions and others*) deemed the case inadmissible. Even if the Court did not find that the right to take industrial action was protected by the right of freedom of association, it still chose to assess whether legislative intervention, if performed, would have been necessary in a democratic society in accordance with Article 11(2). Following a thorough review of the background to the concrete intervention, the Court found that it constituted a necessary intervention in a democratic society.

In 2008, the ECtHR made a striking change of paradigms by recognising the right to bargain collectively as an independently protected right pursuant to Article 11 in its judgment of 12 November 2008 (*Demir and Baykara*). In a judgment of 21 April 2009 (*Yapi-Yol Sen*), the Court also recognised the right to take industrial action as an independently protected part of the freedom of association. Consequently, both the right to bargain collectively and to take industrial action now enjoy the special protection which comes from being an integral part of freedom of association in Article 11(1). Any state intervention against these two rights—e.g. state intervention in industrial conflicts in Denmark and Norway—thus has to be "necessary" in a democratic society and may be tested by the courts and, ultimately, by the ECtHR.

4 Changed Balance Between Legislation and Collective Agreements

A striking feature of the impact of European rules is the fact that the legislature has gained a more prominent role in relation to the social partners concluding collective agreements. Member States have primary responsibility for complying with the EU Treaties, the EEA Agreement and the European Convention on Human Rights. This calls for some kind of legislative framework, especially when directives on employment conditions are to be implemented in national law. Consequently, the ongoing implementation of EU and EEA directives undoubtedly shifts the balance between legislation and collective agreements in favour of legislation.

The impact of EU and EEA law, however, has not resulted in any basic changes to the division of work between the social partners and the legislature in the Nordic countries. Member States have transferred limited regulatory authority to the EU in the field of labour law, while the social partners and the legislature in all the Nordic countries seem to have reached a mutual understanding as to implementing EU and EEA directives in such a way as to minimise clashes with the existing system of labour market regulation. Directives on employment conditions have led to more employment-law legislation in all the Nordic countries, but not to systematic legislation on wages and working conditions. In particular in Denmark, Iceland and Sweden, implementation of directives has led to the adoption of new legislation, while in Finland and Norway directives have largely been integrated into the existing Work Agreement Act and the Working Environment Act, which already regulated a broad range of working conditions.

A special feature of the national rules implementing directives is that their interpretation must continually take account of the interpretation of directives by the European Court of Justice (and the EFTA Court). The Court has widely promoted a more uniform understanding and use of the directives than can immediately be read from the wording of the directives. To an increasing extent, the Court emphasises that directives have the general purpose of improving living and working conditions at an ever increasing level and that the directives specify fundamental rights in the Charter of Fundamental Rights.

The Nordic courts have generally used EU and EEA law loyally and endeavoured to interpret national rules in accordance with EU and EEA law. There are, however, a few examples of cases in which a Nordic court has refused to interpret a national rule in accordance with EU or EEA law, in cases where such interpretation has not been possible within the framework of recognised interpretation principles in national law. A striking example is the judgement of 6 December 2016 (*Ajos*) in which the Danish Supreme Court stated that it was not possible to interpret a provision of the Danish Salaried Employees Act in accordance with the CJEU judgment of 22 September 2014 (C-114/14—*Ajos*). Furthermore, and contrary to the CJEU judgment, the Danish Law on accession to the EU did not provide the legal basis to allow the unwritten principle or Article 21 of the Charter of Fundamental Rights prohibiting discrimination on grounds of age to take precedence over the contested provision of the Law on Salaried Employees. As a result, the Supreme Court concluded that the company could rely on the Danish provision.

5 Conclusion

All Nordic labour law systems interact with a European law system which is becoming increasing unmanageable. European law is developing in a complicated interaction of different types of sources of law, such as general principles of law (treaties) and specific rules (directives). European rules address conflicting considerations, e.g. promotion of free movement and securing basic trade union rights, and the three European courts do not necessarily take the same approach to these considerations. This complex formation of law often makes it difficult to precisely determine European obligations.

Legislation has become more prominent in all the Nordic countries as part of the implementation of European obligations. However, there has been no basic change in the division of work between the legislature and the social partners, and collective agreements still play an important role in determining wages and working conditions in all the Nordic countries. However, the right to free movement of services seems to present special challenges to the Nordic systems and continues to spur political debate as well as lawsuits on matters of principle.

One of the most striking features of the European impact on Nordic labour law systems is the fact that the courts have gained a more prominent role in relation to the social partners and the legislature. The courts have gained more of a law-making function resulting from their duty to interpret the conformity of national rules with the EU, EEA and ECHR. At the same time, they have gained a more rights-verifying role arising from their duty to check whether a challenged legal position is compatible with obligations under EU, EEA and ECHR law. To the widest extent possible, they must interpret national law in accordance with European obligations, which includes the dynamic development of general, vague principles of law.

The courts may also test whether national rules are compatible with European obligations, e.g. whether legislative intervention in a labour market conflict was "necessary". This is bound to continually narrow the political room for manoeuvre and make it more difficult for the social partners to find common ground based on a mutual understanding of national law.

References

Hasselbalch O (2002) The roots—the history of Nordic Labour Law. Scandinavian Studies in Law, No. 43. http://www.scandinavianlaw.se/pdf/43-1.pdf. Accessed 13 July 2018

Kristiansen J (ed) (2015). Europe and the Nordic collective-bargaining model—the complex interaction between Nordic and European Labour Law. Nordic Council of Ministers. TemaNord 2015: 541. Available at http://norden.diva-portal.org/smash/get/diva2:816030/FULLTEXT02.pdf. Accessed 13 July 2018

The International Encyclopaedia for Labour Law and Industrial Relations. http://www.kluwerlawonline.com/toc.php?pubcode=IELL. Accessed 13 July 2018

Public Administration and Good Governance

Olli Mäenpää and Niels Fenger

Abstract The Nordic countries share broadly similar rules and principles of administrative law. Although the administrative laws of Denmark, Norway and Iceland have much in common, they differ in important respects from the public law of Finland and Sweden, so that one may speak of two groups of public law. Executive power and the conditions for its exercise have been regulated in constitutional acts, more so for Finland and Sweden than for Denmark and Norway. In all the Nordic countries legalism maintains its significance in the exercise of administrative functions although in the provision of public services, legalism is somewhat more subdued. All Nordic countries have law on access to documents and were amongst the first countries in Europe to have such legislation.

1 Introduction

1.1 The Structure of Administration

In the Nordic countries, the core of the central state administration is formed by a combination of ministries and independent administrative agencies. It is the general responsibility of the ministries to supervise and control the subordinate state administration, but their duties also include making individual decisions of major importance in a number of administrative activities. Territorial organization is based on provinces and regions at the intermediate level and municipalities and districts at the local level. Provinces and districts are integral parts of state administration while municipalities and the regions constitute units of self-government.

O. Mäenpää (✉)
Faculty of Law, University of Helsinki, Helsinki, Finland
e-mail: olli.maenpaa@helsinki.fi

N. Fenger
High Court of Eastern Denmark Copenhagen, Copenhagen, Denmark
e-mail: NielsFenger@OestreLandsret.dk

© Springer Nature Switzerland AG 2019
P. Letto-Vanamo et al. (eds.), *Nordic Law in European Context*,
Ius Gentium: Comparative Perspectives on Law and Justice 73,
https://doi.org/10.1007/978-3-030-03006-3_10

The national (state) level is primarily responsible for such general public services as research, defence and the police. Local administration, based on autonomous municipalities or regions, is responsible for individual services such as healthcare, social services and basic education. The state administration exercises supervision and evaluation of public services. Moreover, as a rule the central authorities may only intervene in decisions taken by local and regional authorities to the extent that their decisions can be considered illegal.

In other respects, the organization of the administrative apparatus differs. A specific characteristic of Swedish and Finnish administrative law is that administrative structures are not fully centralized. Administrative agencies and public officials are required to act independently and solely on the basis of legal regulation. In the exercise of their authority they therefore enjoy distinctive independence with regard to superior authorities and the instructive power they might want to exercise. Public officials are also individually accountable for their decisions.

Since decisions are made independently, a ministry is considered to lack the power to intervene directly in an agency's decision-making in individual cases or in an agency's day to day operations. Similarly, a public official is expected to use their powers autonomously and without direct interference by a superior official. A ministry which considers that an agency's application of law in individual cases is incorrect or undesirable may try to change it only by amending the applicable rules. The ministry may also issue general policy instructions.

In this respect, the other legal systems follow the more traditional European model, as the general rule in these countries is that a minister may give orders as to how a subordinate directorate should decide an individual case. Moreover, when applying rules that give the authorities discretion, that discretion must be applied in a manner that complies with the policy of the government. within the framework set out by legislation and general principles of law. That being said, in a few fields of administrative law special legislation prescribes that a given case should be decided by an independent agency, with the effect that the minister may not intervene in the decision-making process.

Another major difference between the various legal systems is that Sweden and Finland have special administrative courts whereas Denmark, Norway and Iceland have a single judicial system which, especially in Denmark, is supplemented by a wide range of administrative complaint bodies. See, in this respect, Sect. 5.1.

1.2 The Nordic Welfare Model and Administrative Regulation

The duties and powers of administrative organs vary by their contents and their nature in different fields of administration and in different activities. At the beginning of the 20th century, the main duty of authorities was administrative regulation based on the application and enforcement of law in individual cases. This still has an essential significance in the activity of authorities, but in the welfare state the quantitative emphasis of activities has shifted to providing social benefits and public services. Public administration has also become more involved in economic activities. At the same time the administrative machinery has grown considerably and become more complicated and fragmented.

The forms and procedure used and the lines of action applied by administrative organs depend greatly on what kind of administrative duty is concerned. Administrative regulation is by definition based on unilateral decision-making and characteristically takes the form of written administrative decisions or administrative acts of various kinds such as administrative permits, legitimations and injunctions. Regulatory methods of more general scope such as rule-making, standard-setting and planning are also frequently used.

In addition to regulation, public services form another major field of administrative activity. Public administration still remains the central provider of public services and benefits but in most of the Nordic countries outsourcing has gradually strengthened the role of private actors, procurement and competition. When the administration performs economic functions its procedures have more or less adjusted to the models of private economic operators. This is, to a large extent, subject to competition laws and regulation concerning public procurement.

An essential element of Nordic welfare society is that municipalities play the predominant role in provision of public services. Most of the expenditure of local and regional authorities arises from providing basic community services, such as social services and healthcare, education and cultural services, infrastructure maintenance and environmental protection.

2 Legal Framework

2.1 Rule of Law and the Executive

In many respects, the Nordic countries have broadly similar rules and principles of administrative law. At the same time, however, it is essential to observe certain fundamental differences. Traces of history are clearly discernible in the field of public law. Indeed, although the administrative laws of Denmark, Norway and Iceland share much in common, they differ in important respects from the public law of Finland and Sweden, so that one may speak of two groups of public law. Many of the differences can be traced back to the fact that Denmark and Norway (including Iceland) were united under the same King and ruled from Copenhagen, whereas Finland was part of Sweden until 1809.

A common characteristic of all the Nordic countries is that both French and German law have been a source of inspiration for the development of several principles of administrative law, such as the proportionality principle and the range and limits of judicial review. Moreover, German and French legal literature has afforded valuable methodical patterns for the conceptualization of Nordic administrative law by providing concepts and structures for describing and developing legal principles.[1]

Legalism and strict adherence to law have traditionally occupied a central role in Sweden and Finland, more so than in the other Nordic countries. To be sure, formal legalism has been substituted by more goal-oriented and value-based objectives in the welfare state. Yet in all countries legalism maintains its significance in the exercise of administrative functions. With respect to public administration, the rule of law requires that the executive powers of any administrative authority must possess an express basis in law, while the exercise of public power must be justified on grounds laid down by law. The principle applies especially when an administrative authority (e.g. Ministry, agency, municipality or public official) makes administrative decisions or other acts that directly affect individual rights and obligations. The rule of law is thus a necessary prerequisite in all exercise of administrative authority. In the provision of public services, legalism is somewhat more subdued but a legal basis is still necessary for any social benefit or service.

In practice, the rule of law entails, among other things, that administrative authorities have no general competence to perform their duties. For instance, although the main duty of the police force is to uphold public order and security, any intervention by the police in the sphere of private activities must be supported by an express legal basis in each individual case. The principle of conformity to law also denotes that the decision-making power cannot be based solely on administrative regulations, guidelines, instructions or plans. It is the duty of an authority within its sphere of competence to apply the law. It is another matter that administrative regulations and directives can guide decision-making, provided that this kind of supervision is based on a sufficiently precise rule establishing the power to issue such directives. In addition, internal administrative policy or strategy are to be complied with within the bounds set by law.

Executive power and the conditions for its exercise have also been regulated in constitutional acts, more so for Finland and Sweden than for Denmark and Norway. The constitutionalization of the executive function in the two former countries includes several qualitative requirements of significance. For example, the Finnish Constitution stipulates that all public action must be authorized by law, the law must be strictly complied with in the exercise of any public activity, the executive must comply with the qualitative requirements of good, transparent and accountable administration; in addition, access to the court must be available for any administrative decision concerning a right or duty. According to the Constitution, it is the duty of a public authority (the authorities) to ensure that fundamental and human rights are implemented and protected. In addition, autonomous arrangements, notably in the broad area of municipal self-government, must be respected by both the legislature and the executive, while any transfer of administrative duties to the

[1] Fenger (2004), Revsbech (2016), Graver (2015), Strömberg and Lundell (2014), Bogdan (2010), Mäenpää O (2018), Nuotio (2012).

private sphere can only occur if protection of fundamental rights, good administration and access to justice are duly guaranteed. In comparison, the Danish Constitution is much more silent in these respects and leaves most of these matters to the discretion of the legislator.[2]

Although the above-mentioned requirement in the Finnish Constitution may be said to represent a relatively conventional list by modern constitutional standards, it appears that the basic tenets of that constitutionalized administration have recently been subject to considerable pressures, both domestic and European.

First, the relative autonomy of the administration has been growing, especially with respect to legislative control. This is due to several interconnected factors. Detailed legislative regulation quite simply faces limits based on knowledge, technical exigencies, the need to reach political compromises and the like. Transfer of legislative powers to the European level, public-private partnerships and increased use of private or semi-private regulation have not alleviated these problems. This has all resulted in strengthening the role of the executive as the provider of practical problem-solving based on the interpretation and application of law—not only in the traditional form of unilateral decision-making but more often in a negotiated, horizontal mode based on partnership and participation.

Second, to a varying degree all the Nordic countries share a clear, and perhaps partly concomitant, shift from executive government to public governance. This reflects several significant developments ranging from a change of mindset concerning the role of the "public" in public administration to a transformation of the traditional executive function into public governance. Administration exercising public governance is based, for example, on partnership and association and hybrid forms of decision-making denoting problem-solving in a predominately administrative setting instead of execution of laws. Third, the emergence and strengthening of multi-level European governance based on an interplay between committees, networks, European and national agencies, shared governance and the like has probably strengthened the position of national administrations while simultaneously, in Finland at least, the inter-linkages have weakened national accountability, which is regulated by the Constitution.

It is not apparent that these pressures and the inroads they are capable of making into the constitutional setting of the role and function of public administration have so far been duly recognized. Whether constitutional premises and requirements can accommodate all these transformations, or whether they in fact erode constitutional norms that are designed to ensure administration that is fair, transparent, accountable and based on law, is still an open question. So far, it seems that, perhaps paradoxically, the recent constitutionalization of the administration has been of quite limited significance in this respect.

Additionally, a clear trend is evident towards an increasingly digital administration. First, all Nordic countries have introduced rules that permit, and in some cases oblige, citizens and business to interact with the administration by way of

[2]Christensen et al. (2012).

digital communication. The most far-reaching regime is in Denmark where the administration may, in all types of civil cases, and save for a few narrowly defined situations, send most types of communication to special e-boxes that citizens and businesses are obliged to set up. Moreover, a large number of acts have been introduced according to which the citizen may only apply digitally for permits, services and the like, typically by entering the relevant authority's webpage and filling out an electronic form.[3]

Second, decisions are increasingly taken either solely by a computer, as is the case for more simple tax matters, or via a system where a computer provides support to a physical case handler, e.g. by providing checklists and suggestions as to how a decision should be decided and formulated.

Third, the influence of data protection regulation is to an increasing degree felt in national administrations. In some respects the basic values underlying data protection only corroborate what already follows the traditional principles of administrative law. In other respects a certain tension might arise.

2.2 *Basic Legal Principles of Nordic Administration*

In addition to normative legal regulation, several legal principles enjoy a central role in the administrative activities of all the Nordic countries. These administrative law principles provide a qualitative value basis for administrative authorities in interpreting and applying the law. The principles function mainly as guidelines and constraints in using discretionary administrative powers, but they may also assist in the interpretation of other types of legal provisions. The principles may be relied on by individuals in administrative procedures, and as such they can also be asserted in both judicial and administrative proceedings related to administrative decisions. Administrative decisions taken in breach of these principles may be annulled or revoked by the courts.

Prominent administrative law principles include impartiality, equality, proportionality, prohibition of abuse of power, and protection of legitimate interests. While these principles were originally developed in administrative law doctrine and judicial practice, many of them have gradually been assigned a more binding legal role by elevating them to constitutional entitlements or by regulating them in written legislation.[4]

In Finland, the leading principles have been codified in the Administrative Procedure Act.[5] Pursuant to Section 6, "An authority shall treat the customers of the administration on an equal basis and exercise its competence only for purposes that are acceptable under the law. The acts of the authority shall be impartial and

---

[3]Fenger (2014), p. 89.

[4]See in general Marcusson (2005).

[5]*Hallintolaki/Förvaltningslag* 434/2003.

proportionate to their objective. They shall protect legitimate expectations as based on the legal system." Similar obligations exist more or less implicitly in the other Nordic legal systems.

The general principle of *equality* means that similar situations must not be treated differently, unless an objectively justified cause exists for doing so. Discrimination or favouritism, for example, on the basis of origin, religion, sex, age, political or social views, trade union activity or for other similar reasons is prohibited. A similar procedure and a consistent approach must be complied with in similar cases, although for a justified reason an authority may also change its practice if that practice is to be followed consistently.

Impartiality means that only factors objectively relevant to the case may be taken into account. Decision-making and other official activities of an authority must also otherwise be impartial and independent. This principle has acquired concrete form in, for example, bias provisions emphasizing the neutrality of administrative action. According to these provisions, an official will be disqualified if confidence in their impartiality is at risk for a particular reason.

The principle of *proportionality* requires that a reasonable relationship should be observed in all circumstances between the relative importance of the ends pursued and the means put into operation. Consequently, the exercise of public authority must be determined appropriately in relation to the desired objectives. Such a determination can usually be made on the basis of the general interest involved and the reasonableness of the activity in attaining it.

All *abuse of power* (including discretionary power) is prohibited. According to this principle, the administration must not pursue a purpose other than that for which the corresponding power has been conferred. A decision taken for purposes other than those stated may constitute an abuse of power, even if the decision as such falls within the powers of the authority.

To guarantee *protection of legitimate interests*, administrative authorities are expected to act lawfully and predictably. Administrative decisions can not normally have retroactive effect. However, for example, revocation of a licence or a benefit is possible provided that it has a legal basis. Legitimate expectations may be created by consistent administrative practice and they may also be based on information or advice supplied by an official. A person can rely on justified expectations only if they have acted legitimately, for instance, by submitting correct information.

2.3 European Framework

In the Nordic countries, a significant part of national legislation derives, fully or partially, from European Union (EU) law. It is therefore easy to understand that the public administration of each Nordic country is a quite closely interconnected element of European administration. However, a considerable degree of national autonomy remains with regard to procedures, structures and judicial review. On the other hand, the European Court of Human Rights (ECtHR) has also been active through its case law in defining certain standards for national administrative laws. The focus of its judicial activity has been on issues such as access to justice in cases concerning executive application of the law, the quality of legal protection afforded to subjects of administrative decision-making, and the effectiveness of judicial protection.

Recently, the ECtHR has also held that, in some types of case, the administration has an obligation to hear a party before it takes an adverse decision and to state reasons therefor. Moreover, the ECtHR has held that a right for journalists and certain interest groups to be granted access to documents can be derived from Article 10 of the European Convention on Human Rights covering freedom of speech. Until now, these minimum requirements for good administration have not gone further than already follows from the national legislation of the Nordic countries.[6]

In addition to national Nordic administrations, a distinct sphere of European administration has gradually developed into a transnational and multi-level executive with increased powers and specific procedures. European administration does not necessarily refer only to the transnational administration of the EU. The national administrations of the Nordic States of the EU can also be considered as elements or tools of European administration when they apply, implement and execute EU law.

3 The Right to Good Administration

3.1 Good Administration—Basic Requirements

The Finnish Constitution expressly confers on the right to good administration the status of a basic right. Section 21 guarantees everyone the general right to have their affairs "considered appropriately and without undue delay by a lawfully competent… public authority as well as to have a decision pertaining to his/her rights or obligations reviewed by a court of law". Express constitutional guarantees include openness of proceedings, the right to be heard, the right to receive a decision with stated grounds, and the right to appeal a decision.

The list is by no means exhaustive. Items to add to the list, for instance, might include the right to a fair and unbiased procedure, the right to compensation for harm caused by unlawful administrative activity and the right to initiate proceedings against an official infringing material or procedural norms. Based on its constitutional status, the right also serves as an interpretative guideline for applying more detailed procedural provisions. In the other Nordic countries, these rights are not guaranteed on a constitutional level but ensured by legislation.

[6] Fenger (2018).

3.2 *Procedural Guarantees*

The details of good administrative procedure are laid down in specific acts (Norway[7] 1967; Denmark[8] 1985; Iceland[9] 1993; Finland[10] 2003; Sweden[11] 2017).[12] Public authorities have a general obligation to provide service to all citizens. One of the principal applications of the obligation is the duty to ensure the actual possibility for individuals to comply with their procedural duties. Additionally, authorities and officials are obliged to supply necessary guidance and advice concerning formal requirements in individual cases. They also have to ascertain that the relevant facts are established, although the duty to provide evidence may lie on either the private party or the public authority.

In general, access to administrative procedure is quite extensive. As a rule, standing is granted to those whose own interests are at stake in a relevant manner. Anyone whose rights, interests or obligations may more substantially be affected by a decision are entitled to act as parties and consequently also to use the procedural powers of a party.

The right to be heard before a decision is made is considered one of the fundamental guarantees of good public administration. To guarantee a fair hearing, a party must be reserved an opportunity to reply to claims by others as well as to any evidence that may have an effect on the decision. The right to be heard also establishes a right to submit facts, arguments or evidence that may be relevant in resolving the matter. Parties to an administrative procedure usually also have access to a secret document if the document either has actually affected, or may affect, the outcome of the procedure, although several exceptions apply.

A party must produce evidence in support of its claim and it is the authority's duty to obtain any other evidence. The burden of proof thus lies with the private party claiming a right or a benefit or an otherwise beneficial decision. If the case has been initiated by the authority, it is duty-bound to obtain and provide evidence supporting its claims. In the latter case the burden of proof will generally lie with the authority because the decision sought is likely to be detrimental to the private party.

In Finland, administrative decisions are usually decided on the basis of a report presented by an official. The rationale for the requirement of report-based decision-making is to enhance the correctness of administrative decisions and to extend public accountability even to the preparatory stage. The presentation consists of a document submitted by the reporting official to the administrative body or civil servant whose duty it is to take a decision in the case. The report itself focuses

[7]*Lov om behandlingsmåten i forvaltningssaker* 1967.

[8]*Lov om offentlighed i forvaltningen* 1985 no 572.

[9]*Stjórnsýslulög* 37/1993.

[10]*Hallintolaki/Förvaltningslag* 434/2003.

[11]*Förvaltningslag* 2017:900. Nergelius (2011).

[12]See also: Ahlström (2018), Fenger (2013, 2018), Smith and Eckhoff (2016), Mäenpää (2016a).

on the facts and merits of the case, with a survey of applicable law and a proposal for the decision. It is the duty of the reporter (or referendary) to summarize the facts of the case and the legal norms applicable as well as to express their own opinion on how the case should be decided. The reporter assumes full responsibility for the correctness of the facts and the proposal they make. Even if the decision differs from the proposal, the reporter will share responsibility for it, unless their dissenting opinion is put on record.

A decision by an administrative authority must clearly specify what rights it grants and what obligations it imposes on the party concerned, or in what other manner the case was resolved. A decision that is of detriment to a party, or that does not fully comply with what they have applied for, must also at least state the reasons for the determination by indicating the principal facts and evidence on which it was based and the statutes and provisions that were applied. A decision that qualifies for appeal must enclose appeal instructions. The main purpose of the instructions is to inform the party of the essential prerequisites for lodging an appeal in an administrative court.

4 Nordic Openness

4.1 The Principle of Openness

The principle of access to government documents has a longstanding tradition in Sweden and Finland dating back to a constitutional enactment from 1776 (Act on the Freedom of Publishing and the Right of Access to Official Documents). While it is true that this constitutional principle of openness has been interpreted and applied in a varied manner, the principle itself has prevailed over the centuries.

The right of access to official documents is included as a fundamental right in the constitutions of the two countries. According to the Swedish Constitution "every Swedish citizen shall be entitled to have free access to official documents." Similarly, the Finnish Constitution lays down the principle of openness and freedom of information: "The documents and other records in the possession of public authorities shall be public unless their publicity has been separately restricted by Act of Parliament for compelling reasons. Everyone shall have the right to obtain information from public documents and records." Together with the guarantees of freedom of expression and freedom of information, the right of access forms a vital component of open government.

Significantly, the principle of open access to administrative and judicial documents has been defined as a basic constitutional right and not merely an interpretative principle. Since access to government-held information enjoys constitutional status, the right of access may be invoked by anyone regardless of citizenship or the purpose for which that right is exercised. As a basic right it also takes precedence over ordinary legislation. For instance, if application of a statute would be in evident conflict with the right of access, the access provision in the Constitution would be given primacy in judicial proceedings.[13]

Whereas Denmark and Norway have no constitutional provisions ensuring openness, all Nordic countries nevertheless share the basic idea that openness in administration constitutes one of the cornerstones of democratic government and the public accountability of administrative personnel. Transparency of administration makes it possible to publicly monitor its functioning. It also strengthens public confidence in the administration. In general, government information should be considered a public asset, with the exception of personal privacy, national security matters and such other legitimate interests as may be prescribed by law.[14]

The methods of guaranteeing openness in administration vary depending on the character and form of administrative activity. Basically, three separate methods and areas of openness may be distinguished. First, official documents and information about the working of the administration are subject to the principle of publicity. They are presumed to be publicly accessible, unless express provisions form a restriction.

Second, it is a general obligation of the public authorities to make public information available on equal terms to all individuals requesting it. Should the matter under preparation be of such a character that it may have widespread effects, Finnish law provides that the authorities even have an active duty to make known the information about it. Third, openness extends even to the actual business of preparing and handling administrative matters by the authorities.

4.2 Access to Government-Held Information

Detailed rules governing access to official documents are laid down in specific legislation regulating the scope and limitations of access as well as procedures for gaining access, in Sweden in the Act on access to information and secrecy (2009),[15] in Finland in the Act on access to official documents (1999),[16] in Norway in the Act on the right to see documents held by public entities (2006),[17] and in Denmark in the Access to documents Act (2013).[18]

All four acts are based on the principle of general access to official documents, denoting an assumption of openness covering all documents drawn up or received

---

[13]Mäenpää (2016b).

[14]Fenger and Grønnegård Christensen (2017), Jørgensen (2014).

[15]*Offentlighets- och sekretesslag* 2009:400.

[16]*Laki viranomaisten toiminnan julkisuudesta/Lag om offentlighet i myndigheternas verksamhet* 621/1999.

[17]*Lov om rett til innsyn i dokument i offentleg verksemd* 2006 no 16.

[18]*Lov om offentlighed i forvaltningen* 2013 no 606.

by a public authority or a body exercising official functions. The authorities have not only the duty to respond to requests for access, they also have a proactive obligation to provide information and promote openness by producing and disseminating information on their activities. This is especially the case in Finland, and to a lesser extent in the other Nordic countries.

Under the presumption of openness, access to documents is the predominant rule, whereas secrecy is the exception that must in each case have an express legal basis. Everyone is presumed to have a general right to examine the contents of an official document and obtain the information contained therein, subject only to exceptions provided by law. These exceptions must also be construed narrowly. If only a part of a document is secret, access must be granted to the public part of the document if this is possible without disclosing the secret part. The authorities are also under an obligation to manage their documents and data systems so as to guarantee access to public information without disclosing secret information.

To protect such legitimate interests as personal integrity, commercial confidentiality and national security, access has been restricted with regard to information about, for example, issues falling under the core areas of foreign policy, privacy, and business secrets. One reason for these restrictions is that personal data obtained in the course of government work should be protected because of their sensitivity. The operations of authorities can also not be wholly public in matters dealing with national security or crime prevention. These reasons account for the majority of express secrecy or confidentiality provisions.

In cases where the right to access is denied by a public official, sufficient reasons must be provided for refusal. All decisions taken pursuant to access legislation are reviewable in court.

5 Access to Justice and Supervision

5.1 Judicial Control of Administrative Action

In all the Nordic countries, a general right to challenge the legality of administrative decisions either in administrative courts or in courts of general competence has traditionally been regarded as a fundamental element of the system of legal protection and judicial review. The right to appeal an administrative decision is guaranteed as a basic right, as indeed is judicial reviewability of administrative acts. The review procedure is regulated either in specific acts on judicial procedure in administrative courts or in the relevant country's general act on court procedure.

In Finland and Sweden, appeals against administrative decisions by state or municipal authorities are, as a rule, lodged with administrative courts acting as court of first instance in most administrative matters. The administrative courts review inter alia tax decisions, municipal decisions, building and planning decisions,

decisions concerning the environment, social welfare and healthcare decisions, staff decisions and other administrative decisions.[19]

In Denmark and Norway, cases concerning judicial review of administrative bodies are handled by the general courts. Moreover, especially in Denmark, a wide range of administrative appeal bodies perform tasks similar to those of the administrative courts in Sweden and Finland. The administrative appeal bodies are generally independent from the ministries. Typically, decisions are taken by a panel chaired by a judge and supplemented with specialists such as professors and representatives from interest groups. Decisions by administrative appeal bodies may be appealed to the "normal" courts.

In all the Nordic countries, an appeal for judicial review must, in many cases, be preceded by a request for reconsideration addressed to the administrative authority in question. An authority may, even at its own initiative, reconsider and correct its own decision provided that obvious errors exist in the decision or the decision is materially defective.

In Finland and Sweden, reflecting the general right to judicial review of administrative acts, the court structure also consists of two sections. The general administrative courts form a separate sector within the judiciary. The Supreme Administrative Court exercises the highest judicial power in administrative cases. The general courts, with the Supreme Court as the highest instance, have jurisdiction in civil and criminal cases. General courts lack the power to review administrative decisions and decide administrative disputes. As already mentioned, the court system in Denmark and Norway is based on a one-tier structure with a single Supreme Court that is competent in all types of cases and lower courts that similarly deal not only with judicial review of administrative acts, but also civil and criminal cases.

The right to appeal may be exercised by anyone whose right or legally protected interest is directly infringed or affected by an administrative decision or its consequences. In Finland and Sweden, decisions by municipal authorities may be appealed both by the parties immediately concerned and by any member of the municipality, irrespective of whether the decision has only the slightest impact on their rights or duties. A municipal appeal is thus a combination of both legal supervision and judicial review. In the other Nordic countries only parties to the case may ask for judicial review.

Judicial review may be directed against any act or measure of an administrative authority whereby a matter has been resolved or dismissed. To be appealable, the decision must contain a final and conclusive disposition on an individual case. This entails that no appeal is available against either initial or tentative decisions at the preparatory stage.

As a rule, decisions by all administrative authorities are reviewable. In this respect, no distinction is drawn between administrative decisions and acts of the state. Decisions by the cabinet or the ministries may thus be subject to appeal, even

[19]Lavin (2016), Mäenpää (2008).

if they were based on a very wide margin of discretion. However, investigation of the advisability and expediency of those decisions falls outside the scope of judicial review.

The right to a fair hearing and other guarantees of procedural fairness also apply in judicial proceedings concerning administrative cases. These guarantees include the right to be heard, the procedurally equal status of the parties and public hearing in addition to the essential right of access to a court. In administrative decision-making, the administrative authority acts as the counterpart to the appellant. The authority usually also has superior power compared to a private party. Its superior position is based on several factors, usually including the right to exercise unilateral public power, sophisticated expertise in legal and administrative issues and broader access to government-held data and information. Also of significance is the government authority's general proficiency in conducting the decision-making procedure and participating in judicial procedure. Against this backdrop, material equality is how the requirement of fairness is understood in the law governing administrative-judicial proceedings

In Finland and Sweden, the administrative courts are under a general obligation to actively conduct the procedure and to obtain evidence and factual information on their own initiative. The court is required to review all available evidence and resolve all claims and demands in the matter. Review of legality is also understood to extend to the exercise of discretionary powers. The court therefore has the power to investigate whether an authority has complied with general administrative principles. In Denmark and Norway, the normal rules on civil procedure apply in cases concerning judicial review. Thus, the courts will not examine ex officio whether a decision violates e.g. the principle of equality or the procedural guarantees enshrined in the Danish Public Administration act.

The court has the power to uphold or annul a challenged decision. The court can also refer a case back to the administrative authority for reconsideration. In addition to affirming or annulling the decision subject to review, the court may also partially amend it, although it may not substitute itself for the administrative authority which adopted the contested decision.

5.2 Supervision of Legality and the Institution of Ombudsman

The general control of legality in public administration is the duty of specific supervisory organs or ombudsmen. The Parliamentary Ombudsman, and in Finland and Sweden also the Chancellor of Justice, have a general remit but there are also more specialized ombudsmen to guarantee e.g. equality or consumer protection. Superior administrative organs also exercise control of legality and appropriateness within the subordinate administration. It is considered to be the official duty of any superior authority to ensure that the authorities under its direction observe the law.

Administrative complaint is the ordinary procedure for any individual to bring an administrative irregularity to the knowledge of the superior authority or an Ombudsman. The scope of administrative complaints is extensive. A complaint may include a claim that a subordinate authority has acted in breach of its duties, that it has in some other manner failed to conform to the law or that other faults, irregularities or errors have been committed, or that the authority has failed to act. Besides legality, an administrative complaint may also invoke adequacy, appropriateness and compliance, with the requirements of good administration as a basis. The legality and appropriateness of administrative activity may also be examined by both the specific supervisory organs and by an Ombudsman on their own initiative.

5.3 *Accountability*

Each civil servant is individually responsible for the lawfulness of their acts in office. Official accountability extends to all decisions by an official. In Finland, anyone who has suffered a loss of rights or damage due to the unlawful act or omission of an official or a person responsible for a public duty may demand that the person concerned be punished and that the public authority or the official be ordered to compensate for damage. In Denmark, claims must be directed to the authority concerned, as it is solely up to that authority to decide whether it will bring charges or seek redress against the relevant official.

References

Ahlström K (2018) Förvaltningslagen. Karnov, Stockholm

Bogdan M (ed) (2010) Swedish legal system. Norstedts, Stockholm

Christensen JP, Albæk Jensen J, Hansen Jensen M (2012) Dansk statsret. DJØF, Copenhagen

Fenger Niels (2004) Forvaltning og Fællesskab. DJØF, Copenhagen

Fenger N (2013) Forvaltningsloven med kommentarer. DJØF, Copenhagen

Fenger N (2014) Borgeren og digitalisert forvaltning – hvor går vi? 40. Nordiske Juristmøte, Oslo, 21–22 August 2014

Fenger N, Grønnegård Christensen J (2017) Åbenhed og fortrolighed i den ministerielle beslutningsproces En redegørelse for offentlighedslovgivningens beskyttelse af den politisk-administrative beslutningsproces i udvalgte europæiske lande. http://www.justitsministeriet.dk/sites/default/files/media/Pressemeddelelser/pdf/2017/undersoegelse_af_andre_landes_aktindsigtsregler.pdf. Accessed 12 June 2018

Fenger N (2018) Forvaltningsret. DJØF, Copenhagen

Graver HP (2015) Alminnelig forvaltningsrett. Universitetsforlaget, Oslo

Jørgensen O (2014) Access to information in the Nordic Countries. Nordicom, Gothenburg

Lavin R (2016) Förvaltningsprocessrätt. Wolters Kluwer, Alphen aan den Rijn

Marcusson L (ed) (2005) Offentligrättsliga principer. Iustus, Uppsala

Mäenpää O (2008) Hallintoprosessioikeus. WSOYPro, Helsinki

Mäenpää O (2016a) Hallintolaki ja hyvän hallinnon takeet. Edita, Helsinki

Mäenpää O (2016b) Julkisuusperiaate. Talentum Pro, Helsinki
Mäenpää O (2018) Hallinto-oikeus. Alma Talent, Helsinki
Nergelius J (2011) Constitutional law in Sweden. Wolters Kluwer, Alphen aan den Rijn
Nuotio K (ed) (2012) Introduction to Finnish Law and legal culture. Forum Iuris, Helsinki
Revsbech K (2016) Forvaltningsret Almindelige Emner. DJØF, Copenhagen
Smith E, Eckhoff T (2016) Forvaltningsrett. Akademika, Oslo
Strömberg H, Lundell B (2014) Allmän förvaltningsrätt. Liber, Malmö

Crime and Punishment

Tapio Lappi-Seppälä and Kimmo Nuotio

Abstract Nordic criminal justice systems are based on shared histories and traditions, common model of society (Nordic Welfare State), as well as over 50-year co-operation in legal issues. For some periods, Finland, however, has followed its own paths, as a result of severe political crises in first part of the 20th century. This period was followed by a profound revisions of criminal law and a dramatic decrease in the use of imprisonment in 1960–1990s from over 150–60 prisoners/ 100,000 population. These experiences are worthwhile to study when most countries are still experiencing increasing incarceration rates. And so are the underlying principles of Nordic penal policy, which still rest on the values of Nordic Welfare State and the idea that social policy is the best criminal policy.

1 Introduction

1.1 Early History

From 1200 to 1400 criminal sanctions in the early Nordic lands consisted mainly of monetary penalties. Imprisonment as a general punishment was unknown; corporal punishment was rare; and death sentences were reserved for very few offences. During the period 1500–1600, centralized power became more established and criminal justice gradually became more severe. However, it never reached the level of brutality observable in continental Europe or in England, a point noted by Nordic legal scholars in the late 1800s.[1]

[1] Olivecrona (1891), Forsman (1896).

T. Lappi-Seppälä
Institute of Criminology and Legal Policy, University of Helsinki, Helsinki, Finland
e-mail: tapio.lappi-seppala@helsinki.fi

K. Nuotio (✉)
Faculty of Law, University of Helsinki, Helsinki, Finland
e-mail: kimmo.nuotio@helsinki.fi

© Springer Nature Switzerland AG 2019

P. Letto-Vanamo et al. (eds.), *Nordic Law in European Context*,
Ius Gentium: Comparative Perspectives on Law and Justice 73,
https://doi.org/10.1007/978-3-030-03006-3_11

Explanations for this "early Nordic exceptionalism" range from cultural factors, to social and demographic factors (in comparison to continental Europe, the Nordic countries did not suffer from the mass poverty which contributed to widespread unrest and rebellion to be met with increased penal repression), a combination of geographical factors and penal ideology (the deterrent effect of public executions was deemed to be much more modest in sparsely populated Nordic countries compared to a densely populated European metropolis) and to structural and political arguments. The Nordic countries never adopted full-scale feudal structures, and landowners were never granted judicial powers which would have enabled implementation of criminal law for private interests.[2]

1.2 Modern Criminal Law Reform

The Nordic codes of the late 1600s and early 1700s cannot be classified as inherently reformist. They were based on old provincial codes and subsequent royal legislation. They were products of the age of absolutism, inspired by Mosaic law, deterrence and the *Lex Talionis*, untouched by Enlightenment ideas and legal scholarship which were about to spread across Europe during the 1700s. This development reached the North in the 1800s, at all levels.

In the mid-1800s the Nordic countries carried out comprehensive reforms of their criminal law. Prison played the role of principal punishment for serious offences, replacing corporal punishment. Preparations for a new criminal code started in Sweden in the early 1800s; the first proposal was presented in 1832 and ultimately accepted in 1864. Preparations for a new criminal code in Norway and Denmark started at about the same time. Norway was also the first country to complete the work in the form of a new criminal code in 1842. This first Nordic criminal code was strongly influenced by recent German codes, the texts of Paul Johann Anselm Feuerbach and the French *Code Pénal*. Danish reform took longer. After two unsuccessful attempts to initiate total criminal law reform, a commission appointed in 1850 managed to finalize the task in 1866. The code follows the Norwegian code in many details.

Reform in Finland was stalled by state-political reasons. The first preparations for reform of sanctions and criminal law started in the 1820s, though actual law drafting ceased after the separation of Finland from Sweden in 1809. The Estates gathered for the first time under the Russian regime in 1863 and partial reform covering enforcement of sanctions was accepted in 1866.[3] Total reform of the criminal code was completed in 1889 by enactment of a new criminal law.

---

[2]Lappi-Seppälä (1982), pp. 61–62, Pratt and Eriksson (2013).

[3]See Blomstedt (1964), Lahti (1977), pp. 122–127, Lappi-Seppälä (1982), p. 126 ff.

All the Nordic codes of the 1800s were strongly influenced by German criminal law theory, representing the state of the art in legal thinking at that time. German influence in legal theory and legislative drafting was mostly mediated through Nordic scholars who had studied at German universities or otherwise studied German philosophy and German scholarship. The idealist philosophy of Hegel, an important source of inspiration for nationalistic movements in many parts of Europe, was highly influential in German criminal law scholarship. At the same time, the codes borrowed from each other.

Intra-Nordic influences were evident throughout the drafting process in all the Nordic countries. This was the case with Denmark following Norway in 1866. Finnish reform, while the last European criminal code based on the German classical school of criminal law, was also influenced by intensive co-operation with leading Swedish legal scholars. Indeed, Nordic legal co-operation started to gain more systematic institutional forms in the coming century.

1.3 Nordic Co-operation

As noted in the introductory chapter, Nordic lawyers started convening in 1872. Furthermore, Nordic scholars were active participants in the International Union of Penal Law (I.U.P.L./U.I.D.P.) established in 1889. The first national criminalist association was established in Denmark in the 1890s, and the other Nordic countries followed; their first meeting was held in 1937. Among other activities, these associations have co-published the Scandinavian Journal of Criminal Law and Criminology (*Nordisk Tidsskrift for Kriminalvidenskab*) for over 90 years. The journal has been an important forum for publishing articles on criminal law research and criminology. Nordic lawyers' meetings increased communication between key legal actors. Very likely this also helped transfer ideas. Nordic neighbours also often took into account one another's already-tested solutions, and it became a common practice to refer to the experience of neighbouring countries when drafting new bills.

In 1962, the Scandinavian research Council for Criminology (*Nordisk Samarbetsråd för Kriminologi*) was established by ministries of justice to "further criminological research within the member countries and advise the Scandinavian governments and the Council on issues related to criminology." In the same year the Nordic governments signed the Helsinki-Treaty, according to article 5 of which "state parties should strive towards the harmonization of the norms related to criminal offenses and punishments." This also became the task of the Nordic Committee for Criminal Law (*Nordiska Straffrättskommittén*), established by four Nordic Ministers of Justice in 1960. The Committee continued working until 1992, but its main results were produced in the 1960s and 1970s.

The output of the Committee includes establishment of the Nordic extradition system, which can be seen as a forerunner of the European Arrest Warrant.[4] However, national legislators were not always willing to follow: The Committee was still more like an expert group—not an official committee, and jointly drafted reports were not always politically weighty enough to convince governments and legislative bodies of the benefits of a Nordic solution. One of the topics for which this model of common preparation was tried concerned the rules and principles of exercise of criminal jurisdiction. Finland and Sweden followed commonly drafted instructions whereas Denmark did not, while Norway followed only half-way.

That said, the Committee provided an important platform for establishing joint Nordic policy lines in issues under discussion and national planning tables (see for example the Committee's reports on conditional release and sentencing). This co-operation and exchange of information and experience continued in the form of joint research seminars and annual meetings of criminologists, lawyers and practitioners arranged by the Nordic Criminalist Associations and the Scandinavian Criminological Research Council.

In general, the uninterrupted series of joint Nordic meetings since 1872 has provided a specific environment for legal development in countries that share long common roots but have also experienced different times and different fates in the course of history. Notwithstanding numerous differences in details and legislative solutions, we may with full justification speak of the "Nordic Model of Criminal Justice." This has its foundations in common history and traditions, subsequently in the formation of a specific form of society—the Nordic welfare state—in the latter half of the 20th century, as well as in active co-operation in legal and policy issues during the post WW2 decades. This model—sometimes termed "Scandinavian exceptionalism"—is most notably exemplified in more humane, rational and tolerant sanctioning practices. These practices have received wide international attention among researchers, policy-makers and the media.

1.4 Nordic Criminal Law Distancing Itself from the German Inheritance

Whereas throughout the 1800s and still in the early 1900s the Nordic countries were heavily influenced by changing German legal ideologies (first the classical school and subsequently the "sociological" school), this started to change after WW2. The emergence of criminology and empirical social sciences from the 1960s onwards, fresh and critical notions from legal realists and analytical jurisprudence made German-style conceptual jurisprudence look obsolete and out-dated. Reformers, such as Inkeri Anttila in Finland, saw that the entire criminal justice system needed

---

[4]Council Framework Decision 2002/584 on the European Arrest Warrant and the Surrender Procedures between Member States. Elholm and Feldtmann (2014).

to be rethought.[5] Johannes Andenaes in Norway conducted ground-breaking research in the field of crime control and deterrence that changed the way the mechanisms of general prevention came to be understood,[6] while Alf Ross in Denmark "deconstructed" practically all key concepts developed by the German scholars of the 1800s.[7]

About the same time, a future leading scholar in Sweden, Nils Jareborg, published a monograph on the two fundamental concepts of German legal theory, act and intent (*Handling och Uppsåt*), noting that he would not discuss German theory, "since it stands in this field so uninteresting with all of its self-sufficient and unrealistic concept formation.[8] Subsequently Nordic critical criminologists such as Nils Christie[9] and Thomas Mathiesen[10] gained attention far beyond Europe.

The days when Nordic scholars copied German textbooks are clearly over. The scholarly field had become open and it has become acceptable to search for inspiration pragmatically from a variety of foreign sources. This has also become visible in legislative drafting. To take just one example, in the reform of the general part of the Penal Code in Finland, German scholarship was only regarded as one source of inspiration, but it was not in any way given priority as a model. The act deliberately tried to avoid theoretical commitments. Where this was unavoidable, choices were made on the basis of both pragmatic considerations and national and Nordic traditions. Thus, for example, the definition of criminal intent followed (instead of German models) the probability model which had been developed in the other Nordic countries.[11] Put bluntly, we might conclude that finally the Nordic scholars and the Nordic legislatures saw that they were standing on their own two feet.

1.5 European Legal Integration and the Nordic Model

However, the survival of clever national solutions is no longer self-evident. By the 1990s the European political landscape had changed, and since then new forms of international collaboration and influence have been emerging. In the legal field, Nordic harmonization has been supplemented, partly even replaced, by European harmonization. Besides the European Union (EU), the Council of Europe has also been active in drafting conventions on substantive criminal law as well as collaboration in cross-border cases. The European Convention on Human Rights (ECHR)

---

[5]On Inkeri Anttila's works in English, see Anttila (2001).

[6]Andenaes (1974).

[7]Ross (1975).

[8]Jareborg (1969), pp. 6–7, for further works by Nils Jareborg, see Jareborg (1988) and Jareborg (2002).

[9]Christie (1982, 2000).

[10]Mathiesen (1990).

[11]See e.g. several of the articles in Lahti and Nuotio (1992).

as applied by the European Court of Human Rights (ECtHR) has shaped European criminal procedural systems and to some extent even European systems of criminal law.

The impact of European integration is mostly visible in the field of criminalization. European harmonization has mainly addressed issues of terrorism and organized crime and some other forms of criminality of a cross-border character. As regards systems of sanctions, European harmonization has affected the setting of penalty scales for selected specific crimes. Neither the European Union nor the Council of Europe has seriously tried to address doctrines of penal liability.

Even though a certain tendency of fragmentation is evident in national criminal laws, meaning that international law and international criminal law affect certain parts of criminal law whereas the law of the European Union or the Council of Europe affect other parts of criminal law, it still today falls on national legislatures, national courts and (national) scholars to build a totality of all this which is maximally coherent. In plain words, even in these new surroundings the Nordic countries maintain the possibility to defend and further develop the Nordic Model should they find the political will to do so.

2 Prison Reform and Penal Theories

2.1 Introducing Imprisonment in the 1800s

Preparations to introduce imprisonment as the central sanction started in the Nordic countries in the early 1800s.[12] However, the formal introduction of imprisonment as the principal sanction in Nordic law occurred first in connection with overall reforms of criminal codes, starting with Norway in 1842, followed by Sweden in 1864, Denmark in 1866 and ending with Finland in 1889. All codes defined imprisonment as the principal sanction and abolished corporal punishment (but maintained the death penalty as an option reserved for the most serious offences, mainly for murder). Principles of enforcement were, as a rule, confirmed in separate lower-level regulations.

Early prison reform was characterized by struggles between competing enforcement philosophies: the Philadelphian system, developed in the early 1800s under the spiritual influence of the Quakers; and the Auburn system, developed in New York in the 1820s. The Auburn system assumed that the way to reform was through work in total silence, whereas the Philadelphian system was based on the belief that religious meditation in single-cell solitude paves the way to reform and salvation. Neither of these methods proved especially successful, and alternative

[12] Sections 2 and 3 are largely based on Lappi-Seppälä (2017).

solutions were produced during the latter half of the century, among them the progressive system developed by Irish prison reformist Walter Crofton. The latter may also be classified as a combination of the Philadelphian and the Auburn systems.

The choice between enforcement philosophies was of fundamental practical relevance as it also determined the way new prisons should be built: either as single-cell prisons suitable for continuous isolation or as facilities with space for organized work for all inmates. The Nordic countries followed partly different solutions. Prison construction in Sweden around the mid-1800s followed the Philadelphian cell model. Norwegian enforcement principles were formulated in co-ordination with Swedish reform following the cell system. The Danish plan in 1842 came up with a compromise: short-term sentences were to follow the isolation model, while longer sentences were to be enforced following the Auburn model.

Finnish prison construction started somewhat later due to general state-political reasons. Largely thanks to this delay, the sharpest ideological controversies over enforcement were softened by compromises. Finland never adopted a full-scale Philadelphian single-cell model, but followed a compromise formulated under the 'progressive system' label. This may have been partly a matter of resources: single-cell prisons were far more expensive. However, by the end of the 19th century, doubts about the beneficial effects of long-term total isolation had also started to emerge. The 1889 legislation stressed the aim of rehabilitation, but with religious overtones ("Each prisoner must be provided with spiritual counsel, teaching and advice on how to improve his person and life") as well as work and discipline ("Prisoners must be ordered into hard work, obedience, order and cleanliness", according to the Finnish Act on Sentence Enforcement 1889).

2.2 *Towards Individualized Treatment and Cure*

Plans to redraft the 19th century criminal codes emerged soon after their enactment. In 1902, Norway received a much-appreciated new code, inspired by new ideas from the German sociological school. Denmark enacted a new criminal code, largely based on the same foundations, in 1930. Total reform in Sweden and Finland was postponed, but the principles of enforcement were shaped through partial reform.

Sanction structures in general were revised under the influence of individual preventive programmes of late 20th century criminalist movements. Concrete changes included the introduction and expansion of early release programmes and suspended or conditional sentences, but also the adoption of security measures and specific sanctions for mentally disordered offenders. All the Nordic countries adopted indeterminate confinement of high-risk offenders around the late 1920s. Sweden, Denmark and Norway also established specific institutions for mentally disordered offenders, whereas in Finland the parliament abolished the establishment of a specific "psychopath-institution" for resource reasons, though accepting adoption of indeterminate detention for high-risk violent offenders.

The period from 1930 to 1950 may be defined as the golden years of penal rehabilitation. This applies especially to Sweden. Prison law reform started in the mid-1930s, spurred on by Minister of Justice Karl Schlyter's speech in 1934 (which coined the slogan "Empty the prisons").[13] During the same year a committee started to work with new enforcement legislation. The enforcement decree of 1938 laid the foundations for upcoming total reform that took place in 1945. This act represents the culmination of treatment ideology in Sweden and forms "the foundation of modern prison services in Sweden."[14] The law abolished the cell system and introduced differentiated enforcement and individualised treatment for different offender groups.

Sweden's prison law confirms four central principles, to be later formulated in the coming reforms: the requirements of human dignity, legality, rehabilitation and harm-minimization. These principles travelled quickly to other Nordic enforcement codes: Denmark in 1946, Finland in 1950 and Norway in 1958. Whether, and to what extent, these ideals and reality are actually met in everyday prison practice is another question.[15] As regards Finland, the steep post-war crime wave, lack of material resources and the (then) prevailing conservative and punitive criminal policy ideology among leading law professors prevented further adoption of the Swedish model, despite some isolated attempts towards that direction. Changes in this respect had to wait for some fifteen to twenty years more.

2.3 *The Decline of the Rehabilitative Ideal*

Treatment ideology prevailed in the Nordic Countries from the 1930s/40s until the late 1960s. The position of this ideology was strongest in Sweden and Denmark, and weakest in Finland, which was recovering from the hardships of the first half of the 20th century. In the 1960s things started to change. The Nordic countries experienced heated debate on the results of and justifications for involuntary treatment in institutions, both penal and otherwise.

The extensive use of confinement and compulsory treatment in various institutions (such as in healthcare and in the treatment of alcoholics) was criticized for being both inhumane and ineffective. Critical research findings on the effects of treatment changed criminal policy priorities from custodial sanctions to community alternatives and to open care measures. Justification for imprisonment shifted from individual prevention and treatment towards general prevention.

[13]"*Avfolka fängels*erna", see Petersson-Hjelm (2011), p. 148 ff.

[14]Petersson-Hjelm (2011), pp. 130 and 177 ff.

[15]For critical remarks on this point, see Petersson-Hjelm (2011), p. 262 ff.

The 1960s/70s witnessed radical reforms in the field of social policy, alcohol policy, healthcare, child welfare and criminal policy—of which prison reform was but one aspect. The Nordic countries entered the 1960s from different starting points, and each country had problems of their own. Finland was only now joining the Nordic welfare state family, with much still to catch up on. However, prisoners' rights and prison conditions became a target of political action in all of these countries. Each of them also witnessed the establishment of prisoners' associations in 1966–1968 to improve prisoners' rights and to promote the humanization of prison conditions.[16]

The results of these efforts were realized in a series of reforms around the turn of the 1960s/70s. Major Finnish reforms were conducted in 1971–1975. Swedish prison reform was conducted in 1974. Corresponding Danish reforms were carried out through administrative regulations by a progressive prison director in 1970–1973. In Norway legislative activities were restricted mainly to changes related to indeterminate sanctions.

The decline of treatment ideology did not entail a general shift towards harsher penal regimes and prison warehousing. The core message was to scale down the use of imprisonment and to abolish indeterminate sanctions. The prison reforms that followed at the turn of the 1960s/70s improved the rights of inmates, abolished humiliating disciplinary punishments, introduced prison leave and expanded the system of open facilities.

The resulting criminal policy ideology—"humane neo-classicism"—stressed both legal safeguards against coercive care and less repressive measures in general. In sentencing, the principles of proportionality and predictability became the central values. In sentence enforcement, the principles of normality/normalization and minimization of harm replaced the old progressive principle. In prison construction, strategic decisions were made towards replacing old, larger, closed prisons with smaller open-type facilities. A major change with strong symbolic significance was the abolition of indeterminate sanctions, including preventive detention, during the early years of the 1970s.

For Denmark, Norway and Sweden the period from the 1960s onwards represents a period of fairly stable and low incarceration rates. For Finland this was the beginning of a long-term reduction in imprisonment rates that continued up to the early 1990s, to the point where Finland reached the general Nordic level of around 60 prisoners for every 100,000 inhabitants.[17]

---

[16]KRUM in Sweden 1966, KRIM in Denmark and in Finland 1967 and KROM in Norway 1968, for history and the work these organizations, see Mathiesen (1974).

[17]These changes and their background have been discussed in more detail in Lappi-Seppälä (2007, 2009).

2.4 Prison Reform 2000 and Human Rights

The principles laid down in the 1970s outlined penal reforms for the following fifteen to twenty years. The fourth round of prison law reform took place under a complex mixture of increasing punitive demands, growing rehabilitative aspirations and emerging human rights influences.

The 1990s witnessed growth of politicization in criminal policy even in the Nordic countries.[18] A growing drug problem led to intensification of control and supervision in prison settings. Penal rehabilitation was also experiencing a new return in the form of What Works-thinking. At the same time the growing international human rights movement, the incorporation of the ECHR and the establishment of the ECtHR and the European Committee for the Prevention of Torture and Inhuman or Degrading Treatment or Punishment (CPT) started to influence penal reforms. This influence was visible, not only in national prison laws but partly also on the level of constitutional and fundamental rights. All the Nordic countries revised their prison codes in the 2000s. Denmark[19] and Norway[20] were the first countries to do so in 2000, Finland[21] followed in 2006 and Sweden[22] in 2010. Iceland,[23] too, enacted a new enforcement code in 2005. The code, however, lacks specific provisions related to the general aims of enforcement.

Preparations for a new prison law started in Denmark in 1985. The final bill prepared by the Ministry of Justice was sent to the parliament in 1999 and entered into force in 2000. Prior to the 2000 reform, Danish enforcement legislation was based on administrative regulations alone. The new Corrections Act covers both custodial and community sanctions, as well as enforcement of fines. Perhaps the most important single human rights-oriented change brought about by the 2000 law reform was the introduction of court appeals to replace internal administrative control.

The 2000 Danish prison reform was first and foremost a rule-of-law reform, with the intention of specifically regulating prisoners' rights. The same ideology can be found behind changes that have given the courts a much more active role in the realm of corrections.[24] Instead of substantial changes in enforcement aims and principles, the ideology behind the 2000 act was to "give Parliament the responsibility for the regulation of this in every way important part of the administration of the state."[25]

---

[18]See for discussions Ugelvik and Dullum (2012).

[19]*Lov om fuldbyrdelse af straf mv.* 1999 no 145.

[20]*Lov om gjennomføring av straff mv.* 2001 no 21.

[21]*Vankeuslaki/Fängelselag* 767/2005.

[22]*Fängelselag 2010:610.*

[23]*Lög um fullnustu refsinga No* 49/2005. See also Iceland's The Penal Code, *Almenn hegningarlög* 19/1940.

[24]Greve and Snare (2009), p. 311.

[25]Greve (2014), p. 222.

Norway received a new Prison Law in 2000 to replace its old treatment-oriented code of 1958. Preparations for the law started in 1980 and the first proposal was published in 1988 (NOU 1988:37). The Preparatory Committee discussed the principles of enforcement under the framework of classical theories of punishment. Preparation of the final bill took over ten years and the time-span is also visible in the argumentation. While the 1988 proposal included no references to human rights documents, the bill of 2000–2001 devotes specific chapters to this topic with the general notion that "increased focus on individuals' human rights has led the government to propose changes to the existing prison law."[26] Thus the Norwegian Prison Law 3:38 allows the use of coercive measures "only if the circumstances make this strictly necessary, and less forceful measures have been attempted in vain or will obviously be inadequate." With reference to the decisions of the Human Rights Commission from the late 1980s, the bill also stressed the need to restrict the use of solitary confinement only to cases where it is deemed to be absolutely necessary as a preventive measure, never as punishment.[27]

Sweden reformed its prison law in 2010 on the basis of an extensive committee report published in 2005 (SOU 2005:54). The committee work was inspired by emerging ideas on new rehabilitation (What Works). The proposal laid strong emphasis on the old progression principle and increased individualisation with progress plans, and even re-introduction of the system of privileges attainable through good behaviour. New elements, compared to the previous code from 1974, included increased emphasis on reducing the risk of reoffending and on security. Presumably the most important single change motivated by international obligations and human rights requirements was replacement of the internal administrative appeals mechanism with a court-based system. Compared to the Danish and Norwegian codes, the aims of enforcement and leading principles are also defined in more detail consisting of the general aim of rehabilitation, the aim of harm minimization, respect for human dignity, and the like.

In Finland, preparations for a new prison law started with the appointment of a prison law committee in 1998. The new prison law entered into force in 2006. The reform was much influenced by ratification of the ECHR in 1989 and constitutional reforms carried out in 1995 and 2000. Joining the Council of Europe and ratification of the ECHR at the time of constitutional reform opened the window of opportunity for incorporating human rights as part of fundamental rights in the constitution. This proved to play an important role in revisions of prison law. The constitution imposed stricter demands than before on legal regulation in all decisions dealing with deprivation of liberty. It also obliged the legislator to define the rights and obligations of prisoners in greater detail than before. Additional pressures towards total revision of the prison law emerged from the fact that the old enforcement act had become fragmented and outdated from a penological point of view.

---

[26]See Det Kongelige Justis-og Politidepartement (2000), pp. 12–18.

[27]Despite these notions, the introductory chapter of the bill stresses preventive aims and security.

Preparatory work for the code also used the support provided by recommendations from the CPT, for example on issues related to introduction of a structured enforcement plan, the need for a comprehensive strategy regarding separation of prisoners for safety and security, and prisoners' right to appeal. All in all, the 2006 reform of prison law can be characterized first and foremost as a rule-of-law reform. As stated in the governmental bill, the act "aims to bring the prison law in accordance with the requirements of the new constitution, to define the obligations of prison authorities in more detail, to increase legal safeguards and transparency in prison administration, to reorganize the imprisonment process to a more structured and planned process and increase investments in rehabilitative program- and treatment work and thereby also to reduce recidivism." (Gov Prop 262/2004)

3 Principles of Enforcement

3.1 Rights-Oriented Principles

All codes include declarations of leading principles of enforcement. Some of them can be conceived as penological aims, some as expressions of broader values related to human and fundamental rights to be taken into account in pursuing those aims. Some can also be understood as regulatory principles that define the mode of enforcement in specific areas.[28] The following section gives a brief overview of some of these principles, using Finnish prison law—being the most detailed in this respect—as a point of reference.

The principle of inviolability of human dignity is confirmed in section 1 subsection 2 of the Finnish Constitution[29]: "The Constitution shall guarantee the inviolability of human dignity." It sets human dignity as the basic value behind the other fundamental rights provisions. Subsection 7.2 states that "no one shall be sentenced to death, tortured or otherwise treated in a manner violating human dignity." Section 22 of the constitution, in turn, states that "public authorities shall guarantee the observance of basic rights and liberties and human rights." These requirements have been incorporated in Nordic prison laws since the mid-1940s. They are also repeated in the present codes: The Penal Code of Finland[30] (FPC) "Prisoners shall be treated fairly and with respect for their human dignity" (FPC 1:5.1), The Swedish

[28]Principles alone, of course, are not enough. Their contents need to be specified. This is addressed by separate provisions dealing with issues such as arrival and placement in prison, basic care and accommodation, participation in activities, contacts with the outside world, prison order and discipline and inspections.

[29]*Suomen perustuslaki/Finlands grundlag* 731/1999.

[30]*Rikoslaki/Strafflag* 39/1889.

Penal Code[31] (SPC) "Every prisoner shall be treated with respect for his or her human dignity and with understanding for the special difficulties associated with the deprivation of liberty." (SPC 1:4)[32]

Another principle that should be mentioned is the principle of legality and imprisonment as loss of liberty only.—Offenders are sent to prison as punishment, not for punishment.[33] The message behind this famous phrase has been given different formulations. One formulation can be found in Finnish law: "The content of imprisonment shall be loss or restriction of liberty." (FPC 1:3.1) European Prison Rules (2006)[34] 102.2 states: "Imprisonment is by the deprivation of liberty a punishment in itself and therefore the regime shall not aggravate the suffering inherent in imprisonment." The Danish formulation of 1945 states that "the punishment of imprisonment solely consists in the deprivation of liberty, and that the prisoner otherwise retains the rights and duties of a citizen in society."[35] These formulations embody at least two distinct but interconnected claims: one related to prisoners' position as subjects of rights and another related to the content of imprisonment.

The first claim states that prisoners are no longer "slaves of the state", but that their rights are protected by law like any other citizen. This requirement is constitutionally confirmed in the Finnish Constitution (Section 7.3): "The rights of individuals deprived of their liberty shall be guaranteed by an Act of Parliament." The section rejects the prior "assumption of institutional powers" (or "inherent limitations").[36] Since the rights of persons who have been deprived of their liberty must be safeguarded by an Act of Parliament, all restrictions on these rights must in Finland be based on a parliamentary act, not regulations of lower level statutes or correctional orders issued by the administration according to explicit or implicit broad authorization from the parliament.[37] The second claim is about the content of imprisonment. It is no longer required or allowed to impose extra hardship on prisoners for reasons related to the "aims of punishment" (whether retribution or deterrence). Loss of liberty, as such, is enough.

---

[31]*Brottsbalk* 1962:700.

[32]This requirement is listed as the 1st rule both in the European Prison Rules 2006 and the The United Nations Standard Minimum Rules for the Treatment of Prisoners (the Nelson Mandela Rules) 2015.

[33]Quoted by Ruck 1951.

[34]Recommendation Rec (2006) 2 of the Committee of Ministers to member states on the European Prison Rules.

[35]Greve and Snare (2009), pp. 310–311.

[36]van Zyl Smit and Snacken (2009).

[37]As noted by critics, vague criteria (such as "the demands of security") easily water down the intended legal safeguards. For a criticism of Danish law, see Greve and Snare (2009).

The principle of minimum intervention is linked with the second claim above. Thus, the cited Finnish provision continues, "The enforcement of imprisonment may not restrict the rights or circumstances of a prisoner in any other manner than that provided in the law or necessary due to the punishment itself." (FPC 1:3.1) Swedish law states that "enforcement may not entail limitations of the prisoner's liberty other than those that follow from this Act or are necessary to maintain good order or security." (SPC 1:6.1) According to The Danish Penal Code[38] (DPC), "during sanction enforcement an individual must not have restrictions imposed on his existence other than those provided by law or which result from the sanction itself." (DPC 4 §) Restrictions need to be based on clear authorization by law.

The normality principle occupied the central position as the leading principle of enforcement in Finland in the 1970s. As formulated in the present law: "The conditions in a prison shall be arranged, to the extent possible, so that they correspond to the living conditions prevailing in society." (FPC 1:3) The other Nordic countries lack explicit formulations of the principle, but it forms a clear starting point for the regulation of prison life and conditions in general.[39] In simple terms, the principle calls for the abolition of certain practices followed in prison life only (for example, the requirement to wear prison clothes). In broader terms, the principle affects the ways in which work, education, and training are arranged in prisons.[40]

3.2 Aim-Oriented Principles

The rehabilitation principle belongs among so-called aim-oriented principles. Rehabilitation remains the central aim in enforcement, even if the actual use of imprisonment is based on other motives.[41] All the Nordic codes stress rehabilitative-related aims, but with different wordings. The Finnish Prison Law states: "The goal of the enforcement of imprisonment is to increase the ability of a

[38]*Straffeloven* 1930 no 126.

[39]As noted by Engbo (2017), the normality principle does not have fixed content. He makes a distinction between proactive and defensive approaches. The proactive approach obliges the authorities to arrange conditions enabling prisoners to live as normally as possible inside prison. The defensive approach entails a duty of non-interference in the form of minimum intervention.

[40]For a detailed description of application of the normality principle in Finland, see Hartoneva (2002) and for Denmark Engbo (2005), pp. 44–45 and Engbo (2017).

[41]See the *Lag* (1974:203) *om kriminalvård i anstalt* 4 §: Enforcement of imprisonment shall be carried out so that the prisoner's adaptation to society is furthered and the detrimental effects of the deprivation of liberty are counteracted.

prisoner to lead a crime-free life by promoting the prisoner's potential to cope and his adjustment to society as well as to prevent the committing of offences during the term of sentence." (FPC 1:2) The section covers both more narrowly focused efforts for social rehabilitation and reduction of recidivism, as well as broader attempts to provide social support and networks promoting social adjustment and social survival.

The Danish Corrections Act[42] (3 §) states that "The enforcement of the sanction shall take place with necessary regard both for the execution of the sanction and for the need to assist or influence the convicted person to lead a law-abiding life." Similar elements are to be found in Swedish law: "Enforcement shall be devised so as to facilitate the prisoner's adjustment in the community and counteract the negative consequences of deprivation of liberty." (SPC 1:5.1) However, the law also puts more emphasis on efforts to prevent re-offending: "Enforcement shall, so far as possible and without neglecting the requirement to protect the community, focus especially on measures intended to prevent re-offending." (SPC 1:5.2)

The wording of The Norwegian Penal Code[43] (NPC) is more ambiguous: "A sentence shall be executed in a manner that takes into account the purpose of the sentence, which serves to prevent the commission of new criminal acts, reassures society, and within this framework ensures satisfactory conditions for the prisoners." (NPC 1:2) Furthermore, "sanctions shall be executed in a manner that satisfies the need for security. The substance thereof shall be based on the measures available to the Correctional Services for assisting a convicted person to adjust to society. The Correctional Services shall make suitable arrangements for enabling a convicted person through efforts of his or her own to avoid committing new criminal acts." (NPC 1:3.1)[44] In addition, it does not mention adjustment to society but only prevention of crime.

The aim of minimizing harm can be seen as another re-formulation of minimum intervention (and the normality principle), but with a clearer and more concrete aim. The Finnish code links the avoidance of harmful effects of prison life and maintaining health and social functionality in the same paragraph: "The ability of a prisoner to maintain his health and functional ability shall be supported. The goal is to prevent any detriment resulting from the loss of liberty." (FPC 1:3) The Swedish code combined the aim of harm minimization with the general aim of social rehabilitation (see above SPC 5:1). The Norwegian code discusses this principle in connection with remand prisoners: "In the case of persons remanded in custody the Correctional Services shall make suitable arrangements for remedying the detrimental effects of isolation." (NPC 1:2.2) Efforts to maintain health include equal healthcare services for prisoners (as compared to the rest of the population). Harm

[42] *Straffuldbyrdelsesloven* 2017 no 1491.

[43] *Lov om straff* 2005 no 28.

[44] See further Greve and Snare (2009), p. 316.

may be minimized by providing psychosocial support and treatment and by supporting prisoners' contacts with the outside world.

3.3 Juveniles

The Nordic countries abolished specific juvenile prisons in the 1970s as a reaction against indeterminate sanctions. Since then custodial care orders have mostly been implemented under the child welfare system. Consequently the number of young offenders in actual prisons has remained "too small" to justify establishing specific institutions for juveniles only. This has sometimes aroused critical observations from the CPT.

The response to this criticism is that juveniles are kept separate, provided that this is in their best interest: "When enforcing the imprisonment of juveniles, who have committed their offences when under 21 years of age, special attention shall be paid to the needs arising from the age and stage of development of the prisoner." (FPC 1:5.2) And furthermore: "A prisoner under 18 years of age shall be kept separate from adult prisoners unless otherwise required by his best interests." (FPC 4:8) Similarly the Swedish code states "A prisoner who is under the age of 18 years may not be placed so that he or she is together with prisoners aged 18 or over unless this can be considered to be in his or her best interests" (SPC 2:3), as does the Norwegian code: "Particular importance shall be attached to a child's right of access to his or her parents during the execution of a sanction." (NPC 1:3.2)

4 Nordic Model—Past, Present and Future

4.1 Common Route with Different Paths

When adopted and presented as a replacement for corporal punishment in the early 1800s, prisons were supposed to be frightening places with enough deterrent potential. Nordic prisons were no exception.[45] The principles of enforcement in 19th century prisons were a combination of deterrence, retribution and reform. Rehabilitation, however, was to be achieved, not by treatment and support in our understanding of the words, but either by solitude and discussion with one's conscience, or through hard work and religious teaching. Criminal codes themselves were influenced by the classical German theory of criminal policy with its emphasis

[45]For critical reports on conditions in 18th and 19th century Nordic prisons, see Scharff Smith and Ugelvik (2017), pp. 10–12.

on retribution and general prevention. In the 20th century, religious-oriented enforcement practices, the atonement of sins in solitude, and reform through hard labour were displaced by scientifically informed views about the causes of crime and the effects of punishment, with stress on more individualized and differentiated treatment. Adults and juveniles were kept separately in separate institutions, as were chronic recidivists and offenders suffering from mental disorders.

The process culminated in the golden years of penal rehabilitation in Sweden from the 1930s to the 1950s. This reform was essentially a social-democratic welfare project reflecting both changed conceptions of the tasks and responsibilities of the state and the enhanced social and material conditions of the (Swedish) "peoples' home" providing shelter and support for the weak and those in need.[46] Other Nordic countries followed, some more closely (Denmark and Norway), and some from a distance (Finland).

From the 1960s/70s onwards, social-liberal critics of criminal law raised barriers against treatment without consent, use of indeterminate sanctions and overuse of incarceration in general. While these reforms were conducted largely under the same flag in all the Nordic countries, their starting points were different. For Finland the main target was reduction of the high number of prisoners, in international terms, by use of shorter sentences and alternatives to imprisonment. Other Nordic countries mainly distanced themselves from the overly optimistic ideal of penal rehabilitation, while still maintaining rehabilitative-oriented practices as part of their sanction structures.

In the North the idea of rehabilitation did not fade away in the 1970s. Rather, claims and conclusions were less radical and more modest: to admit that imprisonment should not be used *because* of its rehabilitative potential, to abolish all forms of non-consensual treatment, and to restrict the use of penal confinement based on empirically insecure assumptions regarding offenders' future behaviour.

The Nordic criminal justice systems spent the years from the 1970s to the 2000s in a moderate penal climate, by comparison with changes experienced in other western regions and countries during that period. All Nordic countries had their share of the "new punitive turn", albeit in different form, scale and time. Still, the relative magnitude of these changes—in comparative terms—remained modest to the extent that the Nordic countries still maintained the characterization of "Nordic penal exceptionalism" as part of comparative criminal political analyses.[47]

---

[46]Petersson-Hjelm (2011), p. 361.

[47]Pratt and Eriksson (2013).

4.2 *Nordic Penal Exceptionalism—Does It Exist, and Will It Last?*

The Nordic welfare state, along with its underlying structures, values and practices, has enabled the creation and defence of a criminal political model that today is characterized by internationally low prison population rates, humane prison conditions and a general commitment to rehabilitating and reintegrating offenders into society.[48] The outcome can be characterized by a pragmatic and non-moralistic approach and with a clear social policy orientation. It reflects the values of the Nordic welfare-state ideal and emphasizes that measures against social marginalization and equality also operate as measures against crime.

The survival of this model is by no means self-evident. Nor does a consensus exist among Nordic scholars about the "true nature" of "Nordic exceptionalism", or about the survival of the Nordic welfare state itself. Socio-economic and political structures have experienced radical changes, the hegemony of social-democratic parties is already history, as indeed are the days of centralized tripartite wage agreements that once paved the way towards more egalitarian wage policies. Privatization and market forces are stepping into social service sectors, and populist right-wing protest parties wield increasing influence in national politics.

As regards the content of penal policy, intra-Nordic criticism has challenged many of the flattering characterizations of international observers by pointing out examples of increasingly punitive sanction practices, the toughening of prison control to curb the spread of drugs in prisons, excessively punitive pre-trial practices and the use of solitary confinement, not to mention the general hardening of penal rhetoric. Recent demographic changes and large-scale immigration have changed penal debate in some countries (most notably in Norway), while others have been troubled by specific crime problems (such as motor-cycle gangs in Denmark).[49]

So, is it time to say goodbye to Nordic penal exceptionalism (if indeed it ever existed)? Are we perhaps witnessing the "end of Nordic humane and rational penal policy"? Before answering these questions, some hard facts need to be acknowledged: Children under 15 are not punished and the number of children aged 15–17 in penal institutions is counted in tens; prisoners maintain all their constitutional rights, rights that are defined in detail in the law, monitored nationally and internationally, and protected in practice; a substantial number of prisoners are serving their sentences in open facilities; the use of indeterminate confinement is either

[48]For comparative analysis along these lines, see Cavadino and Dignan (2006) and Lacey (2008). The internal logic between political economy, welfare and social values and their relevance for penal policy formation has been analyzed in more detail in Lappi-Seppälä (2008).

[49]For critical discussion, see Barker (2017), Ugelvik and Dullum (2012), Scharff Smith and Ugelvik (2017), Shammas (2017). For long term analysis of legislative changes in Nordic countries, see Lappi-Seppälä (2016b).

prohibited or limited to a minimum; criminalizations still follow the principle of *ultima-ratio* and rule-of-law, albeit under growing pressure from the European Union; political and criminological discourse about crime prevention takes place within the framework of social- and situational prevention, with only fragmented notions towards criminal law (usually in connection with high-risk violent recidivists or sexual offences); the sanction system has been reformed towards community measures with stress on social reintegration (and not plain control) and with the declared aim of reducing the use of custodial sanctions.

As a result, the Nordic countries have fewer prisoners than any set of industrialized countries in the world. During the last ten years the number of prisoners has also decreased on average by a little over ten percent (and the number of incoming inmates by almost 30%).[50]

These elements can be acknowledged without falling into complacency or into the false belief that this state of affairs is secure in the future. Nor is there reason to assume that Nordic criminal justice systems are functioning without flaws and injustices. We need to be prepared for the possibility that things may take an adverse turn, and we need to maintain a critical view towards our own practices. Affluent societies, such as the Nordic countries, can and must be able to produce penal practices that correspond to their levels of socio-economic resources, pay full respect to human rights, and give true prominence to the social and humanitarian values underpinning the ideal of the Nordic welfare state.

References

Andenaes J (1974) Punishment and deterrence. University of Michigan Press, Ann Arbor

Anttila I (2001) Ad Ius criminale humanius: essays in criminology, criminal justice and criminal policy. Finnish Lawyers' Association, Helsinki

Barker V (2017) Nordic vagabonds. The Roma and the logic of benevolent violence in the Swedish welfare state. Eur J Criminol 14(1):120–139

Betænkning om en lov om fuldbyrdelse af straf mv. Bind I. Arbejdsgruppe nedsat af Straffelovrådet Betænkning nr. 1181/1989

Blomstedt Y (1964) Rikoslakireformin ensimmäiset vaiheet vuoden 1866 osittaisuudistuksiin saakka. Historiallinen Arkisto 59. Turun sanomalehti ja kirjapaino Oy, Turku

Cavadino M, Dignan J (2006) Penal systems: a comparative approach. SAGE Publications, London

Christie N (1982) Limits to pain. Robertson, Oxford

Christie N (2000) Crime control as industry. Routledge, London

Det Kongelige Justis-og Politidepartement (2000) Ot.prp. nr. 5 (2000–2001)

[50]The fall is steepest in Finland from 3776 to 2859 prisoners (−24%), followed by Sweden (from 7196 to 5664, −21%). Norway forms the exception, with sharply increasing numbers of prisoners (3300–3927, +19%, which has also gained the attention of the Norwegian research community).

Elholm T, Feldtmann B (2014) Nordic trends of jurisdiction—an international perspective. In: Elholm T, Feldtmann B (eds) Criminal jurisdiction: a nordic perspective. DJØF Publishing, Copenhagen, pp 149–151

Engbo HJ (2005) Straffulbyrdelseret. Juris-og Okonomiforbundets Forla, Copenhagen

Engbo HJ (2017) Normalisation in Nordic prisons—from a prison governor's perspective. In: Scharff Smith P, Ugelvik T (eds) Scandinavian penal history, culture and prison practice: embraced by the welfare state? Palgrave Macmillan, London, pp 327–352

European Prison Rules (2006) Council of Europe Publishing, Strasbourg

Forsman J (1896) Suomen lainsäädännön historia: sen pääpiirteet. [1.] osa, Luentojakso. Helsinki Söderström

Greve V, Snare A (2009) Ideologies and realities in Prison Law: some trends. In: Wahlgren P (ed) Scandinavian studies in law, vol 54. Stockholm University of Law Faculty, Stockholm, pp 305–332

Greve V (2014) The sanctioning system. In: Langsted B, Garde P, Greve V (eds) Criminal law in Denmark. DJÖF Publishing, Copenhagen pp 100–113

Hartoneva A (2002) Normaalisuusperiaate Suomen vankeinhoidossa. Rikosseuraamusviraston julkaisuja 3/2002. Vammalan kirjapaino, Vammala

Jareborg N (1969) Handling och Uppsåt. Norstedt, Stockholm

Jareborg N (1988) Essays in criminal law. Uppsala, Iustus förlag

Jareborg N (2002) Scraps of penal theory. Iustus förlag, Uppsala

Lacey N (2008) Women, crime, and character: from Moll Flanders to Tess of the D'Urbervilles. Oxford University Press, Oxford

Lahti R (1977) Criminal sanctions in Finland: a system in transition. Scand. Stud. Law 21:119–157

Lahti R, Nuotio K (1992) (eds) Criminal law theory in transition. Finnish and comparative perspectives: Strafrechtstheorie im Umbruch. Finnische und vergleichende Perspektiven. Finnish Lawyers' Publishing Company, Helsinki

Lappi-Seppälä T (1982) Teilipyörästä terapiaan—piirteitä rangaistusjärjestelmän historiasta. Vankeinhoidon historiaprojektin julkaisu, Helsinki

Lappi-Seppälä T (2007) Penal policy in Scandinavia. In Tonry M (ed) Crime and Justice: a review of research, vol 36. The University of Chicago Press, Chicago

Lappi-Seppälä T (2008) Trust, welfare, and political culture. explaining national differences in penal severity. In: Tonry M (ed) Crime and justice: a review of research, vol 37. The University of Chicago Press, Chicago

Lappi-Seppälä T (2009) Imprisonment and penal policy in Finland. Scand Stud Law 54:333–380

Lappi-Seppälä T (2016b) Nordic sentencing. In: Tonry M (ed) Crime and justice: a review of research, vol 45. University of Chicago Press, Chicago

Lappi-Seppälä T (2017) Enforcement principles and Nordic prison reform 1800–2000. Tidskrift Utgiven av Juridiska Föreningen i Finland 2–4:426–449

Manifesto on European Criminal Policy. http://www.europarl.europa.eu/document/activities/cont/201112/20111207ATT33475/20111207ATT33475EN.pdf. Accessed 6 June 2018

Mathiesen T (1974) Scandinavian studies in criminology, vol 4: the politics of Abolition. Essays in political action theory. Scandinavian Studies in Criminology. Universitetsforlaget, Oslo

Mathiesen T (1990) Prison on trial: a critical assessment. SAGE, London

Olivecrona SRDK (1891) Om dödsstraffet. Uppsala

Petersson-Hjelm A (2011) Fängelset som välfärdsbygge. Institutet för rättshistorisk forskning. Rättshistoriskt bibliotek, Band 68, Stockholm

Pratt J, Eriksson A (2013) Contrasts in punishment: contrasts in punishment. Routledge, London

Ross A (1975) On guilt, responsibility and punishment. University of California Press, Berkeley

Shammas VL (2017) Prisons of welfare. Incarceration, social democracy, and the sociology of punishment. Department of Sociology and Human Geography, Faculty of Social Sciences, University of Oslo

Scharff Smith P, Ugelvik T (2017) Scandinavian penal history, culture and prison practice. embraced by the welfare state. Palgrave MacMillan, London

Straffelovrådets betænkning nr. 1355/1998 om en lov om fuldbyrdelse af straf m.v. Delbetænkning III om sanktionsspørgsmål. http://www.krim.dk/undersider/retskilder/betaenkning1355-straffuldbyrdelse.htm. Accessed 6 June 2018

Ugelvik T, Dullum J (2012) Penal exceptionalism? Nordic prison policy and practice London. Routledge, London

Zyl van Smit D, Snacken S (2009) Principles of European prison law and policy. penology and human rights. Oxford University Press, Oxford

Courts and Court Proceedings

Anna Nylund and Jørn Øyrehagen Sunde

Abstract The Nordic courts and court culture have several distinctive traits: (1) a three-tier court hierarchy with little specialisation; (2) judicial discretion and pragmatism; (3) "Nordic" oral proceedings; (4) lay participation; and (5) the role of Supreme Courts and the doctrine of *quasi-stare decisis*. Many of the traits are not uniquely Nordic, yet their combination and small distinctions compared to other legal systems do set them apart. There are also considerable differences between the Nordic countries. The main divides follow the historical division between the historical Swedish, eastern, kingdom, which included Finland; and the historical Danish-Norwegian kingdom, which also included Iceland.

1 Introduction

Nordic courts and court culture feature several distinctive traits. These traits have developed over centuries and are contingent on historical development and development of the role of the courts from public assemblies for resolving disputes to modern courts. Many of the traits are, of course, not uniquely Nordic, yet their combination and small distinctions compared to other legal systems do set them apart. Despite the many similarities, there are also considerable differences between the Nordic countries. Nordic cooperation has been weak at law-making concerning procedural law, although judicial networks are strong. The main divides follow the historical division between the Swedish, eastern, kingdom, which included Finland; and the Danish-Norwegian kingdom, which also included Iceland.

A. Nylund (✉)
Faculty of Law, University of Tromsø—The Arctic University of Norway,
Tromsø, Norway
e-mail: anna.nylund@uit.no

J. Ø. Sunde
Faculty of Law, University of Bergen, Bergen, Norway
e-mail: Jorn.Sunde@uib.no

© Springer Nature Switzerland AG 2019
P. Letto-Vanamo et al. (eds.), *Nordic Law in European Context*,
Ius Gentium: Comparative Perspectives on Law and Justice 73,
https://doi.org/10.1007/978-3-030-03006-3_12

This text presents five distinct features of the Nordic courts and court culture and discusses how they interact to form a Nordic court system and court culture. Differences between the Nordic countries will also be discussed. The five features are: (1) a three-tier court hierarchy with little specialisation; (2) judicial discretion and pragmatism; (3) "Nordic" oral proceedings; (4) lay participation; and (5) the role of Supreme Courts and the doctrine of *quasi-stare decisis*. Under each of these categories, both similarities and differences are examined. Although this text argues that a Nordic procedural culture exists, it also argues that this culture is far from monolithic. Before discussing the five features, a brief historical background is given.

2 Historical Background

In the Early Middle Ages, public assemblies (*ting*) were arenas for both mediation and adjudication. These assemblies were multi-faceted organs that had a legislative and executive function, in addition to offering conflict resolution. They were found at local and regional levels, and in Iceland at—what would today be considered—a national level. However, public assemblies were just one of several instruments for conflict resolution; a fixed order between the different levels of assemblies did not exist in the Early Middle Ages. Consequently, conflict resolution was flexible and rather informal.

The High Middle Ages, from the 12th century, saw a move towards regularity and fixed order that was manifested in compilations and codifications of law as from the 13th century. From this time on, we see the basic structure of the three-tiered court hierarchies of the Nordic countries being shaped, with a local court, a regional court with a quasi-appellate function, and the king as the third and final instance. An array of different instruments for conflict resolution has continued to co-exist with the courts ever since.

From the 16th century on, the Nordic countries were split into a western kingdom consisting of Denmark-Norway (including Iceland) that lasted until 1814; and an eastern kingdom consisting of Sweden (including Finland) that lasted until 1809. Both Sweden and Denmark-Norway were conglomerate states, including colonies. The apparent homogeneity today is thus a consequence of political efforts to unify realms that were otherwise quite heterogeneous. One instrument of unification was the courts. In the Swedish realm, the Svea Court of Appeal (*Svea hovrätt*), established in 1614, was the first Court of Appeal, and would continue to play a role as *primus inter pares* when more such courts were established in order to link the different parts of the Swedish realm to the central government. In the Danish-Norwegian realm, the Supreme Court in Copenhagen, established in 1661, played an important unifying role. The division between the eastern part, Finland and Sweden; and the western part, Denmark, Iceland and Norway, is still apparent from Nordic procedural law.

Trained lawyers in the capacity of judges, advocates and prosecutors first began to dominate Nordic courts from the second half of the 18th century. Legal qualifications did not become compulsory for practising law in the Danish-Norwegian realm until 1736, and in the Swedish realm until 1749. However, it was not until the early 19th century that all legal protagonists had to fulfil this criterion. This means that the Nordic countries were very slow in joining the professionalization process in Western Europe that might be claimed to have started in the mid-12th century. This left relatively wide scope for lay participation and for lay concepts of law in the Nordic courts, and room for judicial discretion and a search for pragmatic solutions.

The absence of the modern (civil) codes, along with relatively weak legal scholarship, left leeway for the courts. Hence, even up to recent times, unification of law also became, in practice, a task for the courts, producing precedent, and for the legislator, producing statutes and other legislative acts. Law remained less systematic and technical and thus did not impede lay participation in the courts. A three-tier system of general courts fits well into this picture—a simple court structure makes it easier to pursue a unifying purpose, with the involvement of citizens.

Procedural rules were archaic until the 20th century. Until then, the old codes enacted in the late 17th and early 18th centuries regulated court proceedings. In contrast to many other western countries, civil and criminal procedure are regulated by a single act of parliament in Denmark,[1] Finland[2] and Sweden.[3] In Finland, rules that solely govern criminal proceedings are found in the Criminal Procedure Act,[4] but rules common to both types of proceedings, such as rules of evidence, are found in the Code of Judicial Proceedings. In Norway, the Dispute Act[5] regulates civil proceedings, the Criminal Procedure Act[6] criminal proceedings, and the Courts of Justice Act[7] the organisation of courts, judges and legal counsel.

3 A Simple Court Structure with Little Specialisation

Like many western countries, Nordic courts generally consist of a three-tier structure. The main exception is the Finnish administrative courts, which consist of only two tiers. In the western Nordic countries, Denmark, Iceland and Norway, the court system consists of general courts; and in the eastern Nordic countries, Finland

[1]Administration of Justice Act, *Retsplejelov* 2016 no 1257.

[2]Code of Judicial Procedure, *Oikeudenkäymiskaari/Rättegångsbalk* 4/1734. Despite its name, the act is not technically a code.

[3]Code of Judicial Procedure, *Rättegångsbalken* 1942:740. Despite its name, the act is not technically a code.

[4]*Laki oikeudenkäynnistä rikosasioissa/Lag om rättegång i brottmål* 689/1997.

[5]*Lov om mekling og rettergang i sivile tvister* 2005 no. 90.

[6]*Lov om rettergangsmåte i straffesaker* 1981 no. 25.

[7]*Lov om domstolene* 1915 no 5.

and Sweden, of general courts and administrative courts. The division between general and administrative courts is based on the tradition of a strong and powerful administration in the Swedish realm, but is not taken from the more separation-of-powers-based system found in France.[8]

Proceedings in administrative courts are of a more ‘investigative’ or ‘inquisitorial’ nature, where the court is more actively involved in investigating the facts of the case, and both parties are, as a rule, obliged to bear their own costs. Administrative proceedings in general courts are treated as civil cases, so that the proceedings are of an ‘adversarial’ nature and the losing party is, as a rule, ordered to compensate the costs of the prevailing party.

Two characteristics set the Nordic court system apart from many other countries. Firstly, there is just one type of first court in the court hierarchy and, with few exceptions, all cases start at the bottom of the hierarchy. Secondly, only a few special courts exist outside the main hierarchy; moreover, the jurisdiction of such courts is largely limited.[9]

The first characteristic has been strengthened in recent decades: almost all cases start in the district courts or first administrative courts. Reforms in recent decades have strengthened the role of the first courts, which in turn has further streamlined the hierarchy. For instance, the Courts of Appeal in both Denmark and Norway were the first courts in serious criminal cases until 2007 and 1995, respectively. Today, practically all cases, smaller and larger, follow the same path through the court system. Another example is the Icelandic court system. Since its independence in 1919, Iceland has had a two-tier court structure, as the second level of courts has been transformed into the Icelandic Supreme Court.[10] In 2016, the parliament voted to introduce a Court of Appeal, which became operational in 2018.[11]

The Danish Maritime and Commercial High Court (*Sø-og Handelsretten*) remains an exception: it functions both as a first court and as an appellate court in commercial matters, and is thus both a first and a second court. Another example is the Finnish administrative courts, which consist of two tiers.

The second characteristic is the limited use of special courts. In recent years, adjudicative functions have been concentrated in the courts in the Nordic countries. In Finland, Water Courts (*vesituomioistuin/vattendomstol*) were abolished in 2000. Their adjudicative tasks were transferred to the ordinary courts. In Norway, the 34 Land Consolidation Courts (*jordskifterett*) had jurisdiction in matters relating to setting and adjusting the borders of real estate properties. In 2016, the Land Consolidation Appeal Courts were merged with the Courts of Appeal, so that land consolidation cases are thus ultimately integrated in the general court system. In

[8]Wenander (2016).

[9]A brief overview at http://www.domstol.se/Om-Sveriges-Domstolar/Domstolar-i-Europa/Domstolar-i-Norden/.

[10]Viljhjámsson (1984). See also Halfdanarson (2008), chapter “High Court”.

[11]Hafstað (2016) and Daðason (2016).

Oslo, there is still a separate County Court, dealing with bankruptcy and several traditional notarial tasks. In other cities, these special courts were merged with the district courts under the court reform in 2006.

Despite the disinclination towards special courts, some still exist. The Danish Maritime and Commercial High Court has already been mentioned. Its jurisdiction covers inter alia marketing law, competition law and patent law, like its Nordic counterparts the Finnish Market Court (*markkinaoikeus/marknadsdomstolen*), and the Swedish Patent and Market Court (*patent och marknadsdomstolen*). Norway does not have a specialised court for these types of cases, but administrative boards act as *quasi*-courts, or tribunals, in resolving these matters. Decisions by administrative boards are subject to appeal to the court system. The Oslo District Court has sole jurisdiction in Norwegian patent and intellectual property cases. Interestingly, the Finnish and Swedish Market Courts transcend the boundaries of civil law and administrative law, as their jurisdiction covers both categories of cases.

Labour Courts are the first and final court for disputes arising from collective labour agreements. The Labour Courts were established in Denmark in 1900/1910, then in Norway in 1915, Sweden in 1929, in Iceland in 1938, and, finally, in Finland in 1946. These courts have all arisen from the specific organisation of the Nordic labour market, whereby collective agreements play a central role as a regulative instrument. General courts enjoy jurisdiction in disputes arising from individual labour contracts. The only exception is Sweden, where the Labour Court fulfils both functions. In cases arising from individual labour contracts, the court forms part of the general court system and functions as an appellate court in the ordinary court system.

The Finnish Insurance Court (*vakuutusoikeus/försäkringsdomstolen*) and the Norwegian Insurance Court (*trygderetten*) handle cases concerning social security benefits, such as unemployment and sickness benefits. Rulings of the Norwegian Insurance Court are subject to limited appeal to appellate courts, while the Finnish Insurance Court is de facto an appellate court, because a tribunal functions as the first 'court'.

With the exception of the Finnish Insurance Court, rulings by special courts can generally be appealed to general and/or administrative courts, making special courts at least partly subject to the jurisdiction of the Supreme Courts. Moreover, apart from insurance courts, the jurisdiction of the special courts is limited to highly specialised issues, many of which concern rights held collectively by a large number of people, or by society as such.

To some extent, specialist courts or divisions within courts provide specialisation, such as the Swedish Patent and Market Court within the Stockholm District Court and the Svea Court of Appeal, and the Swedish Immigration Court within administrative courts. Another form of specialisation is to grant a court exclusive jurisdiction on certain issues. For instance, since 2010 the Danish Judicial Registration Court (*tinglysningsret*) in Hobro has held exclusive jurisdiction over judicial registration and recording, issues that were concentrated here from the other district courts.

The disinclination towards special courts reflects the ideal of judges as generalists. Judges hear all types of cases, civil, criminal and family, and in Denmark, Norway and Iceland, administrative cases too. In some larger courts, however, some types of cases are heard by a specific group of judges. Moreover, the largest courts are organised in divisions, where each division specialises in certain types of cases.[12] Judges rotate between the sections, to ensure that each judge remains a generalist.

In Finland, Sweden and more recently Denmark, judges are often recruited from within the courts. Young lawyers first serve as deputy judges, and then continue as assistant judges and legal clerks, often working in many different courts before appointment as a permanent judge. This ensures training and experience in multiple court settings.[13] Norwegian judges are recruited mainly from outside the courts, since appointments as assistant judges (*dommerfullmektig*) are very limited.

Nordic courts form a pyramid-shaped hierarchy, from the many district courts[14] at the bottom, to rather few Courts of Appeal[15]—one in Iceland, two in Denmark, five in Finland, and six in Norway and Sweden—to a single Supreme Court[16] at the top. Administrative courts in Finland and Sweden follow the same pattern, although there are no appellate administrative courts in Finland.[17] As a result, almost any action brought to court could end up in the Supreme Court or the Supreme Administrative Court. In Finland, a merger between the Supreme Court and the Supreme Administrative Court has been discussed.[18]

4 Judicial Discretion and Pragmatic Dispute Resolution

Judicial discretion and pragmatic dispute resolution are typical traits of Nordic court proceedings. Judicial discretion is reflected in the use of general procedural rules that are applicable to a wide range of different types of cases. Additionally, many procedural rules give the judge ample discretion. For example, time limits are often not set by law, and even when the law sets a time limit, the court is often allowed to

---

[12]Only courts with approximately 15–20 judges or more are organised in sections, such as the district courts in the capitals and the largest urban areas.

[13]European Commission for the Efficiency of Justice (2016), pp. 83–86.

[14]*Byret* in Denmark, *käräjäoikeus/tingsrätt* in Finland, *héraðsdómstól* in Iceland, *tingrett* in Norway and *tingsrätt* in Sweden.

[15]*Landsret* in Denmark, *hovioikeus/hovrätt* in Finland, *landsréttur* in Iceland, *lagmannsrett* in Norway and *hovrätt* in Sweden. The Swedish Administrative Court of Appeal is *kammarrätt*.

[16]*Højesteret* in Denmark, *Korkein oikeus/Högsta domstolen* in Finland, *Hæstiréttur* in Iceland, *Høyesterett* in Norway and *Högsta domstolen* in Sweden.

[17]In Finland, the administrative courts consist of *hallinto-oikeus/förvaltningsdomstol* and *Korkein hallinto-oikeus/Högsta förvaltningsdomstolen*. In Sweden, the administrative courts consist of *förvaltningsrätt*, *kammarrätt* and *Högsta förvaltningsdomstolen*.

[18]Mäenpää et al. (2015).

extend it. For instance, courts set a longer time limit for the defendant to file a statement of defence in a complex case than in a simple case, and courts are more likely to extend the time limit to file a statement of appeal in a cross-border case, where documents must be translated, than in a purely national case.

Although special provisions exist for some types of cases, such as those concerning child custody, the provisions do not form coherent regulation of a specific procedure. Rather, there are only single provisions modifying specific aspects or parts of the proceedings, and general procedural rules apply to all other dimensions.

Judicial discretion requires a high level of trust in the courts. In a European survey of 2012, the five Nordic countries all ranked among the top eight in terms of levels of trust in the courts, with Denmark, Norway and Finland as the first three, Sweden as fifth and Iceland as number eight.[19] The Nordic countries are generally high-trust societies, and trust in the judiciary must be viewed on that basis. Trust between courts and citizens is mutual. For instance, the courts prefer to serve documents by ordinary mail. A receipt slip is sent with the documents and the recipient is asked to note the date of service, sign the slip and return it to the court. In the vast majority of cases, service is successful. The method is cheap, fast and convenient. In some situations, the courts may also serve documents by telephone.

Another example of the quest for flexibility is hearing witnesses by telephone when the court considers this appropriate. Although the court cannot fully ensure the identity of a witness, the method is convenient and in particular increases the availability of experts and expert witnesses. Hearing witnesses by telephone is necessary to maintain the principle of orality, while balancing this with cost efficiency.

Pragmatism is also reflected in the view on settlements in civil proceedings. The judge is expected to promote settlement when appropriate. The judge may inter alia discuss the advantages of settlement, and the cost, delay and insecurity arising from court proceedings, and point to the relatively small differences between the claims of each party. Settlement is also encouraged more indirectly. For instance, an abstract stating the most important claims and facts, both disputed and undisputed, often expedites settlement.[20]

Moreover, many types of dispute are actively directed away from the court system towards other organisations. Consumer dispute resolution is state-sponsored and mostly free of charge for the consumer. The proceedings are time- and cost-efficient, with consumer law experts providing services. In Denmark, Norway and Iceland, many consumer dispute resolution processes result in a binding and enforceable outcome, unless one of the parties instigates court proceedings. In Finland and Sweden, decisions are only recommendations, but the overwhelming majority of companies abide by them voluntarily. Companies that do not follow recommendations are put on a black list by consumer organisations. In Norway and

[19]Arnstad (2017), p. 6. See also Jackson et al. (2011); Spignoli (2016) and the EU 2017 Justice Scoreboard. http://ec.europa.eu/justice/effective-justice/scoreboard/index_en.htm.

[20]Ervo and Nylund (2016).

Sweden, for instance, the general consumer dispute resolution boards consider more than 10,000 cases annually.[21]

Dispute resolution outside the courts is reflected in the modest number of court cases. The Nordic countries have one of the lowest numbers of civil and commercial cases for every 100,000 inhabitants in Europe. Table 1 for the number of cases shows the modest number of cases in Nordic courts. Germany, for instance, has approximately twice as many cases, Portugal more than three times as many, and Belgium seven times as many.[22]

The modest number of cases in second instance courts is a result of two interacting processes. Firstly, Courts of Appeal have instruments to filter appeals, giving them leeway to focus on complex cases and cases involving doubt as to whether the outcome in the district court was correct. Courts of appeal have been given flexible tools to manage at least some of the workload. Secondly, as citizens trust the courts, they are also inclined to be satisfied with the outcome and have faith that the outcome is correct. Both mechanisms reinforce the pyramid shape of the court system.

5 Oral Proceedings—With a Nordic Twist

Court proceedings in the Nordic countries are oral in the district courts. The main hearing constitutes the core of court proceedings. The hearing is concentrated as a single hearing, or in larger cases as hearings on consecutive days. During the main hearing, the parties present their claims and defence, evidence, and legal arguments supporting the claims and defence. All arguments are presented orally directly to the judge or panel of judges hearing the case. Witness evidence is presented directly to the court in the main hearing. As a rule, affidavits and other types of written recordings of witness evidence are not admissible.[23] Even though a concentrated main hearing is the norm, judges are not passive umpires. Particularly in civil proceedings, judges engage actively in the proceedings, often either during the preparatory stage by helping the parties to identify core disputed issues, or at the main hearing, by asking the parties critical questions. Sometimes judges do both.

In administrative courts in Sweden and Finland, an oral hearing is only conducted when required in order to take evidence, or if a party requests a hearing.[24] In Finland and Sweden, written procedure is the norm in appellate civil proceedings. In Sweden, oral proceedings are common primarily in criminal cases, whereas in

---

[21]See http://arn.se/om-arn/statistik/ and https://fil.forbrukerradet.no/wp-content/uploads/2015/10/arsrapport-2016-v.2.pdf.

[22]European Commission for the Efficiency of Justice (2016), pp. 186–190.

[23]See Ervo and Nylund (2016), note 25.

[24]The Swedish Act on Administrative Proceedings, *Förvaltningsprocesslagen* 1971:291, section 9, and the Finnish Administrative Judicial Procedure Act, *Hallintolainkäyttölaki/Förvaltningsprocesslag* 586/1996 section 37.

Table 1 Caseload at different court levels in the Nordic countries in 2017

	District courts		Courts of appeal		Supreme court	
	Civil	Criminal	Civil	Criminal	Civil	Criminal
Denmark[a]	45,833	186,465	5160	5974	105	20
Finland[b]	9701	51,076	2176	5465	60	77
Iceland[c]	5999	2438	0	0	307	94
Norway[d]	15,774	66,563	1987	1192	65	52
Sweden[e]	61,784	86,270	2686	8528	37	29

[a]http://www.domstol.dk/om/talogfakta/statistik/Pages/default.aspx
[b]Oikeusministeriö (2018) and http://korkeinoikeus.fi/material/attachments/kko2/vuosikertomukset/qRmVGSQYR/Korkeinoikeus_teksti_suomi.pdf
[c]https://www.heradsdomstolar.is/tolfraedi/ and Hæstaréttar Íslands (2018). The figures for district courts are from 2016
[d]https://www.domstol.no/no/domstoladministrasjonen/offentlighet-og-innsyn/statistikk/
[e]Domstolsverket (2018) and Högsta domstolen (2016). The figures for the Supreme Court are from 2016

Finland an oral hearing is held in less than one-third of all cases. In Denmark, Norway and Iceland, oral proceedings are the norm in appellate courts in both civil and criminal cases.

In all the Nordic countries, Courts of Appeal apply filtering mechanisms to enable them to rule on appeals in simplified written proceedings. Proceedings in the Supreme Courts are usually written in Sweden and Finland, while oral hearings are held in Denmark, Norway and Iceland. Finland and Sweden are to a greater extent influenced by continental law; while Danish, Norwegian and Icelandic procedural law is influenced by English law.

The prevalence of oral proceedings is also reflected in the number of lay judges. At least in the Nordic countries, the relative number of lay judges corresponds to the prevalence of oral proceedings in district and appellate courts.

6 Lay Participation (in Criminal Cases)

As we have seen, law in general, and the judiciary in particular, were first professionalized in the Nordic countries since the end of the 18th century. It is the generalist, and not the specialist, who is the ideal judge. These two factors feature among several that have opened up Nordic courts to society, and hence the reasons that lay participation is still a characteristic of Nordic courts. However, lay judges are rarely used in civil cases. When the court hears a civil case as a panel consisting of lay judges, the lay judges are often experts in a field relevant to the case before them.

Despite similarities, there are also significant dissimilarities. In Sweden, administrative courts sometimes sit as a panel with lay judges, whereas Finnish administrative courts have no lay judges. In criminal cases, the use of lay judges is declining, particularly in Finland. Today, lay judges participate primarily in serious cases and only in the district court. The number of lay judges is only 1738 (32 for every 100,000 inhabitants) in Finland. Furthermore, neither Finland nor Iceland operates a jury system. In Sweden, the jury is limited to cases concerning freedom of the press.

However, Sweden has lay judges in criminal cases where the accused risks imprisonment for six months or more, in both district courts and Courts of Appeal. In district courts, lay judges form the majority of the panel, with three lay judges and one professional judge. In Courts of Appeal, two lay judges and three professional judges hear criminal cases. There are approximately 85 lay judges for every 100,000 inhabitants in Sweden.[25]

Denmark and Norway have a two-tiered system concerning lay judges in criminal cases. A single professional judge hears the least serious criminal cases, while in other criminal cases the panel consists of one professional judge and two lay judges. A fortified panel hears the most serious cases, however. In Norway, the augmented panel is only present in the Court of Appeal. The augmented panel is reminiscent of the jury system. In Norway, the jury system was abolished in 2017. A guilty verdict requires a qualified majority of the augmented panel: in Denmark, two-thirds of the lay judges and two-thirds of the professional judges must vote for a guilty verdict; and in Norway, five of the seven members of the panel must vote for a guilty verdict. In both countries, lay judges form the clear majority of the panel of judges. Denmark and Norway have 212 and 832 lay judges, respectively, for every 100,000 inhabitants: by far the highest numbers in Europe.[26]

7 A Quasi-stare Decisis Principle

In the Nordic countries, the Supreme Courts function as courts of precedence. Although their rulings are not formally binding on lower courts, Supreme Court decisions have a de facto binding effect on lower courts. Unless a lower court has exceptional reasons for challenging the case law, it treats Supreme Court rulings as *stare decisis.*

The pyramid-shaped court hierarchies and the low degree of court specialisation make the court structures perfect for passing down precedent. With no codes of law through which law is unified, and no long tradition of legal scholarship puzzling together the pieces of legislation produced by the legislator, the Supreme Courts have partly been given, and have partly taken on, the task of unifying law through precedent. As previously emphasised, historically the Nordic courts have played a unifying role, so that this was not a new role for them. At the same time, the Nordic

[25]European Commission for the Efficiency of Justice (2016), p. 90.

[26]European Commission for the Efficiency of Justice (2016), p. 90.

Supreme Courts had traditionally been Courts of Appeal that also produced precedent.

With the introduction of tighter access filters in Sweden in the 1970s, in Finland in the 1980s, in Norway and Denmark in the 1990s, and presently in Iceland, the Supreme Court gained an instrument to concentrate on cases raising important questions of interpretation of the law, viz. cases that serve as precedent. In 2016, the Supreme Court of Iceland heard 432 cases, while the numbers of cases in the other Nordic countries were 123 in Denmark, 135 in Finland, 108 in Norway, and 66 in Sweden.[27] In addition, the Finnish Supreme Administrative Court heard 327[28] cases and the Swedish Supreme Administrative Court 123 cases.[29] In addition, the Supreme Courts heard procedural cases, cases for extraordinary appeal and other cases not requiring leave to appeal. The relatively large number of cases before the Icelandic Supreme Court and the Finnish Supreme Administrative Court reflect their position as a second, not third, court.

Another factor making the Nordic Supreme Courts highly competent as courts of precedent is the relatively low number of judges. The ideal judge is a generalist and the Supreme Court judges are the *crème de la crème* of generalists rotating in chambers dealing with all kinds of cases. The number of Supreme Court justices is low: Iceland has nine Supreme Court justices, Norway 20, Denmark 19, Sweden 16, and Finland 19. The Finnish Supreme Administrative Court has 20 justices and the Swedish 14. Few justices and few cases foster coherence within the Supreme Courts. With only one or two pyramid court structures and few special courts, the Supreme Courts have the opportunity and duty to ensure and develop coherence in the legal system.

8 Conclusion: Nordic Courts and Nordic Judicial Dialogue

Nordic courts are characterised by a three-tier court hierarchy with a low degree of specialisation, judicial discretion and pragmatic dispute resolution, oral proceedings, lay participation, and a *quasi-stare decisis* principle that makes the courts powerful. There are historical reasons for this, and seen in a retro-perspective this appears quite logical. However, the Nordic courts are not a product of organic development predetermined by history. Instead, choices have been made and courts reformed recurrently.

In terms of reforming the courts, there is a long tradition of looking to their Nordic counterparts. Despite marked differences, particularly between the eastern

---

[27]See Table 1 and Sunde (2017), pp. 53–76.

[28]Statistics from the Supreme Administrative Court http://kho.fi/material/attachments/kho/aineistoa/tilastoja/cfq6ZrylD/Valituslupa-asiat_2016.pdf.

[29]Domstolsverket (2016).

and western Nordic countries, comparing and cooperating before making deliberate choices enjoys a long history. The practice has been strengthened by Nordic meetings of lawyers from 1872, regular comparison with other Nordic countries when preparing court reforms in the 20th and 21th centuries, meetings of first Supreme Court Chief Justices from the early 1990s, and then seminars for selected Supreme Court justices from the early 2000s. The result is, firstly, not identical court hierarchies, but common characteristics that make the Nordic courts different from those we find in other regions of Europe. Still, in recent decades the differences have narrowed. Secondly, the courts have been and will continuously be reformed in order to adapt to the society in which they operate. Since the common characteristics of Nordic courts are the outcome of deliberate choices, supported only by a common historical foundation, the shared characteristics we find today might be lost in the future.

References

Arnstad I (2017) Norden har høyest tiltro til rettssystemet. Rett på sak, 4, 6. https://www.domstol.no/globalassets/upload/internett_fillister/da/publikasjoner/rett-pa-sak/2016/rps4_web_oppslag.pdf. Accessed 19 July 2017

Daðason KT (2016) Landsréttur á laggirnar í ársbyrjun 2018. Visir 26 May 2016. http://www.visir.is/g/2016160529185/landsrettur-a-laggirnar-i-arsbyrjun-2018. Accessed 22 May 2017

Domstolsverket (2018) Court statistics 2017. http://domstol.se/Publikationer/Statistik/court_statistics_2017.pdf. Accessed 19 July 2018

Domstolsverket (2016) Domstolsstatistik 2016. http://www.domstol.se/Publikationer/Statistik/domstolsstatistik_2016.pdf. Accessed 22 May 2018

Ervo L, Nylund A (eds) (2016) Current trends in preparatory proceedings: a comparative study of Nordic and former communist countries. Springer, Heidelberg

European Commission for the Efficiency of Justice (2016) European judicial systems. Efficiency and quality of justice. http://www.coe.int/t/dghl/cooperation/cepej/evaluation/2016/publication/REV1/2016_1%20-%20CEPEJ%20Study%2023%20-%20General%20report%20-%20EN.pdf. Accessed 22 May 2018

Hæstaréttar Íslands (2018) Ársskýrsla Hæstaréttar Íslands 2017. https://www.haestirettur.is/library/Files/arsskyrslur/%C3%81rssk%C3%BDrsla%202017.pdf. Accessed 19 July 2018

Hafstað V (2016) Three tier judicial system approved. Iceland review, 26 May 2016. http://icelandreview.com/news/2016/05/26/three-tier-judicial-system-approved. Accessed 22 May 2018

Halfdanarson G (2008) Historical dictionary of Iceland. Scarecrow Press, Lanham, MD

Högsta domstolen (2016) Verksamhetsberättelse 2016. http://hogstadomstolen.se/Domstolar/hogstadomstolen/dokument/Verksamhetsber%C3%A4ttelsen%202016.pdf. Accessed 19 July 2018

Jackson J, Pooler T, Hohl K, Kuha J, et al (2011) Trust in justice: topline results from round 5 of the European social survey. European social survey. Available at: https://www.europeansocialsurvey.org/docs/findings/ESS5_toplines_issue_1_trust_in_justice.pdf. Accessed: 22 May 2018

Mäenpää O, Esko T, Pynnä T, Pitkäranta A, Skog T (2015) Korkeimpien oikeuksien organisatorinen yhdistäminen – Hyötyjen ja haittojen arviointi. Oikeusministeriö, Helsinki. Available at: http://urn.fi/URN:ISBN:978-952-259-421-1. Accessed 22 May 2018

Oikeusministeriö (2018) Tuomioistuinten työtilastoja vuodelta 2017. Oikeusministeriö, Helsinki. https://julkaisut.valtioneuvosto.fi/bitstream/handle/10024/160698/OMTH_11_2018_Tuomiois tuinten_ty%C3%B6tilastoja_2017.pdf?sequence=4&isAllowed=y. Accessed 19 July 2018

Sapignoli M (2016) Confidence in judicial institutions in Europe (draft version). https://eventum.upf.edu/_files/_event/_5261/_editorFiles/file/Michele%20Sapignoli.pdf. Accessed 22 May 2018

Sunde JØ (2017) From courts of appeal to courts of precedent—access to the highest courts in the Nordic countries. In: van Rhee CH, Fu Y (eds) Supreme courts in transition in China and the West. Springer, Cham, pp 53–76

Wenander H (2016) Rättsliga ramar för styrning av förvaltningen i Danmark og Sverige. Nordisk administrativt tidsskrift 93(1):57–74

Viljhjámsson T (1984) Islands Højesteret. Rett og rettssal – Et festskrift til Rolv Ryssdal. Aschehoug, Oslo, pp 79–88

FSC
www.fsc.org
MIX
Papier | Fördert
gute Waldnutzung
FSC® C083411